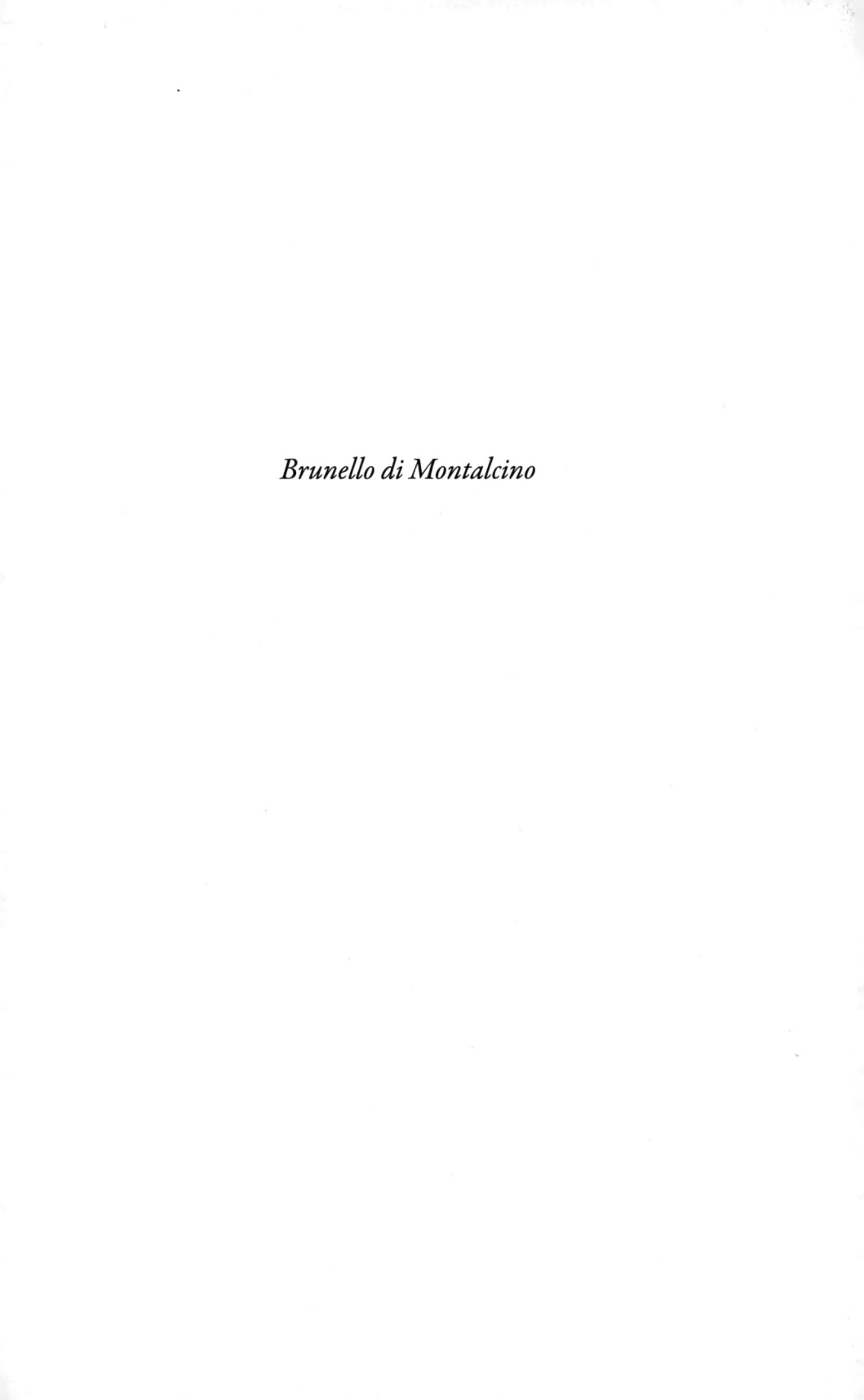

Brunello di Montalcino

Brunello di Montalcino

UNDERSTANDING AND APPRECIATING
ONE OF ITALY'S GREATEST WINES

Kerin O'Keefe

UNIVERSITY OF CALIFORNIA PRESS
BERKELEY LOS ANGELES LONDON

University of California Press, one of the most distinguished university presses in the United States, enriches lives around the world by advancing scholarship in the humanities, social sciences, and natural sciences. Its activities are supported by the UC Press Foundation and by philanthropic contributions from individuals and institutions. For more information, visit www.ucpress.edu.

University of California Press
Berkeley and Los Angeles, California

University of California Press, Ltd.
London, England

© 2012 by The Regents of the University of California

Library of Congress Cataloging-in-Publication Data

O'Keefe, Kerin, 1965–.
  Brunello di Montalcino : understanding and appreciating one of Italy's greatest wines / Kerin O'Keefe.
    p. cm.
  Includes bibliographical references and index.
  ISBN 978-0-520-26564-6 (cloth, alk. paper)
  1. Wine and wine making—Italy—Montalcino. I. Title.
Title: Understanding and appreciating one of Italy's greatest wines.
TP559.I8O38 2012
641.2'2—dc23   2011041259

Manufactured in the United States of America

21 20 19 18 17 16 15
10 9 8 7 6 5 4

*For Terence "Terry" Patrick O'Keefe,
a dear brother and great friend who always
encouraged me to pursue my dreams*

CONTENTS

List of Illustrations ix
Preface xi

Introduction.
Brunello: A Modern-Day Phenomenon of Made in Italy 1

PART ONE
THE PLACE, THE GRAPE,
THE HISTORY, AND THE WINE

1 · Montalcino 9

2 · Temperamental Sangiovese:
Location, Location, Location 19

3 · Birth of a New Wine 38

4 · Brunello Comes of Age 49

5 · Boom Years and the Loss of *Tipicità* 61

6 · The Brunellogate Scandal 70

7 · Brunello Today and Tomorrow:
The Return to *Tipicità,* or Business as Usual? 81

PART TWO
LEADING PRODUCERS BY SUBZONES

8 · Montalcino 95

9 · Bosco and Torrenieri 171

10 · Tavernelle 186

11 · Camigliano 196

12 · Sant'Angelo 205

13 · Castelnuovo dell'Abate 232

PART THREE
BEYOND BRUNELLO:
OTHER WINES AND LOCAL CUISINE

14 · Montalcino's Other Wines:
Rosso di Montalcino, Moscadello, and Sant'Antimo 257

15 · Brunello, Rosso, and Food Pairing 267

Appendix A. Vintage Guide to Brunello 275
Appendix B. Brunello at a Glance 278
Notes 283
Acknowledgments 287
Glossary 289
Bibliography 293
Index 297

ILLUSTRATIONS

MAPS

1. Brunello di Montalcino 2
2. Montalcino, south 96
3. Montalcino, north 135
4. Bosco and Torrenieri 172
5. Tavernelle and Camigliano 187
6. Sant'Angelo 210
7. Castelnuovo dell'Abate 233

FIGURES

1. View of the hilltop town of Montalcino 10
2. The twelfth-century abbey of Sant'Antimo in Castelnuovo dell'Abate 14
3. Montalcino's fourteenth-century fortress 15
4. Panorama of Montalcino's rolling hills and vineyards 39
5. Franco Biondi Santi 99
6. Gianni Brunelli's beautiful Olmo vineyard 116
7. Giulio Salvioni 125
8. Giuseppe Gorelli in his cellar at Le Potazzine 127

9. Large marine fossils found at Paradiso di Manfredi 136
10. The Guerrini family 151
11. Nello Baricci at his Montosoli vineyards 160
12. Emilia Nardi at her Casale del Bosco estate 174
13. The Castiglion del Bosco estate 176
14. Torrenieri subzone 179
15. Gianfranco Soldera at his Case Basse estate 188
16. Santa Restituta church on Santa Restituta estate 192
17. CastelGiocondo 198
18. Sant'Angelo in Colle 206
19. Col d'Orcia's Poggio al Vento vineyard 211
20. Banfi's vinification cellar 220
21. Castello Banfi 222
22. Giuseppe Sesti of Castello di Argiano 227
23. Castello di Argiano property 228
24. Vineyard at Campogiovanni estate with Sant'Angelo in the background 230
25. Castello di Velona 234
26. The hamlet of Castelnuovo dell'Abate 234
27. Mount Amiata 239
28. Stella di Campalto on her San Giuseppe property 247

PREFACE

This book is a drastic departure from the overly generalized coverage currently available on Italian wines. As the title states, *Brunello di Montalcino: Understanding and Appreciating One of Italy's Greatest Wines* is not a survey of the entire Italian wine scene or a sketchy overview of a single region. Instead, the book celebrates one of Italy's most compelling wines, Brunello, its fascinating growing zone and its highly individualistic winemakers, who produce world-class wines of stunning depth and complexity from Italy's most widely planted grape. For it is only in Montalcino that native grape Sangiovese can yield wines with the finesse and seduction usually associated with Burgundy's top Pinot Noirs.

The beginning of my love affair with Brunello coincided with that of another love affair. I first tasted Brunello in 1989 in Montalcino during a summer-long tour of Tuscany with Paolo, my future husband, who not only shared his passion for wine, but whose father, Ubaldo, had an incredibly well-stocked wine cellar filled with Barolos from the late 1950s, 1960s, and 1970s, and Brunellos from the 1970s and 1980s, which he generously encouraged us to open and enjoy. (I have assured Paolo, by the way, that this treasure trove of unforgettable wines was not why I married him, though I think he has his doubts.) While I relished discovering those glorious Barolos, it was Brunello, exceedingly elegant and vibrant, with more complexity than muscle, that won my heart. I moved to Italy in 1991 and immediately began traveling often to the country's famous and lesser-known wine destinations in pursuit of the country's greatest wines, first as a dedicated wine lover, later for a series of short-lived jobs in the trade before becoming a full-time wine writer a few years later. Even though my chosen profession allows me the privilege of discovering and tasting Italy's and the world's most exciting wines, Brunello, with its combination of balance, power, and grace, continues to hold me in thrall. I always return to Montalcino and its Brunellos.

Rather than merely sit in my office and taste thousands of wines every year, I've visited all of the Brunello estates profiled in the following chapters, some several times, and many more that are not in the book. I've spent years researching Brunello di Montalcino for numerous articles in magazines, including *Decanter, World of Fine Wine,* and *Wine News;* and for my previous book, *Franco Biondi Santi: The Gentleman of Brunello.* I've walked producers' vineyards, visited their cellars, and talked for hours with the winemakers and their families. Even though I regularly attend the annual Benvenuto Brunello press tasting, I use this important event to get an idea of the latest vintages, and to discover the growing list of new producers as well as to retry old favorites. But tasting notes and eventual scores have always derived from further investigation, gathered during the frequent and lengthy trips I take to Montalcino every year, and from trying the wines later at home with food pairings, often over a period of a couple of days for each wine.

I would like to address any concerns over the possibility of any conflict of interests. I do not consult for or have any business or commercial relationship of any kind with any of the producers profiled—or with any producers in Montalcino or Tuscany for that matter. I have chosen the producers solely on the merits of their Brunellos.

Regarding quotations, the majority come from field interviews I've conducted as research for this book, or from interviews undertaken for my previous book and numerous Brunello articles I've written over the last several years for various magazines. Otherwise, quotations are cited with a note. And unless otherwise noted, I translated all material from Italian into English.

So, pull up a chair, pour yourself a glass of Brunello, and delve into Italy's most beguiling denomination. And enjoy. *Viva il Brunello!*

INTRODUCTION

Brunello

A MODERN-DAY PHENOMENON OF MADE IN ITALY

Of Italy's twenty regions, none hold more fascination than Tuscany, with its rolling countryside thickly carpeted with vines and olive trees, and with its hilltowns topped with ancient castles and fortresses. Though parts of the region have not been immune to industrialization and development, much of Tuscany's quintessential landscape looks remarkably the same as it did when its hills and cypress trees were celebrated in numerous fourteenth- and fifteenth-century paintings. The cradle of the Renaissance as well as the birthplace of what has become the Italian language, Tuscany is also Italy's most internationally renowned wine-producing region, home to some of the world's most beloved Italian wines, including Chianti Classico, Vino Nobile di Montepulciano, and the greatest of all, Brunello di Montalcino.

Although Chianti Classico and Vino Nobile form part of the trio of Tuscany's most prestigious denominations, they almost never reach the depth and complexity of Brunello, even if they all share the same predominant grape, Sangiovese, and all are produced relatively near each other geographically. Brunello is the only one of these three wines that by law must be made exclusively with this native grape. In fact, Brunello, and its "junior partner" Rosso di Montalcino, are the only wines in all of Italy governed under regulations that demand exclusively 100 percent Sangiovese because the grape excels in parts of Montalcino as nowhere else in Tuscany, Italy, or the world. With their earthy, wild-cherry sensations and full body yet smooth textures, top Brunellos have the body and finesse of the most prestigious world-class bottlings from Bordeaux, Burgundy, and Piedmont. Its longevity is legendary, though market demands for instant-gratification wines have generated a slew of ready-to-drink Brunellos that spurn the wine's reputation for marathon cellaring.

MAP 1. Brunello di Montalcino

Montalcino itself is one of the most captivating wine-producing areas in the world. The growing zone, covered with rolling vineyards and woods, looks as if has been lifted out of a Renaissance painting, and is crowned by the hilltown's imposing medieval fortress. The denomination's flagship wine, Brunello, is, along with Piedmont's Barolo and the Côte d'Or's Pinot Noir, a terroir-driven wine that is fascinating for its diverse expressions, which depend not only on different winemaking styles but on where in the large growing zone the wine originates. While a number of Brunellos rank among the world's finest wines and some labels are among the most expensive bottlings in Italy, all too often some of Montalcino's winemakers make disappointing wines from vineyards in unsuitable parts of the sprawling growing zone, or by relying on invasive cellar techniques that can vinify the authenticity right out of their Brunellos. But when Montalcino winemakers get it right, as many of them thankfully do, the best Brunellos seduce with enticing floral aromas, bright succulent fruit, earthy minerality, and fantastic depth.

Yet Brunello is a very different wine today than it was even just a decade ago. Unchecked planting in the late 1990s and early in the first decade of the new century has led to an explosion in production as these newer Brunellos reach the marketplace. Areas that as recently as the late 1990s had never been cultivated with grapes are now planted with Brunello vines, resulting in evident differences in quality, while winemaking extremes further add to the abundant range of Brunello styles available today. This is where this book comes into play. Before wine lovers invest in a bottle of Brunello, expecting a wine that will be even better after years of laying down in the cellar, they would do well to avoid the more immediate, New World–styled Brunellos from certain parts of the growing zone, and vice-versa for those consumers who want to enjoy their wine right away rather than wait years to tame aggressive tannins and sharp acidity.

Brunello di Montalcino will help wine lovers maneuver their way among Montalcino's minefield of diversity by breaking the vast commune down into seven distinct subzones, ranging from the highest reaches around the town of Montalcino, which yield austere, elegant wines destined for lengthy aging; down to the lower plains in the deep south around Sant'Angelo Scalo, home to immediate, muscular Brunellos with higher alcohol and lower acidity; and to all the other fascinating areas that lie between these two geographical extremes. Chapters on subzones will give readers detailed information including the geography, geology, and climate of each, and what characteristics these parameters impart to Brunello.

While this technical information may sound like a descent into wine geekdom, it is actually necessary to help explain the marked variations among the array of Brunellos on the market today. I should point out these subzones are unofficial, although the ones I use here are widely agreed upon in Montalcino and are the best breakdown of the growing area until official delimitation within the denomination occurs. However, most insiders feel zoning will never be allowed at this late stage because of obvious commercial interests.

Producer profiles accompany each subzone; don't be surprised if some estates that annually rake in top scores from mainstream wine magazines and critics are absent. I have carefully chosen producers, big and small, famous and unknown, who produce excellent Brunellos of *tipicità,* or those that best express the quintessential characteristics of both Sangiovese and the various subzones in Montalcino. I have flagged the very best with a tower symbolizing Montalcino's fortress (♖).

I adamantly do not believe in the "dumbing down" of Italian wine, so have duly avoided the big, black, and inky Brunellos on steroids, often made by one of the country's famed flying enologists, which taste as if they could have been made from any grape variety anywhere in the world. The few producers included whose wines fit into this internationally styled category have been added because of their undeniable impact on the denomination, as will be noted. There will be much more about the various styles of Brunello in chapter 5, "The Boom Years and the Loss of *Tipicità,*" and in chapter 6, "The Brunellogate Scandal."

Montalcino is arguably one of the most dynamic yet controversial winegrowing areas in the world. Its potential for outstanding quality now coexists with unchecked escalation in new plantings and production, compounded by widespread accusations of illicit grape blending. Despite these recent challenges that threaten the denomination, thanks to its inherent class and flair, the greatest Brunellos are as alluring to wine lovers as Ferraris are to car fanatics, and it is no coincidence that Brunello is the enological symbol of the luxury "Made in Italy" campaign designated to the country's most exclusive items. In a relatively short time, Brunello di Montalcino has managed to challenge some of the world's most prestigious and established wines, an incredible feat given that until 1975 there were only 30 producers who collectively made roughly 800,000 bottles of Brunello. Today there are 250 growers and 200 bottlers, annually producing around 8 million bottles of Brunello, with one in every four bottles destined for the U.S. market alone.

To understand this unique wine, the best place to start is Montalcino itself, the spiritual home of Sangiovese, one of the world's noblest yet, at the same time, generally underrated grape varieties. Montalcino is Italy's greatest testament to the existence of terroir, and even though this is perhaps the most abused term in winespeak, it is the only explanation as to why this common vine can yield superlative results in designated parts of the denomination that it never attains elsewhere.

PART ONE

The Place, the Grape, the History, and the Wine

ONE

Montalcino

Brunello's entire production area centers on the expansive commune of Montalcino. This medieval hilltop town, whose name derives from the Italian translation of the Latin Mons Ilcinus (Mount Ilex), the ancient Latin name of the hill on which the town perches, and referring to the ilex or holm oak trees that still populate the surrounding woods, lies roughly 40 kilometers (25 miles) south of Siena and just over 40 kilometers (25 miles) as the crow flies from the Tyrrhenian Sea. Montalcino occupies a central position within the Province of Siena, though it is far away from busy roads and immersed for the most part in unspoiled countryside. Whereas the ancient town center, dominated by its fourteenth-century fortress, is tiny, the entire municipal area, the largest township in the province, includes several hamlets and stretches across 24,362 hectares (60,200 acres), with 70 percent of the area defined as hilly, 29 percent flat, and 1 percent mountainous. Half of the territory is still covered by dense woods and fallow land while 10 percent is dedicated to olive groves and 15 percent to vineyards. The rest is pasture land or is cultivated with various crops, mostly grain. Of the 3,500 hectares (8,645 acres) of vines planted throughout the large territory, 2,100 hectares (5,187 acres) are registered to Brunello, 510 hectares (1,260 acres) as Rosso di Montalcino, 50 hectares (124 acres) planted to Moscadello, 450 hectares (1,111 acres) to Sant'Antimo, and the rest planted with IGT (Indicazione geografica tipica) vines.

Montalcino's rambling surface area resembles a square 16 kilometers (10 miles) wide, delimited by the Orcia, Asso, and Ombrone Rivers. Within these boundaries four major slopes rise to form a ridge, peaking at 667 meters (2,188 feet) above sea level, with Mount Amiata in the southeast protecting the slopes from hail and violent storms. When compared to Chianti Classico

FIGURE 1. View of the hilltop town of Montalcino. Nearly half of the large township is covered by dense woods. Photograph by Paolo Tenti.

to the north and Montepulciano to the east, both further inland, Montalcino enjoys a decidedly more Mediterranean climate. Sangiovese benefits from the warmer summertime temperatures and drier weather that lead to ideal berry maturation, while day and night temperature differences generate complex aromas—perfect ripening conditions for this temperamental variety. It is no coincidence that of all Tuscany's vaunted denominations only Brunello di Montalcino, and Rosso di Montalcino, the denomination's second wine that is made to be drunk young, are required by law to be made entirely with Sangiovese, or as the Italians say, *Sangiovese in purezza*.

However, although Sangiovese excels in select parts of Montalcino, it does not perform as well throughout the whole denomination thanks to the dramatic differences within the large growing zone, which is remarkably diverse for a single township. Among the denomination's vivid variations, vineyard altitude, which ranges from just above sea level to over 500 meters (1,640 feet), is a crucial factor in Sangiovese's performance. Although the variety produces more complex and age-worthy wines in the higher altitudes, when cultivated too high the vine can have trouble ripening in difficult years. Montalcino also boasts several distinct microclimates with sharp contrasts in summer temperatures and annual rainfall, which noticeably affect the grape's ripening ability and dictate when growers start the harvest. In the most scorching areas around Sant'Angelo Scalo, the Brunello harvest begins ten days to two weeks earlier than in the cooler, elevated areas. Subzones also react in remarkably different ways during years with extreme or adverse climatic conditions. Though select areas throughout the entire growing zone can produce beautifully balanced Brunellos in outstanding vintages like 2004, in difficult years like the washout 2002 and the torrid 2003, the vintage will have markedly divergent outcomes in the various subzones, a fact generally ignored by the press, which, in the absence of official zoning, tends to treat the area as a uniform whole.

Montalcino also boasts a phenomenal array of soil types within its confines. Seeing that no denomination-wide soil study has ever been undertaken in Montalcino, it is virtually impossible to say how many types of soils exist, although the Banfi estate, which has performed soil studies in its vineyards, declares that it has identified twenty-nine different soil types on its property alone. As geologists point out, Italy was formed by the collision between the European and African plates. Much of Tuscany forges what is known as a suture of the intercontinental impact, where over a period of millions of years, a stacking up process of the land mass created the Apennine Mountains and the many high hills that dominate this part of the region. While it could be argued that this event largely created the same situation in other parts of Tuscany that are relatively close to the sea, Montalcino is extremely unusual for a unique phenomenon whereby the sea retreated and returned several times, thereby generating a highly uncommon soil composition in parts of the denomination. As a result, according to experts, Montalcino's growing zone boasts one of the most complex and varied soil profiles in the world.

Certainly one reason for Montalcino's composite soils lies in the fact that the celebrated hill was formed in different geological eras. While this makes it difficult to make sweeping generalizations, in the broadest terms the higher reaches of the denomination just south of the town center have the oldest soil since they were the first land masses to rise above the receding oceans that once covered the earth, while the soil in the extreme southwestern lowlands are the youngest soils. Soils in the middle altitudes, on the other hand, are a complex mix of both. The younger soils that dominate the plains in the southwest, comprising alluvial deposits from the relatively recent Quaternary period (up to 1.8 million years ago) and Pliocene epoch, consist of sand, clay, mud, and marine sediment. Heading further uphill, the terrain is clay-enriched with calcareous fossil material usually attributed to the Miocene-Oligocene epochs; while in the upper part of the territory soil is moderately stony, mixed with sand and rich in lime where the well-draining soil is very old (Cretaceous-Eocene) and can restrain the youthful exuberance of productive grapevines.

However, the reality in Montalcino is far more complex than this simplistic breakdown, and the growing zone's pedological (soil) situation is extremely intricate. According to Edoardo Costantini, a professor of pedology and geopedology at the University of Siena for twenty years and the lead researcher of agrobiology and pedology at Florence's CRA-ABP Research Center (Centro di ricerca per l'agrobiologia e la pedologia), not only is Montalcino complex because it was formed in different geological ages, but because parts of the growing zone benefit from a highly rare natural phenomenon. "Usually, land protruded from the sea when the oceans receded, and that was it—end of story. What era the oceans receded in helps define a given area's geological and pedological composition. But in Montalcino, our research demonstrates that the oceans came back again and reclaimed the newly uncovered land masses up to the middle altitudes, roughly 300 to 350 meters (985 to 1,148 feet) above sea level before receding yet again, and that this phenomenon repeated itself several times," explains Costantini.

Costantini, who has compiled a fascinating study on viticultural zoning in the Province of Siena,[1] says that the receding and returning oceans caused massive landslides of an almost unimaginable scale that sent millions of cubic tons of earth crashing down from the higher reaches that mixed in with the marine fossils and sediment deposited by the oceans, and these two events repeated themselves over an extended period. Costantini added, "I don't know of any other wine growing region where both of these occurrences happened together, and it is a major reason why Montalcino has such an intricate soil situation." Costantini stresses that the mixing of the ancient soils from higher up in the growing area with younger soils is found only in certain areas of Montalcino's middle reaches. The lower altitudes, on the other hand, dominated by marine sediment, did not benefit from the massive landslides generated by the returning and retreating seas. Given all these factors, Brunello's entire growing zone boasts a dizzying variety of soils not often found together in a single growing area, or as Costantini says, from a pedological viewpoint, Montalcino is "dynamic, complex, and unique."

According to Costantini and his research team's soil findings, which were achieved through on-site analysis of terrain, climate information, geological surveys, and results from experimental vineyards, with particular emphasis on the most illustrious denominations in the province, there are a number of select areas demonstrating suitable and high vocation for Sangiovese in the immense Chianti Classico zone, whose 70,000 hectares (172,900 acres) spread across nine different townships and include more than 7,000 hectares (17,300 acres) of vines registered to Classico production. The much smaller Montepulciano, on the other hand, with a total surface area of about 16,500 hectares (40,755 acres), generally has less ideal soil than its famed neighbors. "Montepulciano's soil is very uniform, and overall it is too fertile for Sangiovese," explains Costantini. Based on the same research, Montalcino's growing zone boasts many areas with high and very high vocation for Sangiovese, although other parts of the lauded denomination demonstrate downright dismal results, underscoring the necessity of zoning the area for Brunello production.

For more in-depth analysis on the specific conditions in the various parts of the denomination, see the chapters on the individual subzones.

MONTALCINO'S EARLY HISTORY

Based on archeological excavations, we know that the area of Montalcino was inhabited as far back as ten thousand years ago.[2] Excavations throughout the territory have uncovered numerous Etruscan and ancient Roman artifacts, tombs, and ruins, including Roman villas. The most notable find at the Poggio alla Civitella archeological site, just three kilometers from the center of Montalcino, is slowly revealing a fortified Etruscan city that is still waiting to be fully unearthed.[3]

In the Middle Ages, Montalcino prospered thanks to its convenient location along the Via Francigena, the road that pilgrims took from all over Europe for their journey to Rome. They would stop in Montalcino not only to rest but also to visit the Abbey of Sant'Antimo, the beautiful Romanesque abbey that sits in the quiet valley in Castelnuovo dell'Abate. The abbey was abandoned in the mid-fifteenth century, then restored by the Italian government at the end of the nineteenth century when it became property of the state. For many decades the abbey risked becoming merely another museum. Deprived of its clergy for over five hundred years, Sant'Antimo opened its doors as an abbey once again only in the late 1970s, thanks to the determination of an order of Augustinian friars, or more precisely, canons, after they had fought a long battle with Italian bureaucracy to recover the church

FIGURE 2. The twelfth-century abbey of Sant'Antimo in Castelnuovo dell'Abate, now restored to its original glory and inhabited by Augustinian canons. Photograph by Paolo Tenti.

and canonic housing and establish their religious community at the abbey. Sant'Antimo has become famous once more thanks at least in part to the canons' mystical and hypnotic Gregorian chants.

The Sant'Antimo Abbey that stands today among cypress trees and olive groves against a backdrop of vineyards dates to the twelfth century, and was built over another Benedictine monastery originally constructed at the end of the eighth century, which in turn had been erected at the site of an earlier chapel dedicated to Saint Antimo. Though there are various unfounded legends regarding the French king Charlemagne and miracles at the site, it does appear that Charlemagne put his official seal on the partially constructed monastery in 781 when he visited on his way back to France from Rome. In 814 Charlemagne's son and successor, Louis the Pious, granted the abbey his protection and donated it gifts, ensuring not only that it would become an important religious destination for pilgrims, but also that both Sant'Antimo and Montalcino would serve as main rest stops for merchants and soldiers. Montalcino's fortunes continued to rise when, in 1462, the town was elevated to the then highly coveted status of *città* (city) by Pope Pius II, a member of the illustrious Piccolomini family from nearby Pienza.

Montalcino also played a crucial role in the incessant and violent conflicts

FIGURE 3. Montalcino's imposing fourteenth-century fortress protected the Republic of Siena from Florence and her Spanish allies during a ruthless siege between 1555 and 1559. Photograph by Paolo Tenti.

between the Republics of Florence and Siena. Montalcino, annexed to Siena in 1260 after Siena won the Battle of Montaperti, became the last stronghold of the Republic of Siena. When Florence and her Spanish allies conquered and occupied Siena in 1555, the heads of Siena's tattered city-state, along with thousands of its citizens and its allied French troops, fled to Montalcino. There, protected by the town's fortified walls and its impenetrable fourteenth-century fortress, they withstood a brutal siege that lasted for four long years and ended only when Spain and France signed a peace agreement in 1559. Montalcino, and the remains of the Republic of Siena, went under the control of Florence's Cosimo I de' Medici, and became part of the Grand Duchy of Tuscany. Today Montalcino locals proudly point out that their town and their ancestors literally held down the fort for the peninsula's last independent republic; it is an episode that underscores the fiercely independent and individualistic nature that the town and its people boast even today.

Due to the grueling four-year siege, Montalcino never benefited from the Renaissance that illuminated so many other cities and towns in much of Tuscany. The thousands of militants and refugees from Siena drained the town's resources and destroyed the local economy. Montalcino entered into a state of limbo, and would only begin to shake off its stagnation after the unification of Italy in 1861, when the state began building an infrastructure of roads and bridges across the country, and more importantly, railroads. The first train arrived in one of Montalcino's hamlets, Torrenieri, in 1865, connecting the isolated town to the rest of Italy and civilization. It was at about this time that a few of Montalcino's wealthy gentlemen farmers, most of whom already made a well-known sweet white wine called Moscadello, began experimenting with red wine, eventually leading to the creation of Brunello.

Economic relief didn't last long, however, and hard times returned to Montalcino by the early twentieth century. The town had always been dependent on agriculture and the many products it derived from its surrounding woods, including charcoal made from carbonized wood, produced with an antique and laborious method, which fueled fires to heat homes. Montalcino's craftsmen also used local wood to make numerous goods, including baskets and other wicker products that were once essential household items in rural parts of the country. The two world wars generated crippling economic depressions, and as peasant farmers were called to arms, farms lay neglected for years, wreaking further havoc on Italy's agrarian economies that produced little or nothing during the wars and in their immediate aftermath. Already in a sorry state, Montalcino's countryside was further laid waste in June 1944, when the Allies passed directly through the town, liberating it from the occupying Germans.

The first half the twentieth century proved almost fatal for Montalcino's nascent Brunello production. In addition to the catastrophic wars of the period, there were also outbreaks of phylloxera, the root-eating aphid that nearly destroyed winemaking throughout Europe. Only a handful of Montalcino estates were making Brunello at the beginning of the twentieth century, when production was nearly thwarted during the First World War. After the Great War, all of Italy was immersed in poverty and there was little request for quality wine. Montalcino's vineyards lay in ruins. Tancredi Biondi Santi, whose family had created Brunello at the end of the nineteenth century, saw local wine production plummet and realized that Montalcino's winemakers needed to work together to keep the sector alive. In 1926, he founded the Cantina Sociale Biondi Santi e C., a cooperative cellar headquartered in the center of town. He invited other local growers to join him, offered them use of his cellars and equipment, and encouraged them to replant their forsaken land with Brunello vines. The united growers began replanting their ruined vineyards, but yields were understandably low those first years before vines reached full maturity. Just as the new plants began yielding better fruit and production started increasing, the most devastating wave of phylloxera attacked Montalcino's young vineyards in 1930. The area had barely recovered when Italy entered the Second World War in June 1940. By 1944, with demand for quality wines once again nonexistent and most vineyards abandoned for the second time in just a few short years, Tancredi and the other members dissolved the Cantina sociale.

The aftermath of the Second World War was even more devastating than the postwar years of the earlier conflict, and would be felt for decades. Montalcino, as all of rural central Italy, was dependent on the *mezzadria*, a sharecropper system dating from medieval times that would not be completely phased out until after a 1967 law prohibited all new contracts under this feudal arrangement. The *mezzadri*, or tenant farmers, worked a plot of land and gave a large share of everything they cultivated or profits from crop sales to the landowner. They were not specialized farmers but grew a bit of everything they needed to subsist under the system known as *coltivazione promiscua* (also called *coltura promiscua*), where rows of vines would be planted between rows of olive and fruit trees and rows of wheat that would then be cleared as soon as possible each year to make small plots of pasture land for the one or two heads of cattle the small farms possessed.

Yet by the 1950s these centuries-old traditions began to change, as Italy began its transformation from a feeble agricultural economy into an industrialized nation. Suddenly, small sharecroppers working a handful of acres could no longer survive due to the development of industrialized and specialized farming enterprises that muscled out the region's tenant farmers. The younger generation of *mezzadri*, better educated than their usually illiterate fathers and grandfathers, chafed at what was essentially a class system. Further advances in technology also destroyed the steady living of Montalcino's woodsmen, as electricity and oil replaced wood for home heating, and oil-based products, namely plastic, replaced wooden and wicker goods. This steep decline in Montalcino's two main sources of employment and revenue dragged down the local craftsmen: carpenters, tailors, and cobblers closed their doors.

While much of Italy's countryside was going through the same challenges, Montalcino was hit particularly hard. Throughout much of the 1950s, based on per capita income, Montalcino was ranked the poorest commune in the large Province of Siena, and was one of the poorest communes in the entire region. It is nearly impossible for anyone who has recently visited

Montalcino's beautiful and luxurious estates of restored stone villas and immaculate cellars surrounded by manicured vineyards, often with the owner's brand new Mercedes or Porsche parked out front, to fathom the utter misery that engulfed the area only five decades ago. In 1959 the Montalcino newspaper, *La Fortezza,* published the results of a survey on the state of local farms: "210 farms were in bad condition, 281 had no toilets, 243 were without electric lights, 281 had no drinking water, and 135 were without acceptable dung-pits."[4]

Unable to live in these repulsive conditions, a few sharecroppers courageously broke free and somehow managed to buy their own small farms, relying almost wholly on the recent access to financing. Far more farmers, however, abandoned the countryside altogether and moved to the cities to find more lucrative work and better living arrangements. If, in 1951, the consensus registered 10,203 inhabitants in Montalcino, by 1971 there were only 6,297; and this figure dropped to just 5,520 residents in 1981.

By the mid-1980s, however, Montalcino, formerly the poorest commune in the Province of Siena, had become the richest municipality in the province, thanks to the area's liquid gold: Brunello.

TWO

Temperamental Sangiovese

LOCATION, LOCATION, LOCATION

The next step to understanding Brunello is to look at Sangiovese, the sole grape allowed in Brunello di Montalcino. Though a grape with attitude—stubborn, temperamental, and difficult to tame—under the right conditions Sangiovese can yield inimitable, world-class wines, making this late-ripening variety one of Italy's most noble native vines. And although it is the country's best-documented grape, it is also the most controversial—even after a century and a half of academic studies, including recent DNA profiles, in many ways Sangiovese remains a mystery. There is still no definite word on the grape's precise origins, and Sangiovese's dizzying diversity, known as "intravarietal variability," means this grape variety demonstrates marked differences, not just from clone to clone (in viticultural terms a clone is a plant that has been reproduced directly from a bud or a shoot of a superior vine without a seed—guaranteeing the offspring will be biologically identical to the parent), but even from plant to plant. Consider also the grape's infuriating track record of wildly oscillating and therefore unpredictable results, even within the same vineyard among like clones, and it is easy to understand why Sangiovese challenges, exasperates, and intrigues winemakers and viticultural experts alike. Why then would anyone want to cultivate Sangiovese? Because when the fickle variety's numerous demands are met, as they are in select parts of Montalcino, Sangiovese offers wine lovers magnificent and memorable wines with unparalleled aromas, flavors, and intensity.

Sangiovese is often compared to Pinot Noir, not only because it is difficult and unforgiving in both the vineyard and the cellar, but also because it can yield complex, long-lived wines. The two grapes are notoriously site-sensitive, needing perfect and very specific growing conditions in order to excel, and only then do they produce luminous, ruby-garnet-hued wines of extreme elegance and depth. While Pinot Noir arguably has its ideal home in select parts and parcels of Burgundy, Sangiovese yields truly superlative wines in prime parts of the Montalcino growing zone. Thanks to its propensity to flourish at certain vineyard altitudes and in distinct microzones blessed with just the right combination of sunlight and soil composition, Sangiovese, like Pinot Noir, is a decidedly terroir-driven grape as opposed to more robust varieties, such as Cabernet and Merlot, that perform uniformly well the world over. Or as famed consultant enologist Paolo Vagaggini, a native of Siena who spent much of his early career working abroad with international varieties and who now specializes in Brunello and Sangiovese, summarizes, "When compared to Sangiovese which is tricky and easily damaged, Cabernet and Merlot are as resistant as tanks." Vagaggini cautions that anyone wanting to grow Sangiovese has to be willing to accept that this precarious grape will always suffer more than most other varieties in harsh vintages, despite even the best vineyard-management techniques. "There are going to be vintages that are too cold, too wet, or too hot and dry when no matter what measures are taken, Sangiovese won't reach ideal ripening. In such unfavorable harvests, growers have to put up their hands and just accept and work with what Nature sent down that year. Although this type of derailment is rare with most international grapes, it is part of the whole Sangiovese package," elaborates Vagaggini.

Even when vintages are favorable, Sangiovese, which is ubiquitous in central Italy and planted in varying amounts throughout the country, rarely yields the enviable combination of complexity, balance, and structure it attains in select areas of Montalcino.

Seeing that it is extremely vigorous, the vine was grown almost everywhere in Italy to fuel the country's quantity-driven wine industry that dominated the national wine scene from the 1960s until the 1980s. As a result, Sangiovese is still often associated with a myriad of uninspiring and diluted bottlings from the plains of Romagna, in the eastern half of the Emilia Romagna region, and with weedy Chianti sold in straw bottles, both of which are of little interest to wine lovers. Today, Sangiovese is still the most cultivated red grape in Italy, covering 70,000 hectares (173,000 acres) across the country and accounting for more than 10 percent of the country's total vine plantings. It is cultivated in seventeen of the peninsula's twenty regions, is mandatory in eighty-eight DOCs and DOCGs (Denominazione di origine controllata, Italy's appellation system whereby origin is controlled and regulated by the government; and DOCG, Denominazione di origine controllata e garantita, the most rigidly controlled appellation that is further guaranteed by a tasting commission), and is present in the composition of 388 DOCG, IGT (Indicazione geografica tipica, a more flexible designation than DOCG), and table wines combined.

Yet despite the grape's primary role in so many Italian wines, only Brunello di Montalcino and the town's second wine, Rosso di Montalcino, are required by law to be made exclusively with Sangiovese, confirming that the moody grape has a predilection for Montalcino's growing environment.

Sangiovese has fascinated observers for centuries. Its predominance in Tuscany, where it is mandatory in twenty-nine of the region's DOCG wines, and the fact that the variety has been given many synonyms within the region, have led many academics over the years to surmise that it is of Tuscan origin and that it has perhaps been around since the Etruscans first began fermenting grape juice. Its first written mention appeared back in 1590, in Giovanvettorio Soderini's treatise *Trattato sulla coltivazione delle viti*. Soderini, described by historians as "a gentleman from Florence," wrote that "Sangiogheto is juicy and overflows with wine" and that as a grape it "never fails,"[1] although this seems an unusual statement given the grape's notoriously fickle nature. In 1726, Cosimo Trinci referred to "San Zoveto" as "a grape of outstanding quality" in his *Agricoltore sperimentato in 1726;* while in the latter half of the eighteenth century botanist Cosimo Villifranchi defined "San Gioveto" in his *Oenologia toscana* "as the protagonist" of great Tuscan wines.[2] At approximately the same time that Villifranchi wrote about San Gioveto's primary role in Tuscan enology, poems and dithyrambs were being penned in nearby Romagna, celebrating the grape's crucial role in that region's nectar. Writers' interest in the grape continued to develop over the centuries, so that by the early nineteenth century Sangiovese had become one of the most recorded grape varieties in Italian viticultural and botanical literature.

While everyone agrees that Sangiovese is the king of central Italian wines, there has been a lot of debate over the variety's origin, with producers in both Romagna and Tuscany long proclaiming their respective regions as the vine's native home. In 1834, much to the chagrin of the Romagnoli, botanist Count Giorgio Gallesio affirmed the vine's Tuscan roots in his milestone 1834 publication, *Pomona italiana,* an in-depth catalog of Italian fruit and fruit trees. After noting the presence of Sangiovese in Romagna and its "generous wine named after the vine,"[3] Gallesio goes on to declare that despite its presence in Romagna, "Sangiovese is ... thoroughly Tuscan, and is perhaps the most prized grape in this land so dear to Bacchus."[4] The dispute has dragged on for centuries, but most authorities on the subject have sided with Tuscany, including ampelographer Girolamo Molon. In his 1906 *Ampelografia,* Molon wrote, "All ampelographers believe this vine originated in Tuscany."[5] Molon further specified that some of his esteemed colleagues even pointed to Chianti as the vine's birthplace.

However, advancements in technology have apparently uncovered the secrets to the vine's lineage that have surprised growers and researchers in both Tuscany and Romagna. Jose Vouillamoz, a researcher from Trentino's famed Istituto Agrario di San Michele all'Adige, together with several colleagues, including Professor Attilio Scienza of the University of Milan, raised eyebrows and perhaps more questions than answers several years ago when, after carrying out DNA testing on almost two thousand cultivars from an international database, they claimed that all the evidence proved Sangiovese is the offspring of another Tuscan grape, Ciliegiolo, and an obscure grape found in Campania called Calabrese di Montenuovo. These same researchers also speculated that Sangiovese is a spontaneous progeny, or that its creation occurred naturally via self-pollination and without human intervention.

In a twist one might expect in a *CSI* episode, however, more recent genetic research disputes these earlier paternity findings. In 2007 scientists at the University of Florence teamed up with their counterparts from the French Institut national de la recherche agronomique (INRA), and performed DNA testing using a far larger database of 2,786 cultivars from around the world, with a particular focus on Tuscan grapes, to try and discover the parentage and history of Sangiovese. While they agreed that Ciliegiolo is one of the closest relatives in Sangiovese's kin group, they did not accept that it is Sangiovese's father but rather the contrary. "Based on our analysis, it is far more likely that Ciliegiolo is actually an offspring of Sangiovese, and not the other way around," argues Maurizio Boselli, one of the researchers who performed the tests and who is currently a professor of viticulture at the University of Verona. Boselli and his colleagues concluded that Sangiovese's own parents are either extinct or so obscure that they were not present in the large test group. Even more surprising is that the 2007 study deduces that Sangiovese's roots lie wholly in Italy's deep south, either in Calabria or Sicily, based on close kinship with several ancient cultivars including Gaglioppo from Calabria and Nerello Mascalese from Mount Etna.[6] Despite these latest findings, one thing is certain: Sangiovese has been present in Tuscany for hundreds of years, and perhaps far longer, hypothetically transported to the region as seedlings by migrating populations any time between the tenth century B.C. and the Middle Ages.

A GRAPE BY ANY OTHER NAME

There are numerous assumptions as to how Sangiovese came about its unusual name, and one of the most common that pundits as well as historians point to is its similarity to the words *sanguis* and *Jovis,* or "the blood of Jove." This is the explanation usually given by wine producers, perhaps to impress consumers with the romantic appeal of a mystical connection to the gods, but the truth is that no one knows for sure how the name really came about. Sangiovese boasts an impressive list of over thirty accepted synonyms, with the majority hailing from Tuscany. This profusion of individual names for Sangiovese within the region has led many twentieth-century ampelographers to agree with their eighteenth- and nineteenth-century predecessors in assuming that the grape originated in Tuscany. Even today, despite strong DNA evidence to the contrary, some of Italy's most respected viticultural academics remain convinced of the grape's Tuscan roots, including renowned Sangiovese expert and pioneer into Sangiovese clonal research Dr. Roberto Bandinelli, formerly a lecturer and researcher at the University of Florence and currently vice president of the Associazione Toscana Costitutori Viticoli (TOS.CO.VIT).

Whether it originated in the region or not, Sangiovese performs the leading role in Tuscany's most illustrious denominations, where it also still goes by several aliases. It is known as Morellino in Scansano, the denomination in the region's southern Maremma zone; as Sangioveto in Chianti Classico; Prugnolo Gentile in Montepulciano; and of course as Brunello in Montalcino, where it is also known as Sangiovese Grosso. The many aliases, however, are not simply local dialect names for Sangiovese, as is often presumed. Instead, back when these remote growing areas were isolated from each other, what we now consider mere synonyms for Sangiovese were for centuries believed to be distinct and individual grapevines that had no connection to each other, or with Sangiovese for that matter. Not only do Sangiovese's numerous pseudonyms provide a fundamental link to the vine's unusual history, they firmly underscore Sangiovese's chameleon-like attributes.

This brings us to one of Sangiovese's most fascinating albeit challenging traits: its incredible variability in nearly every aspect, including morphology or form, site sensibility, evolution during cultivation, and of course, final results. According to Dr. Bandinelli, who began his groundbreaking clonal research back in 1967, "Sangiovese does not have the genetic stability of other grapes. While variations among clones of other varieties, including Cabernet and Merlot, are very subtle, the differences among Sangiovese's numerous clones, and even differences among individual plants of the same clone, especially in terms of its performance, are extraordinary." Bandinelli remembers hunting for and finding both ungrafted Sangiovese and Prugnolo Gentile toward the close of the 1960s in far-flung parts of Tuscany's most illustrious denominations, remarking, "The strong differences in the leaves alone of these two biotypes were remarkable." These notable inconsistencies in Sangiovese help explain why Montalcino's nineteenth-century grape growers all believed their own local vine was unique rather than part of the extended Sangiovese family.

History shows that until the late nineteenth century the vast majority of growers, winemakers, and ampelographers were utterly convinced that Brunello and Prugnolo were individual cultivars. In his 1866 report on grape cultivation in Montalcino, Cesare Toscani, who was part of an agricultural commission dispatched to the town the previous year, wrote, "In general the most common varieties are Canaiolo, Brunello, and Aleatico for red grapes," adding, "We would have liked to have seen, and in large quantities, Sangiovese, of which in all the places we visited, we didn't find even a trace."[7] Though we now know that Brunello is Sangiovese, the shape of its leaves and the size of both the grapes and clusters were presumably very different to those of Sangiovese in other areas. While most nineteenth-century researchers agreed with Toscani, a few had nevertheless noted a strong resemblance between Brunello and Montepulciano's Prugnolo Gentile, including Count Gallesio while he was conducting research for his *Pomona italiana*. In 1833, after studying the famed local Brunello vine in Montalcino, Gallesio wrote in his travel journals, "I believe it to be Prugnolo of Montepulciano."[8] Still others wrote of parallels between Prugnolo Gentile and Sangioveto.

To resolve the increasing questions regarding the similarities between these three varieties, in 1876 the Commissione ampelografica della Provincia di Siena (the Province of Siena's Ampelographic Commission) planted Brunello, Prugnolo, and San Gioveto (*sic*) in the same experimental vineyard. Based on their evolution in the vineyard and the characteristics of the transplanted vines, the commission concluded that notwithstanding their different names, the three vines were in fact all the same single variety. In 1879 the commission further validated their findings after they compared the wines made by each of the three vines.[9] The researchers surmised that changes in the physical appearance of the plants were generated by the specific growing conditions in individual areas. Although growers in their respective zones continued to call their vines Brunello, Prugnolo, and Sangioveto, and some continue to do so even today, the 1879 commission decided that San Gioveto (also spelled as Sangioveto) would be the variety's designated title since this was the most widely diffused name for the vine. Later, numerous other vines were also proven to be none other than Sangiovese, including Morellino di Scansano and Calabrese, grown near Arezzo. In the late eighteenth and early nineteenth centuries, the pervasive grapevine was called both Sangioveto and Sangiovese, but by the early twentieth century, Sangiovese had become the variety's official name, which should have greatly simplified things.

However, nothing is ever simple when it comes to this grape. Even though dozens of Tuscan grapes had been definitively recognized as Sangiovese, disputes over the existence of two distinct family groups of the variety still rankle growers, enologists, and academics alike. In 1825, a botanist named Acerbi wrote of two kinds of Sangiovese: Sangiovese Grosso, or big Sangiovese, and Sangiovese Piccolo, little Sangiovese. Subsequent researchers confirmed this classification, including Perrin in 1834 and Lawley in 1870,[10] though sources differ as to whether the names refer to the size of the berries or the size of the bunches. A conclusive answer seemed to come in 1879 when the Comitato Centrale Ampelografico (Central Ampelographic Committee) formally divided the variety into San Gioveto Grosso and San Gioveto Piccolo in the committee's grape guide, *Ampelografia italiana*. San Gioveto Grosso was considered superior in quality of the two, while San Gioveto Piccolo didn't mature as well and was less cultivated according to the same report. Back in Montalcino, after experiments had proven that Brunello was actually a clone of Sangiovese, both local growers and ampelographers immediately designated the Brunello vine as Sangiovese Grosso.

Many famed twentieth-century professors firmly believed in the presence of Sangiovese Grosso and Piccolo, such as Nino Breviglieri and Enrico Casini, who sustained the two family groups in their 1965 treatise on Sangiovese in *I principali vitigni da vino coltivati in Italia*. Present-day professors of viticulture still distinguish between Sangiovese Grosso and Piccolo, including Antonio Calò, president of Italy's Accademia della Vite e del Vino (Academy of Vines and Wine) and his colleagues, who confirm the existence of the two classifications in their catalog of Italian grape varieties, *Vitigni d'Italia*.

Calò and his colleagues also supported the division in their published paper "Caratterizzazione molecolare, ampelografica e ampelometrica di 30 accessioni di Vitis Vinifera L. riferibili al 'Sangiovese.'"[11] However, a growing number of critics disagree that the grape has two distinct cultivars, Grosso and Piccolo, and today, especially in Montalcino, producers are divided among those that insist their indigenous clone is Sangiovese Grosso, and therefore different (as in superior) from what they consider "mainstream" Sangiovese hailing from other areas of Tuscany and central Italy, and those that say there is no such thing as Sangiovese Grosso or Piccolo, but only Sangiovese.

Bandinelli agrees with the latter camp, affirming, "These days we feel there is only Sangiovese. We've performed trials where we have taken what is known as Sangiovese Grosso directly from Montalcino's vineyards, Sangiovese from other areas in Tuscany, as well as samples of what local growers are convinced is Sangiovese Piccolo, and planted them all in the same experimental vineyard. When grown together in the same place, any differences that may have distinguished them in their original areas disappear and they are clearly all just Sangiovese, with berries and clusters that are similar enough in size to defy any distinctions of big or little." The Brunello Consorzio agrees with the "Sangiovese only" school of thought, and in 1992 the growers' union modified the section of the production code stipulating Brunello's grape composition from the original wording of "100 percent Brunello (Sangiovese Grosso)" to "100 percent Sangiovese" (known as Brunello in Montalcino). However, Bandinelli adds that the many historic references to Grosso and Piccolo made by leading academics of the nineteenth and twentieth centuries cause him to hesitate before denying that perhaps in the past there were indeed two distinct cultivars populating central Italy. "I've never found any grapes that are similar to the Sangiovese Piccolo that have been described in great detail by many esteemed researchers, but I cannot rule out that it may have existed at one time. I have an active interest in finding it someday, even if so far I never have," admits Bandinelli.

Whether Montalcino's illustrious grape is Sangiovese Grosso or simply Sangiovese, Bandinelli does agree that original clones taken directly from Montalcino's oldest estates are the best suited for Brunello production when compared to newly selected clones coming from other parts of Tuscany or Romagna. "Clearly those clones that have had centuries to adapt to Montalcino's growing area have ancient and unique genetic compositions. They usually excel in their particular environment and can best express their terroir," explains Bandinelli. Examples of these exclusive clones selected in Montalcino's historic estates, usually in collaboration with the top universities and then propagated at leading nurseries, most often the Vivai cooperativi Rauscedo (Rauscedo Nursery Cooperatives) in Friuli, include BBS 11 from Biondi Santi's Greppo vineyards, VCR 5 and VCR 6 ("VCR" standing for Vivai cooperativi Rauscedo) from Il Poggione, CDO 4 from Col d'Orcia, and an array of clones selected in Banfi's vast vineyards including Janus 50, Janus 10, and BF 30.

INVASION OF THE CLONES

Even though clonal research into Sangiovese actually began on a very small scale, conducted mostly at the academic level at the end of the 1960s, it didn't take off until 1988 when Chianti Classico's *consorzio,* in collaboration with the Universities of Florence and Pisa, embarked on an ambitious mission to improve quality within what had turned into an ailing denomination at the time. The project, known as Chianti Classico 2000, lasted sixteen years and studied all aspects of cultivating Sangiovese, which by law must account for a minimum 80 percent of that denomination's wines, although the research has greatly benefited Sangiovese growers everywhere. Besides experimenting with vine planting densities, rootstocks, and training systems that would boost quality, the Chianti Classico 2000 campaign marked the first widescale effort to identify and select the best clones of Sangiovese, a far cry from the isolated efforts of just a handful of individuals who had funded much of the research themselves, like Biondi Santi, who aligned with the University of Florence forty years ago. As Bandinelli states, "In 1970 when I began selecting top performing Sangiovese clones in Montalcino, those from vineyards on Biondi Santi's Greppo estate, most other Tuscan growers were not interested in the research or even in the concept of trying to select individual plants. Even though the goal was to advance quality, most growers at the time felt that I was merely recovering 'old' or 'outdated' plants that couldn't possibly improve winemaking. But even more importantly, the vast majority of winemakers at the time had no interest in improving quality anyway because from the 1960s until the 1980s Sangiovese was grown almost exclusively for its quantity." Bandinelli adds that wine producers across the country greatly benefited from generous government subsidies at the time, further stimulating intentional overproduction and effectively obliterating any incentive to produce quality wines. This all changed by the mid-1980s, as consumers around the world turned away from easy drinking plonk and instead demanded structured wines of higher standards. Measures to better winemaking began in earnest across Italy, eventually leading to methodical clonal research into the peninsula's native grapes, with Sangiovese taking the lead.

There are now eighty-nine registered clones of Sangiovese, more than any other variety cultivated in Italy. Notwithstanding that all these clones have been rigorously selected for quality wine production, they are all highly individual, and their staggering disparities were highlighted at a symposium on Sangiovese held by leading Tuscan firm Ruffino in 2006, where journalists analyzed samples of microvinified wines made with single clones of Sangiovese. The wine made with clone R 24, considered the best clone from Romagna, showed bright, lightly hued ruby red colors with lovely floral aromas accented with hints of earth and spice, and vibrant wild-cherry aromas balanced with bracing acidity and firm tannins. In striking contrast, the sample made from Janus 50, one of several clones selected in Banfi's vineyards, was dark and nearly impenetrable, with marked spicy aromas and plum flavors, accompanied by noticeable alcohol and lacking in fresh acidity. It was nearly impossible to fathom that the astonishing range of aromas, flavors, and colors had all come from the same grapevine, and one wonders just how far severe clonal selection should go before varietal character is smudged. Bandinelli agrees, and during our interview cautioned that "clones should respect the intrinsic character of the vine while improving varietal defects, but they should not alter the essential character of the variety."

The most important goal of clonal research into Sangiovese is improving and stabilizing quality in what is undeniably a capricious and at times an infuriating variety. Disease control is the main focus, and identifying individual plants with looser bunches is crucial because less compact bunches allow air and light to pass through, thereby offering better resistance to many fungus diseases. Looser bunches have the added benefit of allowing in more light, giving even berries in the middle of the bunch a chance to reach full phenolic ripeness. Choosing less productive clones that naturally provide higher concentration in this prolific variety without resorting to costly yield-reducing labor, like green harvesting, is also critical, as is choosing biotypes that ripen earlier in order to avoid damage brought about by autumnal storms that can wreak havoc on late-ripening Sangiovese, which is particularly susceptible to rot thanks to its thin skin. Though combating these singular and vexing problems with Tuscany's celebrity grape is an urgent motive for conducting extensive clonal research, another reason frequently cited by producers is to "improve" Sangiovese's natural color. On this point, I strongly disagree.

While Brunello should never be as delicately colored as, say, a humble *rosato,* by the same token it should never be forced into the black, inky distortions that for years have reaped the top scores from several self-acclaimed critics, who, despite their supposed expert status, evidently don't know the first thing about Sangiovese. Like Nebbiolo and Pinot Noir, Sangiovese simply does not contain naturally high levels of anthocyanins, which are what give grapes, and then wine, their color, but this does not mean that wines made exclusively with Sangiovese are defective lightweights. On the contrary, a fine Brunello's power, finesse, and aging potential are undeniable. Judging a wine then by universal standards that apply to many international grapes, as tasters do in most international wine competitions, can unnecessarily penalize many great wines made entirely or predominantly with Sangiovese, as well as wines made with Nebbiolo and Pinot Noir. In these competitions, where the tastings are blind, judges have no idea what is in the glass before them. Using the color criteria for a quintessential Cabernet can prove catastrophic for Brunello. Case in point: while a bright, deep ruby or garnet color is the perfect shade for young and modestly aged Sangiovese, respectively, these would be weak showings for Cabernet, Merlot, or Syrah, and even more so for Sagrantino di Montefalco from Umbria, all of which have high anthocyanin levels, hence their deep violet, and oftentimes almost opaque appearance.

Judging all wines by universal benchmarks set by international grapes has caused Brunello and other pure Sangiovese wines to be castigated by many critics for not having a more Cabernet-like appearance, when in reality they ought to be praised if they have an exemplary shade of their natural color and instead penalized when they are purple and nontranslucent, since this is a defect for pure Sangiovese, demonstrating either severe overextraction during vinification or, more likely, blending with other grapes. Sangiovese's natural color is characterized not only by its cherry-colored hue but also by its intense luminosity. Wines made entirely with Sangiovese, as Brunello is (or at least, as it is supposed to be), should be bright ruby red in their infancy, deepening toward garnet and tending toward brick hues after years of aging, with the best Brunellos keeping a more youthful appearance even as they age.

At its best expression, a well-made Brunello's natural color is like that of a precious gemstone, with a dazzling, light-reflecting brilliance, while many of those purple, stagnant, and impenetrable wines so often lauded by some of my colleagues instead look like tawdry costume jewelry when compared to the vivid ruby-garnet beauty of Sangiovese. Ironically, consumers have been nearly brainwashed by the media into assuming densely pigmented, nontranslucent wines are of superior quality and that more delicately hued wines are weaker or inferior. Nothing could be further from the truth when it comes to Brunello. Bandinelli agrees: "It is time consumers realized that darkly colored, opaque wines do not guarantee top quality."

Even though some of these newer superclones have pushed Sangiovese to the darker limits of its natural color, overall the new generation of biotypes, widely planted for only a few years, have already helped smooth out the sometimes angular and astringent characteristics that can plague Sangiovese. Yet despite the great strides in clonal research and better vineyard management, Sangiovese remains an irritatingly demanding grape. It can still produce wines that suffer from excessive acidity and green, unripe characteristics when planted further inland in cooler, wetter climates, or can yield excessively jammy, tannic, and one-dimensional wines when cultivated in hot, low-lying plains. It is interesting to note that while native grape Nebbiolo is showing what a number of winemakers around the world (excluding the proud Piedmontese of course) consider interesting results, Sangiovese planted internationally in places like California and Australia has generally disappointed despite the new clones, which do not offer a quick fix for would-be growers. Unsurprisingly, most New World producers have stopped experimenting with the exasperating variety. Even Tuscan winemaking scion Piero Antinori has apparently given up his Sangiovese dream for California. Antinori, who spent years hunting for just the right Napa Valley property that he believed would make a good host to Sangiovese, thought he had found the perfect location at Atlas Peak, a rugged piece of land that reminded him of his native Tuscany, where he planted Sangiovese clippings reportedly taken from Montalcino. After nearly fifteen years of trying, he has publicly admitted he was unsuccessful with Sangiovese in California and has since converted nearly all of his Sangiovese vineyards to Cabernet and Chardonnay.

So while the newly selected clones, combined with rigid vineyard management practices that should include planting several different clones of Sangiovese in the same vineyard, have greatly improved quality in areas that already showed a high or at least suitable vocation for growing the fickle grape, they have not enabled Sangiovese to produce quality wines everywhere in Tuscany, in other regions, or outside of Italy. In other words, clones will never eradicate the fundamental role that growing areas play in Sangiovese cultivation, especially apparent in Montalcino, where Sangiovese excels in select areas but not in others despite the new superclones.

Terroir, that ambivalent term borrowed from French and which refers to the importance of the vineyard's natural environment, may now be the most overused term in winespeak. Opinions vary as to the significance and even the existence of terroir, but the importance of place and what it imparts to Sangiovese is irrefutable. Whether because of its warmer Mediterranean climate that favors ripening, or thanks to the higher altitudes that generate a slow ripening season, which in turn creates intense aromas, or as a result of the extremely complex soils that yield structure, Sangiovese grapes grown in Montalcino's best sites produce wines with an unbeatable combination of power and grace that the variety grown elsewhere, even in other parts of the denomination, can never match.

The large production zone itself boasts marked contrasts in growing conditions and these have a profound effect on local hero Sangiovese, still further testament to the indispensable role of terroir. Immediately south of the tiny walled town, Montalcino's oldest wine-producing estates are located among the highest reaches of the denomination and are noted for making complex Brunellos of great longevity. In stark contrast, Brunellos hailing from more recently planted low-lying vineyards in the far southern expanses are rounder and fuller-bodied with markedly higher alcohol content and lower acidity. Approachable sooner, they are generally not as age-worthy as their northern or high-altitude relatives.

Even taking into account the striking disparities between Montalcino's various subzones, growers throughout the denomination tend to use many of the same tried and true vineyard techniques, from vine training to rootstocks.

BRUNELLO VINEYARD MANAGEMENT

Although it is nearly impossible to generalize on just about any other aspect of Brunello production, because a producer's individual stylistic preferences will ultimately dictate many of the specific techniques winemakers employ, vineyard trellising is a common denominator in Montalcino. The favored vine-training system for Brunello production, and the most common for Sangiovese throughout central Italy, is *cordone speronato,* the low, spurred cordon method also called cordon spur, where a permanent branch, the so-called cordon, is trained horizontally along a wire stretched between poles.

The cordon, which is never pruned completely down, sprouts fruit-bearing canes that are then cut back each year, or spur pruned, and most Brunello producers generally leave two nodes known as spurs that generate new fruiting canes each year. Even though one of the primary benefits of this training system is that it facilitates mechanized pruning and harvesting, many of Montalcino's estates still perform most if not all vineyard maintenance by hand, although more and more producers are now using some mechanization for pruning and canopy management. However, just about all of Montalcino's firms claim to rely on an entirely manual harvest for Brunello, though some of the largest firms with extensive tracts of flat and low-lying vineyards do say they resort to mechanical harvesters for their Rosso di Montalcino and for their Sant'Antimo bottlings.

According to Tenuta Le Potazzine's Giuseppe Gorelli, who like all the best Brunello estates works his vineyards and harvests entirely by hand, the spurred cordon system is preferred in Montalcino not so much for its suitability for mechanized vineyard management but because it "best regulates the plant's production of grape bunches." Although both the double and single cordon techniques are diffused in Montalcino, Gorelli, a trained enologist and agronomist and one of Montalcino's most dynamic young producers, uses a single branch trained along a wire off to one side of the trunk of the grapevine, as opposed to the double cordon that stretches in both directions on either side of the trunk. "I prefer the single cordon because the grapevines are much closer to each other with this method, about 70 to 80 centimeters apart, while with the double cordon the distance between grapevines is about 140 to 150 centimeters apart. With the plants so close to each other using the single cordon, the roots compete for water and nutrients, and this naturally regulates and controls the plant's grape production," explains Gorelli. For Laura Bernini, an agronomist who works throughout central Italy including at Montalcino's Gianni Brunelli estate, another advantage of the spurred cordon is that it "favors a uniform leaf canopy, as well as encouraging mature vines to produce smaller bunches."

While spurred cordon now dominates in Montalcino, according to Gorelli, Guyot training was widely present in the growing area in the 1970s and 1980s, but has long since been abandoned because it pushed Sangiovese to produce too many clusters and too many berries, even though it had interesting results in terms of ripening and vine health. Most experts agree with Gorelli. An experiment between Sangiovese trained on spurred cordon and Sangiovese trained on Guyot conducted over a two-year period at leading

Chianti Classico estate Isole e Olena confirms that cordon spur gives superior results for Tuscany's preeminent variety. According to a thesis written by Alessandro Moretto, who conducted the research for his Ph.D. earned at the University of Pisa, "Spurred cordon, even at different densities, produces superior grapes when compared to those trained with Guyot."[12] Moretto specifies that based on the trials, the Guyot-trained grapes produce heavier bunches, while spurred cordon yields smaller grapes with more polyphenols and much more anthocyanins when compared to the Sangiovese trained with Guyot.

Andrea Macchetti, the managing director, enologist, and agronomist at Mastrojanni, a foremost Brunello estate, may have found the solution to Guyot's previous defects although at the moment he is one of the very few advocates of the technique in Montalcino. Although spurred cordon is used in the firm's older vineyards, vines planted after 2002 are now trained on a modified Guyot trellis system. "For all new plantings, I now use a type of double Guyot that is reduced to three buds on each side, giving it the appearance of a fork," says Macchetti. "Guyot designed like this reduces the number of bunches, making it easier to control production and to accurately select the bunches, overall leading to more stable quality. Spurred cordon on the other hand doesn't produce great quality in the first few years, and after just fifteen years, it starts to lose some of its positive characteristics and ages faster," argues Macchetti. He further points out that while the cordon was "born from the desire to use more mechanization in the vineyards, the fork-designed Guyot can only be worked manually."

Planting density is also crucial for quality wines, and while many of France's best appellations have planted at very high densities for many years, even up to ten thousand vines per hectare, Tuscany lagged dreadfully behind on this issue although it has caught up over the last few decades. Planting at high densities entails cultivating more vines per hectare, and the increased competition among so many plants forces the vines to produce fewer and less compact bunches, reducing the amount of grapes per plant. The lower number of bunches per vine increases sugar content and concentrates both color and tannins in the berries, which are also smaller because they contain less water. Up until the 1980s, the days when grape quantity rather than quality was the guiding principle in all of Italy, low planting densities dominated across the country and in particular central Italy, where plants were loaded down with numerous bunches of large, swollen grapes that unsurprisingly produced watered-down wines. Lower densities were also more common back then thanks to the large distance left between rows, up to 3 meters (10 feet), enough to allow the far larger and bulkier tractors from this period easy access to the vineyards. These days, producers across Italy plant their vineyards to maximize quality rather than to accommodate farm equipment, which has adapted over the years to the decreasing space among rows. Most producers in Montalcino plant new vineyards at densities far higher than the days of yore, and a number of estates are experimenting with very high densities, though on the whole Brunello growers stay well under the 8,000 to 10,000 vines per hectare now common in other wine-growing zones.

In fact most Brunello producers cite 5,000 vines per hectare (2.47 acres) as the optimal density for Montalcino, saying this gives Brunello the best balance. Many of Montalcino's oldest vineyards, like those planted in 1936 at Biondi Santi's Greppo, or even those planted in the 1960s and 1970s at Il Poggione and Case Basse, were planted at old densities ranging from 2,220 to 3,300 vines per hectare, though these are now the exception, and the advanced age of the vines has also regulated these plants to produce fewer grapes that in turn yield very concentrated juice. For new vineyards, Brunello growers say 5,000 plants per hectare is enough to give Brunello its concentrated flavors and structure, but not so high as to cause severe water or heat stress, an important consideration given that irrigation, even emergency irrigation, is not permitted for Brunello production.

According to agronomist Laura Bernini, high-density planting is key to quality because it also encourages reduced vigor of the canopy, and she adds that a small, balanced canopy, which favors optimal photosynthesis, is essential for optimizing grape quality. The canopy also protects grapes from excessive sunlight, again crucial for Brunello due to the lack of irrigation. So what is Bernini's ideal density for Brunello? "There is no single, perfect planting density for Sangiovese, which is very sensitive to soil, climate, and microclimate," states Bernini. She does concede, however, that, as a very general rule, "A standard range for Sangiovese is fixed between 5,000 and 7,000 plants per hectare. Within this spread, the final density depends on specific growing conditions. In Montalcino between 5,000 and 5,800 plants per hectare is usually recommended for those microclimates or soils that are at risk from summer heat and water stress, while in the higher, fresher areas growers can plant a maximum of 7,000 vines per hectare," elaborates Bernini. She further emphasizes that at densities exceeding 7,000 plants per hectare "Sangiovese is more difficult to manage and is more exposed to the problems generated by heat and/or water stress."

Giuseppe Gorelli, whose average plant density at his Le Potazzine estate is 5,000 vines per hectare with his newest vineyards planted at a higher rate of 5,952, agrees that 5,000 is the benchmark in Montalcino. "In Montalcino this is generally considered the ideal number for producing the right amount of grapes per hectare. For example, in 2009, our vines produced about fifty-six quintals per hectare, which averages out to less than one kilo per plant," says Gorelli. He adds that some producers have experimented in Montalcino with extremely high densities, even up to 12,000 plants per hectare, but due to the fierce competition among vines, it has taken over fifteen years for the vines to adapt to these extreme conditions before they began to show results.

Choosing the right rootstock is still another fundamental decision for growers. Ever since phylloxera, the voracious aphid that was accidentally imported into Europe on American grapevines in the latter half of the nineteenth century, munched its way across the entire continent and nearly wiped out Europe's wine production, European *Vitis vinifera* grapes have been grafted onto American rootstocks, the only solution to phylloxera. Until just thirty years ago, there were very few rootstock choices available, and once again, it was the Chianti Classico 2000 project that conducted cutting-edge research into testing and selecting new rootstocks, and above all in combining the right clone with the right rootstock based on specific growing conditions. Some of the most interesting results include rootstocks that increase sugar production, such as 110 R and 41 B. In Montalcino, however, 420 A is still the most common for Brunello production and has actually been used in the zone for years because, according to growers, it is one of the best at keeping Sangiovese's infamous vigor in check, even in chilly years and in cool, loose soil, conditions that can fuel Sangiovese's natural tendency to overproduce. While 420 A is the rootstock of choice for most of the denomination, in parts of the growing zone where vines are planted in dense, compact clay, known locally as *crete,* growers also use Paulsen 775, which helps curb the massive tannins Sangiovese develops when planted in very thick clay.

GREEN HARVEST, HARVEST, AND HANG TIME

Reducing yields by removing leaves and shoots as well as by cutting off already developed bunches to increase quality and keep vines within their strictly regulated production limits is now a common practice in much of Italy and has become a standard technique for prolific Sangiovese. The main reasoning behind the technique is that when plants send all their energy into a few remaining bunches they generate more concentrated juice, whereas when they disperse their resources among a high number of grapes more-diluted wines result. If just a few short decades ago most growers or their farmhands, who were just emerging from the poverty that had gripped rural Italy for generations, refused to throw out perfectly good fruit, reducing yields in this manner has become almost an obsession for many Brunello estates that have gone to the other end of the spectrum, enthusiastically thinning out grape bunches in order to attain overly intense concentration. Recognizing that severe green harvests can produce unbalanced wines with low acidity and very high alcohol, some Brunello producers are instead turning to other methods to reduce production that don't compromise the plant's natural balance. Besides the better clones, higher planting densities, and more suitable rootstocks described above, other yield-reducing techniques include canopy management, very short winter pruning, bud removal, and drastically cutting down on or even banning fertilizer, allowing plants to regulate themselves.

In Montalcino, Sangiovese usually reaches ideal ripening between mid-September and mid-October, although, according to producers, climate change that has slowly pushed temperatures higher over the last decade or so has pushed the harvest forward by a couple of weeks across the denomination. These higher summer temperatures have actually helped ripening in the cooler elevations, while they are accelerating the growing season in the hotter southern reaches with low-lying vineyards, producing wines with higher alcohol and lower vibrancy and complexity. When exactly a producer begins harvesting for Brunello strongly depends on the various subzones, with grape picking in the hottest parts of Sant'Angelo commencing on average about ten days to two weeks earlier than in the higher, fresher areas of the original growing area closer to Montalcino.

These days, nearly all producers decide when to harvest on the basis of analytical tests conducted on grapes that measure not only sugar and acidity levels but also phenolic development, which indicates ripe tannins and the amount of anthocyanins that help growers determine the best time to harvest. The final choice of when to harvest also hinges on what style of wine a firm wants to produce. For example, producers looking for longevity and finesse prefer to pick not only when tannins are ripe but also when acidity levels are still rather high, since fresh acidity is one of the main factors behind the marathon longevity of the most vaunted Brunellos and Riservas.

Other producers, however, pick when acidity is far lower, wanting their wines to be more approachable upon release even if this means they sacrifice some aging potential. Since about the mid-1990s, many of Montalcino's producers have been crafting bigger, overripe Brunellos that many winemakers feel are favored among the media and New World palates. To further exaggerate this extreme style, some producers leave their grapes on the vines well after optimum ripening, an extended hang time if you will. While this method, and the massive tannins and bracing alcohol it produces, may work for many wines around the world, I think most connoisseurs, hence Brunello lovers, are seeking not only power but also balance and finesse, which are eclipsed by overmaturation of Sangiovese. It is just one of the ways that Brunello's *tipicità* or quintessential character is becoming compromised.

When the Brunello harvest finally does begin, even the largest estates in Montalcino say theirs is strictly a manual harvest. Though for the denomination's numerous smaller and mid-sized estates, costly machine harvesters are out of the question for economic reasons, Montalcino's producers cite quality as the motive for handpicking when it comes to Brunello. Despite the vast improvements in the newest machine harvesters, when it comes to selecting only the best grapes to go into Brunello, technology is still no match for the human eye.

DISEASES

Sangiovese across central Italy is particularly prone to several fungus diseases, particularly oidium, also called powdery mildew, and Brunello vines are no exception to the ravages of the disease, which growers keep under control with sulfur-based treatments. Another fungus disease, *mal dell'esca* (also known as black measles in the United States), is perhaps the most devastating of all the diseases afflicting Sangiovese, and in Montalcino it seems to target the oldest vines. At present there is no cure, and this fatal condition is one of the major reasons why some of the denomination's oldest vineyards have been replanted with more resistant clones in recent years.

THREE

Birth of a New Wine

Brunello di Montalcino is far younger than its once more eminent neighbors, which have been vaunted for several centuries or even two millennia. For example, Montepulciano was already referred to over two thousand years ago when Livy wrote in his *History of Rome* that the Gauls had been lured to the area because of Montepulciano's wines; and eighth- and fourteenth-century documents attest to Montepulciano's thriving wine industry, producing what we now call Vino Nobile di Montepulciano. Chianti also has a long, rich history. The area's famous wines spurred Cosimo III de' Medici, the Grand Duke of Tuscany, to delimit the Chianti zone in 1716, along with three other winemaking areas, Pomino, Carmignano, and Val d'Arno, creating Italy's and the world's first controlled wine denominations.

Montalcino had been celebrated for its white Moscadello as far back as the sixteenth century, long before Brunello would catapult it to the forefront of the Italian wine scene and into the hearts of wine lovers around the world. In 1550, Leandro Alberti, a friar from Bologna, wrote that Montalcino was "well known for its good wine that comes from those pleasant hills." Though Alberti doesn't specify red or white, based on later chronicles we can surmise that he was probably referring to Moscadello, the sweet white wine for which the town became famous. In the seventeenth century, several accounts extolled the hilltop town's golden nectar. In 1644, while on his way from Siena to Rome, English traveler John Evelyn wrote of "Monte Alcino, celebrated for its rare Moscadello." The most important recognition came in 1685, when Francesco Redi lauded the "Divine Moscadello of Montalcino" in his dithyramb *Bacco in Toscana* (Bacchus in Tuscany), which celebrated Tuscany's most illustrious wines, including Chianti and Vino Nobile. Between 1676 and 1677, the Grand Duke of Tuscany sent an auditor by the name of

FIGURE 4. Panorama of Montalcino's rolling hills and vineyards taken from Church of Madonna del Soccorso in Montalcino. Photograph by Paolo Tenti.

Gherardini to the Province of Siena on a routine inspection of the different communes. According to the report, Gherardini noted that Montalcino's Moscadello boasted "delicacy and subtlety" and that the Moscadello grapes were grown in terraced vineyards along the steep hill just beneath the city. Gherardini made no mention of red wine, and (a surprising detail) he alluded to grapes grown in dedicated vineyards rather than in fields of mixed agriculture that dominated the Tuscan countryside under the *mezzadria*.[1]

The first records of a wine actually called Brunello, on the other hand, hail only from the 1860s. Clemente Santi, a pharmacist and renowned writer of natural history and agricultural practices, spent most of his time at his Greppo estate in Montalcino, where he not only made award-winning Moscadello that received honorable mention in 1867 at the World's Fair in Paris, but also experimented for years with red winemaking. In 1854, at the Esposizione dei prodotti naturali e industriali della Toscana (Exhibition of Natural and Industrial Products of Tuscany) held in Florence, Santi presented two bottles of his "vino rosso puro 1852," or pure red wine, which presumably meant that Santi did not include any white grapes in the blend. This was a significant breach of custom; adding white grapes was a common practice for red winemaking in Tuscany until a surprisingly short time ago, and although it seems unthinkable, white grapes are still permitted today in some of the region's red DOC and DOCG wines, but more on that later in the chapter.

Brunello's earliest and perhaps most significant recognition came in 1869, when Clemente Santi won two silver medals for his "vino rosso scelto (brunello) del 1865," at Montepulciano's agriculture fair, as the award diploma on display today at the winery attests. This addition of the term *Brunello,* the first written documentation that referred to a wine and not the grape, begs the question of whether the wine was made exclusively with Sangiovese, which was then called Brunello in Montalcino and for years was thought to be a distinct grape variety. Unfortunately, we will never know for sure, but it is safe to say that the variety at least made up a very strong percentage of the wine given the addition of the name Brunello to the wine.

What is clear, however, is that Santi's passion for viticulture, combined with his background in chemistry, allowed him to greatly improve on the primitive vineyard practices and winemaking methods of the period, which proved to be fundamental for Brunello's future. In the many letters and articles he wrote during his lifetime for the leading academic agricultural journals of the day, Santi criticized several contemporary vineyard practices, such as completely stripping the grapevines of their leaves, presumably after the harvest, which not only harmed the plants for future vintages but robbed the soil of potassium from fallen and decomposed leaves. Santi also warned against methodically harvesting too soon, before grapes were fully ripened, another routine custom that lasted well until the latter half of the twentieth century in central Italy. Peasants harvested early primarily to get the grapes in before roaming thieves helped themselves or before autumn storms destroyed the harvests. The tenant farmers also picked early in order to turn the harvested rows into makeshift pastureland, a common practice under the mixed agriculture system of the times.

Though *coltura promiscua,* mixed cropping, predominated in Tuscany in the nineteenth century and the better half of the twentieth, it was clearly understood even then that rows of vines planted in the middle of fruit and olive trees, surrounded by wheat, did not beget quality grapes. In his research on Montalcino's agriculture, *Sulla cultura dell'agro montalcinese e specialmente quello che sono e che potrebbero essere le vigne,* published in 1866, Professor Cesare Toscani wrote, "In the most densely cultivated areas, not even an inch of land benefits from the sun's rays." He further notes, "With the exception of a small example on one of signor Santi's farms, a real vineyard cannot be found in the entire territory of Montalcino." Vittorio

Degli Albizi, of a noble Florentine family and who grew up in Burgundy, realized the drawbacks of mixed agriculture when he returned to claim his Tuscan properties, including the magnificent Pomino estate, now part of the Frescobaldi empire because Albizi's sister (and heir) had married into the Frescobaldi family. In his treatise on Italian wine published in 1867, Albizi noted that "rarely has Nature been so generous in terms of climate, sun exposure, and in the varied soils and slopes" that Tuscany boasted.[2] The reason behind the general inferiority of Tuscan wines was due to the mixed cultivation, according to Albizi, who declared, "To make good or fine wine you need good or fine grapes, which can only be possible with exclusive grape cultivation." Contemporary records show that Clemente Santi, who according to Toscani's report already had at least one dedicated vineyard as of 1866, analyzed other parts of his property in 1869 for potassium levels, most likely as an indicator of where to plant a vineyard. Still other records show that by 1875 Santi was selling vine cuttings to other producers, a sign of an increased and specialized grape production.

While the lack of exclusive grape cultivation in real vineyards suppressed quality winemaking, the rudimentary cellar techniques of the first half of the nineteenth century also played a key role in the prevailing mediocrity that enveloped the region's wines. One of the biggest challenges of the day was the exceedingly short life span of Tuscan wines. As Ignazio Malenotti wrote in his *L'agricoltore istruito dal padron contadino,* published in 1815, "the only defect of Tuscan wine is that of having a very brief life; it dies in its infancy." For Montalcino, one of the most isolated areas in the entire region, this meant that wines could not survive the arduous trip to Florence let alone travel by ship to distant or foreign markets. While winemakers across the region and particularly in Chianti and Montepulciano tried to rectify this problem with the *governo* (also known as *governo all'uso toscano*) method of refermenting wines with partly dried grapes to raise alcohol and beef up structure that would give wines some short-term durability, Clemente Santi instead advocated improving quality through fundamental changes in basic winemaking techniques. He disagreed with the enological wisdom of the day that called for a brief fermentation, which Santi argued was fine for white wines, especially if they were sweet, but was not suitable for red wines. Reds, he contended, need a complete fermentation on their skins to impart color, structure, and stability, all of which are essential to extend a wine's life span.

Santi's enlightened methods of winemaking, which also included experimenting with barrel aging, were obviously successful, judging from the accolades he amassed for both his red and his white wines. In 1871, Santi and other leading farmers of the town, including Galassi and Giuseppe Anghirelli, united and formed a wine society, the Società Enologica di Montalcino. That same year, all three producers, represented under the banner of the Società along with their own names, won prizes for their individual Brunellos at the Fiera Italiana, held in Florence, and at other national wine fairs. Other Brunello producers of note appeared at about this time, including Tito Costanti, who presented a red wine, also referred to as Brunello, at a wine exhibition in Siena in 1870. No one knows, however, what grapes were in these early Brunellos. In addition, the term was applied equally to wines four and even five years old and to wines that were only a year old. However, in 1876, an important agricultural journal referred to a "wine made solely with Brunello in 1875—Collina di Montalcino (Montalcino Hill)—by Giuseppe Anghirelli—tasted after one year,"[3] leaving no question that this wine was made exclusively with Brunello (or Sangiovese) grapes.

Despite these pioneers, Ferruccio Biondi Santi, Clemente Santi's grandson, is credited as the father of modern-day Brunello. Ferruccio, who as an adventurous seventeen-year-old volunteer fought with Garibaldi's forces at the infamous Battle of Bezzecca in 1866, was a fascinating figure, and was obviously used to taking risks. A highly accomplished painter and a man of undeniable culture, he did not, however, leave many detailed records of why he decided to concentrate all his efforts on red wine production in an area so famed for its white wine. The young enologist, who was already running the Greppo estate before his grandfather's death in 1885 and who later united the names Biondi and Santi in honor of his maternal grandfather, learned a great deal from Clemente's experiments. With this unparalleled knowledge base Ferruccio took both viticulture and winemaking to the next level.

On several occasions, in academic journals and in his published letters, Clemente Santi had expounded on the ravages that oidium, or powdery mildew, inflicted on the Moscadello grape, and this may be one of the reasons why Ferruccio focused on red grapes. Other observers speculate that perhaps Ferruccio thought that Sangiovese would be more resistant than Moscadello to the looming threat of phylloxera. What is known for certain is that Ferruccio identified Greppo's best-performing and most disease-resistant plants of a particular cultivar of the Brunello vine that grew on the estate. The grape at the time was known locally as Brunello, meaning "small dark one," because of its size and because of the deep color the skins developed on fully ripened berries. Until the late nineteenth century Brunello was thought to have been a distinct variety, but research later proved that the Brunello grape is part of the extended Sangiovese family and biotypes originating from Montalcino are also called Sangiovese Grosso (see chapter 2). Once Ferruccio singled out the healthiest and top-performing Brunello grapevines, he then carried out a massal selection by taking cuttings from these plants to propagate a new generation of vines. Unlike clonal selection, vines hailing from massal selection are the progeny from a number of vines, and while they may be from the same family and share the same genetic material, plants are not identical.

The young aristocrat conducted his avant-garde experiments during one of the most challenging and frightening times in European viticulture. In the latter half of the nineteenth century, oidium and then peronospora, two fungal diseases imported from America on vine cuttings, ravaged Europe's vineyards. But these diseases would seem like child's play once phylloxera, a root-sucking parasite also imported from America, munched its way across the continent. By the end of the nineteenth century, the louse threatened to wipe out all of Europe's vineyards and its entire wine industry. At the time that Ferruccio was busy concentrating on producing full-bodied red wines with longevity, most growers and producers across Europe were spending all their energies and resources on trying to defend their vineyards.

Reports and documents compiled by the Monte dei Paschi bank in Siena indicate that Ferruccio applied for and won one of eight places in a competition financed by the bank to plant dedicated vineyards. The bank's reports indicate that in 1877 Ferruccio cleared a hectare of his land north of Montalcino and planted his Scarnacuoia vineyard exclusively with "Sangioveto e Brunello," as was stipulated by the conditions attached to the bank's financing of eight experimental vineyards throughout the Province of Siena in an attempt to improve the local winemaking industry. While Ferruccio planted Sangioveto and Brunello, other vineyards financed by the bank were apparently planted with Sangioveto and Canaiolo.[4] For Scarnacuoia's Brunello vines, it is presumed that Ferruccio used the best clones that were the offspring of the mother vines he had singled out by massal selection, confirmed by the bank's reports in 1879 that state the vineyard was cultivated with "grapevines originating from shoots" and that "the plants were well selected." The bank's records further demonstrate that Ferruccio's vines were trained low, "to capture the heat accumulated in the soil," and that planting densities were very high for that time.[5]

Planting vineyards exclusively with "Sangioveto and Brunello," which furthermore were clearly separated in two distinct sections of the vineyard, was a milestone for Tuscan wine, not only because nearly all farms in the region at this time adhered exclusively to the mixed cropping system, but also because the majority of farmers customarily planted a mix of grapes, field selections if you will, of both red and white varieties interspersed within the same vineyard. It is not specified, however, if Ferruccio in 1877 had already grafted his carefully chosen Brunello clones and his Sangioveto onto American rootstock, the only remedy against phylloxera, especially given that (according to contemporary chronicles) the louse had not yet arrived in Tuscany, although by 1877 it was widely known that the insect had already wreaked havoc in France.

It is quite possible that Ferruccio and his grandfather, who was still alive at the time, would have been carefully following the well-publicized events in France as well as the experiments and promising initial results of grafting native vines onto American rootstock. It is highly likely that the forward-looking young landowner would have already grafted his vines on American rootstock in Scarnacuoia when he planted in 1879. Records show that, in 1882, Ferruccio, who was already short pruning his vines down to only two buds to control vigor, found several vines that had mysteriously died. Fearing phylloxera, either because the vines were ungrafted or because this experimental method was still not an entirely proven solution, he notified the local ampelographic commission, which determined that the vines had not been attacked by the aphid but had instead died because the recently dug drainage system was too deep.[6] While the latter vineyard remains somewhat of a mystery, it is certain that by the end of the nineteenth century Ferruccio had indeed replanted his other vineyards with his selected estate clones of the Brunello vine grafted onto the wild American rootstocks. More than a century before it would become an accepted practice in other denominations, Biondi Santi began making full-bodied wines from 100 percent Sangiovese, defying the Tuscan tradition of making wines by blending several grapes, both red and white, that were intended for immediate consumption.

This was, after all, the period when Chianti, then the region's and perhaps Italy's most famous and lauded wine, was made according to Baron Ricasoli's "recipe," which called for a mix of red Sangiovese and Canaiolo grapes to be blended with white Malvasia, which would later be substituted by the inferior and extremely vigorous Trebbiano variety that was cheaper and easier to cultivate. At that time red wines were extremely harsh as a result of antiquated winemaking methods of the day, which included vinifying the entire grape bunch—even the stalk—since the vast majority of Tuscan winemakers had never considered destemming, and malolactic fermentation was unheard of, making the use of white grapes a necessity to soften what were highly tannic and angular red wines, especially if they were to be consumed young. Given the enormous advances in winemaking knowledge and technology that have greatly improved red (and white) wines since Baron Ricasoli's day, it is shocking that white grapes were not merely allowed, but remained mandatory in Chianti Classico until 1996. When Classico broke away from the larger Chianti denomination that same year and created its own appellation, it immediately began phasing out white varieties, banning them altogether starting with the 2006 vintage. Perhaps even more surprising, white grapes, though no longer mandatory, are still allowed for both Chianti and Vino Nobile, although very few producers would admit to using them these days.

Realizing a century ahead of his contemporaries that great red wines could not be made by adding white grapes, Ferruccio Biondi Santi not only shook up the status quo by making red wines solely with Sangiovese; he also made naturally full-bodied wines with aging potential without resorting to the aforementioned *governo* process, which was widely diffused in the region at the time. Instead, Biondi Santi destemmed his wines before pressing the grapes (his son Tancredi and grandson Franco used this same late nineteenth-century wooden destemmer for a number of years), and began aging his wines in large Slavonian oak barrels for years to tame aggressive tannins. A few of these ancient casks, meticulously maintained, are still in use at the winery today. Ferruccio Biondi Santi bottled and commercialized his Brunello, decades ahead of other winemakers, who either made wine just for family consumption or sold their ready-to-drink wines in bulk by the barrel or, more commonly, in large glass demijohns. The oldest bottles of Brunello in existence today are Ferruccio Biondi Santi's 1888 and 1891 Riservas, still in excellent shape in 1994, the last time a few of the remaining bottles were opened and tasted by the press at a vertical tasting held at the estate, which is still run by the family.

At the turn of the twentieth century, according to the 1902 edition of the *Guida vinicola della Toscana,* only three producers were making Brunello: Ferruccio Biondi Santi, and Raffaello and Carlo Padelletti. According to numerous award diplomas, however, Riccardo Paccagnini was another pioneering Brunello producer, winning several important competitions in both Italy and France, including a gold medal in Bordeaux in 1904 for his 1894 Brunello. Paccagnini, who was born in Montalcino in 1854 and graduated with a degree in agriculture from the University of Rome, went on in 1907 to publish a highly acclaimed treatise on grape growing and winemaking, *Trattato teorico: Pratico di agricultura ed enologia,* based on his thirty-six years of experience in Montalcino. Although no one knows why, this trailblazing producer who won over forty awards for his wines sold his farm in 1917 and moved away from Montalcino.[7] Of the original Brunello makers who presented their wines along with Clemente Santi at fairs across Tuscany and Italy in the 1870s, Galassi and Anghirelli had also disappeared by the turn of the century, or at least their Brunellos had. Costanti's Brunellos also vanished from record at the beginning of the century, but the family would eventually revive their Brunello making in the mid-1960s.

What appear to have been trials or just a fleeting moment for other landowners had instead become a serious business for Ferruccio Biondi Santi, who consistently made Brunello from at least 1888 until his death in 1917, at which time his son Tancredi, by now a trained enologist who also held a degree in agronomy from the University of Pisa, took over. Although Tancredi spent much of that first year away fighting in World War I, upon his return in 1918 he not only continued to make Brunello but also implemented even more rigid standards than his father's. The wine's rarity and costly production inspired Tancredi's steep price tags that made Biondi Santi Brunellos and, even more so, the estate's Riservas the most expensive bottlings in Italy at the time—and the Riservas remain so today. That Tancredi was able to implement such strict quality measures and maintain stratospheric prices during one of the bleakest periods in Italy's history, during and after the two world wars, is not just extraordinary; it underscores the enologist's single-minded determination as well as his undying confidence in the remarkable quality of his Brunellos.

According to data obtained by the Consorzio, in 1929 Montalcino boasted a whopping 925 hectares of specialized vineyards, though no one can say for sure if these were all planted with Brunello, and 1,243 hectares of vines in promiscuous fields, before nearly all were razed in 1930 by phylloxera. Montalcino's many small *poderi* (farms) lay in ruins and the town's wine production was at a standstill. During this difficult period, in 1926 Tancredi and other local growers , including Fratelli Crocchi, Padelletti, and Tamanti united together and formed the Cantina Sociale Biondi Santi e C. This cooperative cellar, which used Tancredi's well-furnished vinification and aging cellars in the center of town, made Brunello until 1944, but no Riservas because the majority of the other winemakers wanted quicker returns. The

Cantina Sociale had its share of success and was already exporting Brunello to the United States in the early 1930s, as soon as Prohibition was appealed.

In 1932, a delegation formed by Italy's Ministry of Agriculture came to Tuscany to outline the boundaries within the Chianti zone, and while they were in the area they also visited Montalcino. In its follow-up report, the commission declared that Brunello was "a recent creation of Dr. Ferruccio Biondi Santi of Montalcino."[8] From the late nineteenth century to the years following World War II, less than a handful of wineries produced Brunello, and most of these only sporadically. According to records, local historians, and local storied producers, it appears that only the Biondi Santi family has steadily produced, bottled, and commercialized Brunello since the end of the nineteenth century.

In the early 1930s several of Montalcino's leading firms staged a comeback. Besides Biondi Santi e C.'s cooperative cellar, La Fattoria di Sant'Angelo in Colle (once a single estate comprising what is now Il Poggione and Col d'Orcia), Fattoria dei Barbi, Fattoria di Montosoli owned by Guido Angelini, and Fattoria di Argiano all began presenting their wines, including Brunello, at numerous wine exhibitions in Tuscany and other parts of Italy. The Brunello revival was exasperatingly short-lived, however, as Italy's entry into World War II in 1940 once more stymied production. Not only were local farms again neglected by farmers who had been called to serve in the conflict but in 1944 the Front passed right through Montalcino, laying waste to the countryside before the occupying Germans moved further north with the Allies close on their heels. Thankfully, earlier that same year Tancredi and Franco Biondi Santi walled up the family's old Riservas to protect them from marauding soldiers, an episode that was related for the first time ever in my book *Franco Biondi Santi: The Gentleman of Brunello*. Surprisingly, no one had ever asked Biondi Santi how he protected these precious bottlings, and he apparently hadn't given the episode much importance. Yet hiding these aged Riservas would prove crucial to the denomination's future, when, years later, these rarities were opened during exclusive vertical tastings at the estate, perfectly demonstrating the uncanny aging ability of Brunellos from select areas of Montalcino.

In 1944, with virtually zero demand for quality wines and the vineyards in shambles yet again, Tancredi and the other members of the Cantina Sociale disbanded, and that same year Tancredi built a new cellar at his Greppo estate. While the other producers apparently ceased production, or in the case of Padelletti suspended it for decades, Biondi Santi carried on at his new winery at Greppo, and 1945 brought one of his finest Riservas. Economic recovery was slow, and very little solid evidence exists of producers besides Biondi Santi making Brunello from the mid-1940s until the mid-1950s, yet by the latter half of the 1950s other producers, including Fattoria dei Barbi, had begun producing Brunello. Despite the miniscule production, by the mid-1950s people in high places had not only heard of Brunello; they demanded it for their special occasions—including Amintore Fanfani, the prime minister of Italy, six different times between 1954 and 1987. According to Marco Trimani, one of Rome's leading wine merchants, in 1954 Fanfani, a proud Tuscan by birth, decided to serve Brunello di Montalcino at an official luncheon at Rome's Villa Madama. "The problem was that the caterer had never heard of Brunello di Montalcino, and asked us to get it. I was dumbfounded because I had never heard of it either, and I thought I knew all the best Italian wines," laughs Trimani today. After searching all of Rome and coming up empty-handed, Trimani explains that the only reference he could find was in a 1932 *Guida gastronomica d'Italia,* published by Touring Club Italia, and decided to take a train to Florence to find "this rarity." After a lengthy search, Trimani found it and shipped the needed quantity of the only Brunello he could find, Biondi Santi, to Rome. "My father was not at all pleased, because at the time I paid 950 lire per bottle of Brunello, when a top Chianti Classico was around 150. He told me I was insane!" recounts Marco. Yet again according to Marco, the quality of the wine was so exceptional and the feedback from the luncheon so enthusiastic, Trimani, after meeting with Tancredi, was soon selling the wine in his shop in Rome, finally exposing Brunello to the capital's many connoisseurs.

FOUR

Brunello Comes of Age

Information for the late 1950s and early 1960s is scarce and fragmented, but according to local history, between ten and fifteen growers were cultivating Brunello grapes by the close of the 1950s and a few more producers effectively joined ranks with Biondi Santi and Fattoria dei Barbi by eventually making and bottling the wine, including Poggio alle Mura, then owned by the Mastropaolo family, and Il Poggione. Brunello's growing production and fame coincided with Italy's first serious effort at reining in the nation's fragmented and hitherto largely uncontrolled wine sector. In 1966, Brunello was among the first tier of elite Italian wines to be controlled under the country's new DOC (Denominazione di origine controllata) system, the government's attempt to regulate quality wines modeled after France's AOC (Appellation d'origine contrôlée). Besides Brunello, other celebrated Italian wines that formed part of this original lineup included Piedmont's Barolo and Barbaresco and neighboring Vino Nobile di Montepulciano. While the advent of the DOC was met with enthusiasm in all of these other illustrious denominations and encouraged investments in their respective areas, ironically production initially went down in Montalcino. If, in 1967, a year after Brunello became DOC, there were 76.53 hectares (189 acres) of vines registered to Brunello production, by 1968 the number had fallen to 56.24 hectares (139 acres), and remained stationary in 1969. In 1970, this figure rose to 74.84 hectares, and in 1971, burgeoned to 156.50 hectares. What finally convinced local farmers and growers to invest in Brunello?

Many local historians, such as Ilio Raffaelli, Montalcino's mayor from 1960 until 1980, and several storied producers (and not just the Biondi Santis), refer to the publicity generated by a now legendary state dinner, held at the Italian Embassy in London in April 1969, that apparently compelled a number of farmers to become Brunello growers and producers almost overnight. Giuseppe Saragat, then president of Italy and well known as a wine connoisseur, decided to serve Brunello Biondi Santi 1955 to the attending dignitaries, one of whom was Queen Elizabeth. According to press reports following the event, the wine was a sensation among all the guests, including the queen. A number of small farmers and larger landowners, who so far had seemed deterred by Brunello's rigorous production code, which included buying expensive oak casks and aging the wine for more than four years before release, evidently took notice of the publicity and became ardent Brunello producers, hoping to cash in on the wine's success and promising future. The sudden explosion in vines registered to Brunello production in 1970 and 1971, four and five years after the DOC took effect, certainly supports the hypothesis that it was this now storied dinner in 1969, and not the newly imposed DOC, that finally spurred Brunello production.

From the outset, Brunello has been controlled by one of Italy's strictest production codes, and in terms of mandatory aging before release, Brunello's production code is still perhaps the most demanding in the world. When it first became DOC, in 1966, Brunello had to be aged for a minimum of four years entirely in wooden casks. Even in 1966, Brunello's vinification and aging had to take place exclusively within Montalcino's territory to guarantee origin. However, while Brunello DOC, in place from 1966 until 1980, had to be made with "grapes of the Brunello vine" (Sangiovese Grosso), producers were also permitted to "correct" the wine with "up to 10 percent must or wine from other zones."

This measure was fought by Montalcino's established producers but in the end was passed in order to allow those growers and bottling estates that had only recently planted and whose young vines did not yet generate enough sugar concentration in the grapes to reach the minimum 12.5 percent alcohol stipulated under the production regulations. This measure also helped those producers who still had inferior vines planted in the old *coltura promiscua* fields that had not yet been grubbed up and replanted as specialized vineyards, which also suffered problems with grape maturation and reaching the minimum alcohol level. Although Brunello's pioneering 1966 regulations prohibited Brunello vineyards from being higher than 600 meters (1,968 feet), due to the difficulty in grape ripening at this altitude, the rules unfortunately did not set a minimum altitude for vines, perhaps the gravest mistake of the otherwise demanding regulations. However, the original production code did specify that only "hillside vineyards of Eocene origin are considered suitable," which by definition automatically excluded lower terrains generated in more recent geological eras. For better and for worse, several of these original rules were changed in 1980 once the DOCG regulations came into effect and in subsequent modifications to the production code (about which I will have more to say later in this chapter and in chapter 5).

After the advent of the DOC, Montalcino's growers and producers formed an association, the Consorzio del Vino Brunello di Montalcino, that would not only promote Brunello in Italy and abroad but whose main role would be to monitor production—and above all quality—in a farsighted attempt at safeguarding the wine's prestige. The Consorzio became active in 1967; the majority of its twenty-five founding fathers (listed in appendix B) had been tenant sharecroppers only a few years before. For the most part these ex-*mezzadri* were completely inexperienced in the art and technique of quality winemaking, but what they lacked in experience they made up for with driving ambition and determination. According to a few of the still surviving original members, the group needed twenty-five members to create the growers' union, and several of those who initially joined did not even have vineyards at the time but only wheat fields, others a mixed bag of promiscuous cultivation. Fortunately the newly formed association included several small and medium-sized landholders who were already bottling and selling Brunello, made either with their own grapes or with the vinified wine they bought from the Brunello growers that they then aged and bottled in their own cellars.

The majority of the estates that created the Consorzio are still producing Brunello, proudly considering themselves part of the ranks of Montalcino's "historic" firms that were already established Brunello producers years if not decades before the denomination became overrun by outside investors. Surprisingly absent from the lineup of the Consorzio's founding fathers is Tancredi Biondi Santi, who had played a major role in writing up Brunello's stern production code that formed the backbone of Brunello's DOC regulations. Originally Tancredi Biondi Santi had been called upon to preside over the developing *consorzio*, but right away a controversy arose that soon became a battle. The majority of emerging producers fought to have a second wine that would also fall under the protection of the Consorzio. Seeing that most of these peasant-farmers-turned-Brunello-producers had little in the way of winemaking equipment or aging barrels that they had to purchase in order to set up their new activity, the economic sacrifice of waiting over four years before they could sell Brunello made their dreams of becoming producers of

Montalcino's flagship wine nearly impossible. Many of the growers in 1966 also had to wait while their newly planted Sangiovese vines reached maturity before they could produce berries with enough concentration to meet Brunello's minimum alcohol and dry extract requirements, pushing the first economic returns from eventual Brunello sales even further into the future.

The group members decided among themselves that producers should be permitted to make a second wine from the same Brunello plants that could be released only a year after the harvest and that had no mandatory wood aging, allowing faster economic returns—especially important during this crucial start-up phase. While Tancredi agreed with the concept and the necessity of a second wine, its name evidently infuriated him. The other united producers voted to call this less prestigious bottling, the precursor to today's Rosso di Montalcino, "Vino Rosso dai vigneti di Brunello" (Red Wine from the vineyards of Brunello). Believing that this blatant exploitation of the good Brunello name for what was then a humble table wine would confuse consumers and damage Brunello's burgeoning reputation, Tancredi proposed the name Rosso di Montalcino. When his suggestion went unheeded, Brunello's most storied producer left the Consorzio just before it became active in April 1967.

Back in these formative years for Brunello production, the Consorzio members realized that they needed guidance, seeing that the majority lacked winemaking knowledge and preparation. In the early 1970s, the group enlisted the services of Giulio Gambelli, one of the most respected and well-liked figures in the Italian wine world, who would consult for the Consorzio members until the end of the 1990s. Surprisingly modest given his enormous talent, Gambelli is without a doubt a Sangiovese genius. Known in Italy as the *maestro assaggiatore,* or master taster, in reference to his extraordinary palate, as of 2011 the eighty-six-year-old Gambelli was still consulting for cult Brunello firms Case Basse, Poggio di Sotto, and Il Colle, as well as the celebrated Montevertine firm in Radda in Chianti. Gambelli is not officially called an enologist, for the simple fact that he never had any academic enological training, but was instead discovered while still a young teenager by the late Tancredi Biondi Santi. It seems that Tancredi was so impressed by the fourteen-year-old's tasting capabilities that he hired him as a cellar assistant, first at the Enopolio cooperative winery in Poggibonsi, where Biondi Santi consulted, and later at Greppo, giving Gambelli his unique and unsurpassed training as a Sangiovese specialist.

During the first of his many years working for the Brunello Consorzio,

Gambelli was joined by yet another venerable Montalcino personage, Bruno Ciatti, a trained agronomist who worked for the agricultural inspectorate. In the mid-1960s, Ciatti organized courses in Montalcino, at which he taught farmers and property holders the delicate arts of pruning and grafting vines—which at that time were done directly in the fields rather than at the nurseries. Ciatti was the first person to run the Brunello Consorzio, starting in 1967, and continued to do so until the organization created the official role of director some years later. He went on to become president of the Consorzio from 1974 until 1982. Veteran producers retain fond memories of working with both men, and several have underscored the crucial role Ciatti played in keeping production in check during his time with the Consorzio. As Nello Baricci of the eponymous winery surmises, "Over the years the Brunello growing zone expanded too much. Under the direction of Dr. Ciatti, many areas were deemed unsuitable for Brunello cultivation, but by the early 1980s several of the larger firms were able to have their way and plant where they wanted since they wield a lot of power within the Consorzio."

The two technicians would visit Montalcino's cellars, together or separately, and offer assistance and advice. Gambelli, whose main job was to try the wines and consult on the winemaking process, has always claimed that besides avant-garde vinification techniques, perhaps the most fundamental rule he learned from Tancredi Biondi Santi was the absolute importance of hygiene in the cellar, knowledge that we now take for granted but that was a groundbreaking concept in Italy back in the 1970s and even the 1980s, and a rule that Gambelli passed on to Montalcino's incipient Brunello makers. As he recalled in an interview with Italian journalist Andrea Gabbrielli about his early days in Montalcino, "I used to go from one winery to the next to taste the wines: at the time they were mostly transformed stables and stalls, with all the imaginable problems. Above all, there was still the odor of livestock but also of salami and ham because many people back then had the custom of seasoning these meats in their *cantine*. Slowly, growers built new, modern wine cellars."[1] According to Stefano Campatelli, who has been the Consorzio's director since 1990 and who occasionally accompanied Gambelli on his visits, "Giulio would visit all the cellars at least once a year, and we organized his visits for the spring, when he would visit over a hundred wineries in less than two months. His advice was very much appreciated even by firms with in-house enologists, but since most wineries at the time did not have an onsite enologist, Giulio's advice was a crucial moment for the producers to review the evolving wines."

At about the time that Ciatti and later Gambelli were advising and training the burgeoning winemakers, international critics were discovering the greatness of Brunello. In 1966, British wine writer Cyril Ray wrote in his landmark book *The Wines of Italy,* "Brunello is so big that it is aged in cask for five or six years before bottling, thus acquiring more staying power, and is then kept in bottle for two years before being put on the market." Famed Italian writer, film director, and wine connoisseur Mario Soldati, in the first volume of his cult series on Italian wines, *Vino al vino,* published in 1969, wrote of Biondi Santi's Brunello, "In its category their product has no rivals, not even among the most celebrated Barolos and Burgundies." By the early 1970s, according to several accounts published by Burton Anderson, a celebrated American wine critic, Brunello's fame began to spread beyond Italy's borders. Anderson's tasting of Biondi Santi's 1964 Riserva in 1971 inspired him not only to write his first wine article, "Wine for People with Patience," published that year in the *International Herald Tribune,* but to eventually transfer from Paris, where he had been writing for the leading international newspaper, to Tuscany, where he dedicated himself full-time to writing about Italy's wines.

Wine lovers and collectors were hunting down the few available bottles of Brunello, and investors began rushing to the hilltop town to cash in on the wine's flourishing reputation. Brunello production skyrocketed and for decades its only direction was up. While there were only thirteen bottlers in 1967 making an estimated 150,000 bottles, in 1975 a total of 800,000 bottles were made by thirty producer-bottlers, and by 1979 these figures jumped to 1,500,000 bottles made by forty-three wineries.[2]

BRUNELLO: COMING OF AGE

A rather sanitized version of Brunello history, often reported by more than a few estates in Montalcino and by many factions of the international press, goes something like the following.

In the 1960s and 1970s, Brunello was an obscure wine being made by a number of small estates that struggled with quality issues. On top of this, Montalcino's winemakers had no marketing skills; hence the world knew nothing about the wine and probably wouldn't have liked it anyway, because even the best Brunellos needed years to soften up before they could be approached. All this changed when, in 1978, two American brothers of Italian origin swooped down on Montalcino, practically jumping out of their low-hovering helicopters just before they hit the ground in their unbridled enthusiasm to teach the natives a thing or two about modern winemaking and promotion, and because they were so eager to start making easy-drinking but high- quality wines for the American market. In doing so these two brothers heralded a new era for Montalcino that saved the denomination from oblivion. Later, the enormous winemaking firm founded by this same pair began the most advanced clonal research, hitherto a foreign concept in the denomination, the results of which they generously shared with their neighbors, while their commitment to safeguarding the environment has always been downright commendable. Thanks to massive investments in vineyards and the construction of an industrial-sized cellar, the firm began turning out technically perfect Brunellos on a scale never seen before, making Brunello one of the most sought-after Italian wines in the world.

As with all myths and legends, there is both some truth along with a good measure of invention, convenient forgetting, rewriting, and even denial in this now widely accepted version of Brunello's recent history, although to be fair no one has ever even hinted that anyone had ever jumped out of a still-hovering helicopter. Though the reality of this period is somewhat different than the PR-generated press releases, it is an undeniable fact that the arrival of John and Harry Mariani, founders of Villa Banfi, later renamed Castello Banfi, opened a new chapter in Brunello's history and that Banfi not only brought the Brunello name to wine lovers and wine drinkers across the globe, but that it also brought a hitherto unimagined cash flow into the denomination and generated countless local jobs. However, the firm also set what has become a dangerous precedent in the denomination of cultivating vines in unlikely areas, and in almost unthinkable quantities for Brunello. It could be argued that the firm initiated the era of the good, the bad, and even the ugly in Montalcino—depending on one's point of view.

By the time the Mariani brothers, who had made their fortune importing cheap and easy-drinking Lambrusco into the United States, arrived in Montalcino in 1978 with their Piedmontese enologist and managing director, Ezio Rivella, other large firms had already set up operations in the denomination. These included a group of European investors who began making Brunello at CastelGiocondo, as well as the Marone Cinzano family, who had acquired Col d'Orcia in 1973, not to mention the considerable volume already generated by historic producers Fattoria dei Barbi and Il Poggione. The Marianis' immense firm in the extreme southwestern corner of the denomination, in an area known as Sant'Angelo Scalo, eventually totaling 2,830 hectares (6,990 acres), with a total of 850 hectares (2,100 acres) under vine producing a total of 10 million bottles a year of various wines, would dwarf them all. The Marianis bought vast tracts of land, most of which according to locals had never been under vine before but had instead been cultivated with crops. These observations are supported by an exhaustive thesis on land cultivation in Montalcino, which reconstructed land usage for 1822, 1954, and 1994. While the 1822 interpretation relies on land registers, the 1954 and 1994 maps were created based on aerial photos and maps. According to the authors, in 1822 and 1954, most low-lying land in this extreme southwestern area was in fact dedicated to crops and pasture land, while the more elevated areas were covered with woods. The 1994 map demonstrates great expanses of vineyards in the same areas.[3]

After acquiring the land, the ambitious brothers promptly got to work on bulldozing and leveling the hills in order to have easier-to-manage vineyards in a landscape they seemed to model after parts of California, much to the consternation of other landowners and residents. Italian opinion makers of the day, including influential wine critic Luigi Veronelli, were horrified, as were the other local producers—and rightly so. Geologists who have analyzed the effects of vine cultivation in Montalcino say razing the hills in this corner of the growing zone has wrought dire consequences, namely an increase in soil erosion, already a primary concern throughout the denomination. Land leveling also caused other, more immediate damage as well. As Professor Edoardo Costantini told me in an interview, moving large quantities of soil "caused a strong decrease in landscape and bio-diversity, the alteration of water-table equilibrium, and a general increase in soil vulnerability." He added that because this section of the denomination dates from the Pliocene epoch, it is very rich in marine deposits, and that drastically manipulating the soil has forced this underlying salt up to the surface, creating "a less than ideal environment for grapevines." It should be pointed out that Brunello was not Banfi's main focus when the Marianis first came to Montalcino and snapped up vast acreage of low-lying land in the hottest part of the township. Their original intention was to specialize in yet another easy-drinking wine, a sparkling Moscato that they wanted to call after Montalcino's native Moscadello, and which they thought would be perfect for the U.S. market. Accordingly, they planted a reported 350 hectares (865 acres) of Moscato vines sent down from Asti (located in Piedmont) and dedicated only a fraction of their vineyards to Brunello vines, much to the ire of local winemakers who had been working relentlessly to promote Brunello. Not only did the imported Moscato vines suffer in their new environment; to make matters worse, American tastes took a sharp and evidently unexpected turn toward full-bodied red wines. Despite having geared nearly every aspect of their ambitious Montalcino project for mass white wine production, in the early 1980s, the firm regrafted its "Moscadello" vines with Sangiovese and other varieties. Quality eventually improved, in part thanks to the firm's purchase of the Poggio alle Mura property in 1984 and its cru-worthy vineyards, and later thanks to the results yielded by Banfi's intensive clonal research into Sangiovese.

Montalcino's winemakers were quick to point out, however, that the majority of the firm's low-altitude vineyards, accompanied by Sant'Angelo Scalo's scorching temperatures, were not ideal for Brunello vines, and further grumblings soon began within the denomination in reaction to the anticipated consequences of mass Brunello production at the industrial-sized Banfi, leading some of Montalcino's estates to perhaps fear the possibility of a "Brunello on ice, how nice" advertisement campaign. The firm's planting of massive amounts of international grapes in many of their lowest vineyards, as well as the creation of irrigation pools, did not help alleviate the locals' suspicion and anger, but many newcomers, by now flocking to Montalcino, applauded Banfi's business and marketing approach.

BRUNELLO INAUGURATES THE DOCG

The 1980s were a pivotal time for all of Tuscany, and while the "Super Tuscans" from Bolgheri and the Chianti Classico zone may have broken down barriers with their rebel wines that shook up antiquated wine laws and seemed to dictate Italy's winemaking future, Brunello continued to captivate wine lovers and critics from around the world. In 1980 Brunello was the first wine promoted to Italy's brand new designation, DOCG (Denominazione di origine controllata e garantita), a move that had been in the works since 1973 once Brunello producers realized that the DOC was already hopelessly outdated and inadequate, having become more a question of politics rather than a safeguard or guarantee for quality wine regulation.

Besides undergoing an analytical tasting test and stricter controls, other key changes that came with the DOCG's production code when compared to Brunello's original DOC regulations included the reduction in maximum grape yields from 100 quintals per hectare to 80, while the maximum yield of grapes to wine after aging was reduced from a minimum of 70 percent to 65 percent. The DOCG also reduced mandatory wood aging from four to three and a half years. Yet the most fundamental change was the elimination of the stipulation that had previously allowed the addition of up to 10 percent wine or must from other zones to "correct" Brunello. However, under Italian law, which does not allow chaptalization (adding sugar to increase alcohol levels), producers can add concentrated musts to increase alcohol content up to 2 percent, and each year the individual regions decide whether the practice should be allowed or banned depending on vintage conditions. Tuscany nearly always allows the practice.

Brunello's regulations do not specify that concentrated musts have to come from within the Montalcino denomination, as is clearly stated in the regulations of other top denominations, including Chianti Classico and Barolo, but according to the Brunello Consorzio specifying this is not necessary seeing that the laws governing all DOC and DOCG wines ban the use of concentrated musts from outside the denomination of origin, and in Brunello's case, from vines other than Sangiovese. However, Brunello and all other DOC and DOCG wines can use rectified concentrated musts from anywhere because these concentrated musts are processed to become completely neutral in terms of color, taste, and aromas. Yet according to most producers, since the start of this century, thanks to gradually rising temperatures and drier conditions during the growing season, naturally reaching the minimum alcohol levels is far less of a problem than in the past and as a result they are using concentrated musts to a lesser degree or forgoing them altogether.

After Brunello's inaugural and prestigious "promotion" to Italy's ambitious DOCG with its stricter quality controls, investors, entrepreneurs, and industrialists flocked to Montalcino to try their hand at making Brunello. By the late 1980s, Brunello's distinctive status and panache perfectly embodied the pride of the Made in Italy campaign, promoting the good taste and élan of the best quality products made in the country, giving it the aura of a luxury item. Real estate prices for vineyard land within the denomination, as well as prices for the wine itself—both already high compared to the rest of Tuscany and most of Italy—soared. Translated from Italian lire into euros, if a hectare of Brunello vineyards cost €11,730 in 1977, by 1987 this figure jumped to €50,140.

The 1980s brought a heightened wave of investment to Montalcino: in 1968 there were fewer than 80 hectares dedicated to Brunello but by 1988 nearly 875 hectares had been planted with registered Brunello vines. In terms of production, in 1968 the denomination produced little more than 2,000 hectoliters of Brunello from thirteen producer-bottlers. In only twenty years, eighty-four producer-bottlers were turning out nearly 40,000 hectoliters, though some of this was most likely declassified to Rosso. By the end of the decade, demand outstripped supply, only adding to the wine's allure. Brunello had become the gold standard of Italian wines and seemed destined to remain a hard-to-get yet much-sought-after commodity. As Burton Anderson noted in his 1990 *Wine Atlas of Italy*, at the end of the 1980s, "Sales seem to be leveling off at 1.5 million bottles per year, little more than half the quota of Barbaresco and a quarter of Barolo." It should be noted that these sales figures correspond to vintages produced earlier in the decade that were released at the end of the 1980s.

Brunello had become the buzzword in Italian wine, and eager producers wanted to make and sell as much wine as the market demanded. In the mid-1990s, now considered Brunello's golden era, 125 producers were churning out on average more than 3 million bottles a year, and though the amount varied according to the vintage, it seemed unlikely at the time that this figure would rise significantly. Then, in 1997, with the market clamoring for still more Brunello, producers successfully petitioned to reopen the denomination's sealed vineyard registers. This gave each estate the possibility of expanding their Brunello plantings by a further 8 percent of a firm's total amount of land already cultivated with registered Brunello vines, though all estates were automatically guaranteed a minimum increase of 1.5 hectares (3.7 acres). While this expansion was most likely sufficient to satisfy the seemingly insatiable demand, unfortunately for the denomination, that same year the European Union passed EU Regulation 950/97.

The decree, also known as the Law for Young Entrepreneurs, was designed to attract a new generation into Europe's waning agricultural sector, and gave planting rights and grants for land to those under forty. Both the 1997 opening of the Brunello vineyard registries as well as EU 950/97 were duly exploited in Montalcino, especially the latter, not only by new investors but even more so by already established wine estates, whose owners sold or handed the firms over to their children and divided the land and assets among them, creating two, sometimes even three separate firms, and in turn applied for their increased acreage allowed under the new statutes. The subsequent period of unchecked planting that followed between 1997 and 2002 quickly brought proven vineyard areas to the saturation point, and growers began cultivating areas never before considered adequate for Brunello production, most notably on the plains but also just above riverbanks, next to railway lines, and even in the dense, compact clay in the northeast of the denomination. Add to this the growing influence of the Super Tuscan phenomenon, which suddenly garnered the brightest media spotlight in Italy, and the latter half of the 1990s began a period of intense changes for Brunello.

FIVE

Boom Years and the Loss of Tipicità

By the 1980s and 1990s, when more and more affluent Italians, foreigners, and highly successful wine producers from other parts of Tuscany, such as the Frescobaldis and later the Antinoris, were investing in Montalcino's golden slopes, parcels and plots of land in the original growing areas around Montalcino had become increasingly difficult to acquire. Many turned their attention to the more southern areas lying between Tavernelle and Sant'Angelo, as well as to the southwest around the hamlet of Camigliano and to Castelnuovo dell'Abate in the far southeast. Seeing the sudden interest in their districts, many local farmers who had never before cultivated grapes on their land also decided to plant Brunello vines rather than sell up. Some of these newly exploited parts of the growing zone, particularly in and around Castelnuovo dell'Abate, have proven capable of yielding gorgeous Brunellos with delicious ripe fruit that make them quite friendly while still boasting complexity and aging potential. Brunellos originating from the low and lower lying areas to the extreme south and southwest around the railroad stations of both Sant'Angelo Scalo and around Pian delle Vigne-Camigliano hailed the advent of a discernibly different version of Montalcino's famed wine that was naturally darker hued, with ripe black fruit sensations, noticeably higher alcohol, and less fresh acidity and therefore less vibrancy, all due to the lower altitudes and hotter temperatures. This new breed of Mediterranean Brunello proved to be much bigger, softer, and more approachable sooner than its more northern counterparts from the middle and high altitudes closer to town, which were generally more elegant, austere, and age-worthy. To complicate what was becoming an increasingly confusing wine scene in Montalcino, confusing because at the time almost no one ever discussed the need to start zoning within the vast territory (a subject that remains nearly taboo even in 2011), the emergence of distinct Brunello styles that stemmed from widespread expansion into new parts of the denomination coincided with the advent of drastic winemaking preferences that were to have a radical effect on all of the region's wines.

As the first order of business after snapping up property, the wealthy newcomers who landed in Montalcino in the 1980s and 1990s built modern wineries outfitted with the most advanced equipment, including temperature-controlled stainless steel fermenting tanks and climate control throughout the cellars. Having little if any regard for local tradition, the majority of the rich industrialists-turned-winery-owners, as well as several of the renowned producers arriving from outside of the denomination, opted for new 225-liter French *barriques* that were increasingly becoming the fashion. Seeing that they were often absent from the wineries for long periods while they ran their empires elsewhere, and could not closely follow their new winemaking activities, the majority of recent arrivals hired outside *consulenti*, the jet-setting enologists that for a price could make any style of wine the owner wished. All of this stood in stark contrast to Montalcino's typical late 1960s- and early 1970s-era wineries, some of which were still housed in former-stalls-turned-*cantine*, and to the modest operations set up by ever more *montalcinesi* (people from Montalcino) joining in the local gold rush. But if the older generation of Montalcino winemakers was aghast, especially at the new French barrels and flying winemakers, members of the younger set were intrigued. By this time a number of growers and producers had passed their farms and wineries down to their offspring, who not only had more education and winemaking skills than their parents but, thanks to Brunello, more funds. The 1980s and 1990s saw a good number of the denomination's second-generation producers completing fundamental cellar renovations or slowly building new facilities, and some of these young and ambitious producers also made their way to France. Their trips, almost always to the great châteaux of Bordeaux rather than the small estates of Burgundy, with the exception of the illustrious Domaine de la Romanée-Conti, inspired Montalcino's post-sharecropping generation with big aspirations and new ideas, including the conviction that international varieties should at least be experimented with, while more than a few became convinced that Tuscany's traditional botti (large Slavonian oak casks that impart less wood sensations than smaller French barrels) had had their day.

Besides being held up as the ultimate quality benchmark, that Bordeaux and its wines and later those from Bordeaux-inspired California monopolized the attention of wine critics around the world was surely a fundamental reason why so many of Tuscany's winemakers showed such an elevated interest in the illustrious region. Estates in Bolgheri as well as various producers in Chianti Classico were already having some success trying to emulate Bordeaux blends, often adding native Sangiovese to the mix, and were perhaps well on their way toward Super Tuscandom when winemakers across the region received final proof that Tuscany + Cabernet + other international grapes + barriques = worldwide success.

While it may be too simplistic to cite any one event as the final push toward Super Tuscan mania that catapulted so many wine critics and winemakers into the kind of gushing enthusiasm that teenage girls usually shower upon the latest teen idol, it is no coincidence that when Sassicaia 1985 won almost ecstatic worldwide acclaim upon its release in 1988, the Super Tuscan craze suddenly invaded not just all of Tuscany but nearly every region in Italy. Both new and storied estates across the region and later the country threw themselves headlong into planting international varieties. In near record time, in the country with the most native grape varieties in the world, producers were not only planting countless acres of Cabernet, Merlot, Syrah, and Chardonnay, but they were often grubbing up their indigenous varieties in order to so.

American wine critics and, later, other international wine writers, perhaps daunted by the vast array of uniquely Italian wines made by indigenous vines they knew little or nothing about, were soon favoring these new wave wines made with international grapes or international grapes blended with Sangiovese. Dubbed the Super Tuscans, these darker-colored wines aged in French barriques had similar aromas, flavors, and full-bodied structures of quintessential Bordeaux-inspired Napa Valley wines. They were therefore easily recognized and embraced by these influential palates that were, however, inexperienced in Italian vines and wines.

Phrases such as "inky black," "jammy," and "massive" appeared as glowing praises, along with "awesome," "fruit bomb," and "oaky." The most influential Italian wine guides followed the cadre of international critics and apparently agreed that these new world wannabes and Bordeaux imitations were far more interesting than their own great Brunellos, Barolos, and Barbarescos. Collectively, these wine writers dedicated huge amounts of space loaded with admiration and praise on the country's bottlings made in part or wholly with international grapes that boasted the layers of wood-driven vanilla, coffee, and chocolate flavors these critics adored. The more an Italian bottling tasted as if it hailed from Napa Valley, the more the critics raved about it. Winemakers across Tuscany, hoping to cash in on all the success, were quick to plant French varieties and trade in their botti for all new barriques, which in those early years they used unwisely to say the least. Barriques soon became the wood of choice for any winemaker who wanted the coveted ninety-plus points from those wine writers who associated pronounced wood sensations with good winemaking, and wide use of the small French barrels automatically spilled over into the traditional denominations. In the case of Sangiovese, the intense chocolate, vanilla, and toast nuances of new oak weighed down the variety's vibrant, cherry-berry, and mineral sensations, while the drying wood tannins imparted by exclusive use of new oak, clashed with the grape's naturally bracing tannins. What most winemakers and wine drinkers now consider an outworn trend—not to mention overblown and evident winemaking—was conceived as "modern" and innovative at the outset. More importantly, this blustering style virtually guaranteed critical acclaim and success.

Even though the phenomenon was not confined to Tuscany, storied denominations in other regions showed more resistance to what a strong core of producers in their respective wine zones saw as intense pressure to dumb down their wines to suit the perceived preferences of international palates. In Piedmont, for example, where it is notoriously difficult to obtain land because of the intense attachment inhabitants there have to even a lone surviving row of a long-abandoned vineyard, most Piedmontese would rather die than sell property to outsiders. The result is that the majority of Piedmontese producers today tend to be third- or fourth-generation grape farmers as well as the only winemakers at their small estates, and while traditions in the region are often violated, they are rarely dismantled overnight without a battle, despite some legendary though isolated exceptions. Throughout Tuscany, on the other hand, newly arrived entrepreneurs and outsiders with no attachment to tradition easily acquired land from locals who were more than eager to sell. For these reasons, if by the early 1990s Barolo was in the heated throes of what later became known as the Great Wine Wars—where a host of defenders of classically crafted wines dug in and defended their age-old customs against a new generation of younger winemakers advocating internationally styled Barolos—in most of Tuscany it was more a question of mass surrender.

BRUNELLO TAKES A WALK ON THE DARK SIDE

Brunello—for decades the darling of the Italian wine world—was not immune to the trend, though it was one of the few Tuscan denominations where a strong minority bravely resisted the pressure to change course and to invest in anonymous wines and winemaking. These dedicated Brunello producers included Franco Biondi Santi, Gianfranco Soldera, the Lisini family, and even relatively recently arrived Piero Palmucci of Poggio di Sotto, as well as a host of lesser known producers who until the middle of the first decade of the new century had almost been completely shunned by the press, including Alessandro Mori of Il Marroneto, Florio Guerrini of Il Paradiso, Maurizio Lambardi of Lambardi, and many others. Even if the Super Tuscan phenomenon can be justly credited with waking up many groggy Italian denominations from their hangovers brought on by decades of bland industrial winemaking—such as Chianti Classico, which reacted by breaking away from the Chianti denomination and revamping its own regulations to focus on quality rather than quantity—it is a gross overstatement diffused by many producers and journalists that the movement "taught" Italian winemakers how to make quality wine. I found that my father-in-law's well-stocked wine cellar of majestic old Barolos and Barbarescos from the late 1950s, 1960s, and 1970s—many of them made by little-known firms—and of those few but magnificent Brunellos from the 1970s and early 1980s, revealed stunning, world-class wines. And the numerous vertical tastings I've attended for Brunello, Barolo, Barbaresco, and even Taurasi, the latter going as far back as the 1930s, have amply demonstrated their outstanding quality. That these wines were the exception is of course true, but then again up until two or three decades ago, quality wine was always the exception rather than the rule—even, dare I suggest it, in some of the lauded appellations of France.

These days, with better knowledge, hygiene, and equipment, technically perfect wines are made almost everywhere. Defective wines are now a rarity in Italy and in most of the already established winemaking countries across the globe. Instead, these days, unique and delicious wines that taste like no other offerings in the world, and that also boast breeding and balance, class, and complexity, are the rarity. Fortunately for wine lovers, a host of Montalcino estates have never stopped crafting delicious and inimitable Brunellos that cannot be confused with any other wine in the world, and many other producers are returning to a more classic style now that the euphoria of "the black and the inky" has faded.

Changes in Montalcino's wine regulations clearly reflect the strong influence the Super Tuscan phenomenon had starting around the 1990s and that is still felt today. Montalcino's producers pushed for and received a new and separate denomination in 1996: Sant'Antimo DOC. This flexible designation allows wines to be made from almost any grape variety and now accounts for 450 hectares (1,111 acres) of international varieties planted throughout Montalcino, alongside but not in registered Brunello vineyards, at least not legally. It is worth noting at this point that Montalcino also has about the same amount of hectares dedicated to IGT production, a practically open-ended designation with few restrictions. Even if, in theory, IGT-designated vineyards may be planted with Sangiovese, the vast majority of these acres are dedicated to both red and white French varieties.

Not only did Montalcino's winemakers begin making their own Super Tuscans under Sant'Antimo DOC and IGT Toscana, but a number of Brunellos were also transformed. By the new millennium, darkly exotic, instant-gratification Brunellos that seemed more like Super Tuscans wrapped with Brunello labels emerged alongside of classically crafted Brunellos that suddenly appeared almost ethereal in comparison. While those in favor of barriques and the Super Tuscan–styled Brunellos unanimously defended them as being "what the market wants," and accused that "other style" of being criminally "old-fashioned," other local winemakers have said all along that these contemporary Brunellos had lost their *tipicità,* as the Italians call it, or their quintessential character that had made the wine so famous. As Gianfranco Soldera, one of the denomination's most plainspoken and colorful winemakers, states, "Barriques are only for deficient wines that don't get enough tannins and flavors from the grape and need to make up for this lack with oak sensations." Alessandro Mori, a passionate defender of traditionally styled Brunellos, agrees, and told me under no certain terms what he felt. "Barriques, which are not part of Italy's winemaking customs, destroy the fundamental character of Brunello. Barriques and consulting enologists, who use the same methods everywhere to make what tastes like the same wine, are a menace to Brunello and Italian wine in general, and are turning winemaking into an industry mass producing just another beverage." Mori went on to say what many other Brunello producers were beginning to realize by the early years of the new millennium, that these Brunellos "of enormous structure are flat and lifeless. Elegance has been replaced by explosive fruit and high alcohol, and these wines are made just to please critics and get high scores."

By the 1997 vintage, hailed at the time as the Greatest Vintage Ever in all of Italy by the majority of wine critics, who inexplicably could not taste beyond the vintage's very forward and overripe nature, a good number of Brunellos were of the darker, softer, and rounder kind, with excessive toast and oak sensations. What proved even more damaging for the denomination was that not only did critics bestow their highest scores on these impenetrably hued, wood-driven Brunellos, but at the same time, some of them openly slammed traditionally styled Brunellos from top producers as "tired" and "dull,"[1] effectively damaging sales back when these self-proclaimed experts wielded an inordinate and frankly ridiculous amount of power over the evolving palates of their readers. Many readers of mainstream wine magazines and specialized newsletters were consumers just beginning to drink wine, and if they thought they were finding guidance they had found instead taste dictators who were reluctant to stray from their own comfort zones of familiar tastes.

The threat of economic damage from poor sales that followed scathing criticism convinced a relatively high number of Montalcino's estates that embracing this international style was the only way to survive in those score-obsessed years, from roughly the mid-1990s through about 2005. For years there has been debate as to whether the Brunellos made under this more turbo-charged style would improve over time, or if they would even stand up to aging, particularly crucial for Brunello since the wine's marathon aging potential is one of the reasons the wine has attracted so much attention since the 1960s.

A now infamous press tasting of Brunello vintages from 1964 to 1997, held in 2007 by the Consorzio to celebrate its fortieth anniversary, laid any doubts to rest. Of the twelve 1997 Brunellos presented at the *quarantennale* anniversary tasting, seven were past their prime with almost no noticeable fruit remaining, but instead only wood and alcohol aromas that carried over to the palate along with drying wood tannins. Most of these seven dead Brunellos were among those that had received the highest scores of the vintage just five years earlier when they were first released, and were made under the guidance of some of the most influential consulting enologists in the country. Of the other five, only two were very good, boasting delicious fruit and staying power. Not only had these two Brunellos been traditionally crafted, but they also hailed from the denomination's higher reaches, where grapes benefited from cooler temperatures during the very hot 1997 growing season. Montalcino's highest vineyard areas undoubtedly yielded the best wines of this overrated vintage, which did not deserve its official five-star rating bestowed by the Consorzio. The other three 1997s were not yet over their prime but they were not going to get any better either, due to low acidity and domineering alcohol. The lone 1996 entry and four of the five 1995 entries, among them once again high-scoring Brunellos upon their release six and seven years earlier from leading properties, were equally uninspiring, with little fruit to support the massive wood, tannins, and alcohol.

The same scenario is repeated back to vintages from the mid-1980s: wines that upon their release had counted among the most celebrated Brunellos made by highly and consistently lauded estates, by 2007 tasted like dried-up lumber marinated in moonshine. A turning point was reached with the vintages from the mid-1980s and earlier—these had more vibrancy and fruit than Brunellos a decade younger. Not only were the vast majority of these wines made according to more Sangiovese-friendly methods, but the most outstanding of the older Brunellos all came from tried and true parts of the denomination.

The change in Brunello is also reflected in three modifications made to its DOCG production code in the 1990s. The first, in 1991, reduced Brunello's minimum wood aging from three and a half years to three, although the wine still had to remain in estate cellars for at least four years starting from the first January after the harvest, five for Riserva. The collective thinking behind this reduction in barrel aging was that most producers, supported by even many Brunello purists, felt that so much time in wood was drying out the bright fruit harvested from younger, recently planted vines, and that Brunello would benefit instead from more bottle aging. The 1991 amendment also reduced minimum overall acidity. If in 1966 and 1980, Brunello was required upon release to have a minimum acidity of 5.5 per 1,000, this minimum went down to 5 per 1,000, reflecting the trend away from vibrant acidity to accommodate the softer, sweeter Brunello, which often, however, bordered on flabby. This same modification also substituted the name "Sangiovese Grosso" for Sangiovese.

The next change came in 1996, the most fundamental alteration being that mandatory wood aging, still set at a minimum of three years, could be carried out in "oak containers of any size." Up until now barrel aging had been required to take place in oak or chestnut botti, the traditional large casks, although most Brunello producers using botti had only been using Slavonian oak and not chestnut barrels for years. This modification was an obvious concession to the use of barriques, which, although they had been in use for a while, were technically violating the production code. The updated regulations also called for a minimum period of at least four months of bottle aging for Brunello, six months for Riserva. Another critical adjustment to the rules governing Brunello was that up until this point all the previous regulations had considered only land of Eocene origin as suitable for Brunello vines; the 1996 revision changed this crucial clause to "land formed between the Cretaceous period through the Pliocene epoch," an obvious acknowledgment and acceptance of the hitherto new or uncultivated areas that were now under vine for Brunello production throughout the denomination. The same 1996 modification also stipulated that all new vineyards and replantings must have a minimum planting density of 3,000 plants per hectare.

Still not satisfied, in 1998 the majority of producers, or rather, the largest producers that command the most voting power within the Consorzio, once again demanded and received yet another ratified version of the laws governing Brunello. The most critical change this time was the reduction from three years mandatory wood aging to two, retroactive back to the 1995 harvest, still in estate cellars. While a host of more conservative producers, most of them small-sized, fought against this measure, Franco Biondi Santi, the stalwart of tradition himself, at the time surprisingly supported it. He now admits, however, "That was a mistake. I agreed that three years in wood was too much for those producers with very young vines because wine made from young vines suffers from too much wood aging. My decision was based on the fact that the overall minimum aging period in estate cellars would remain fixed at over four years after the harvest. But this measure has since set off a series of attempts to shorten the minimum cellaring period from four years to three, and to further reduce wood aging from two years down to one. A good wine made from Sangiovese Grosso needs four years to stabilize; otherwise it needs to be forced chemically and physically."

Barrique aging alone did not cause all the very pronounced changes to Brunello's *tipicità*, however. The large number of dusky-colored Brunellos with exotic flavors and aromas that appeared from the 1990s on caused a new generation of critics to suspect illicit blending with grapes other than Sangiovese for Brunello. Very few serious wine writers and dedicated Brunello fans were surprised at what happened next, but most were indeed shocked that it took so long to come about.

SIX

The Brunellogate Scandal

Under its production code, Brunello is required to be "intense ruby red tending toward garnet" and have "intense and characteristic aromas." While it can be argued that the production code's stipulated "characteristic aromas" is somewhat vague, there can be no misinterpreting the clearly defined color, nor should there be: 100 percent Sangiovese swings from ruby red to deep garnet. And as any serious-minded Brunello producer or winemaker anywhere in Italy who works with Sangiovese will tell you, "If it's inky black, it ain't Sangiovese." Clearly as the numbers of suspiciously dark, concentrated, and exotically perfumed Brunellos increased over the years, so did speculation of illicit and widespread blending with other grapes. In an article published by *Wine News* in 2003, I wrote that many of the 1997 Brunellos I had tasted in 2002 "were so jammy it was hard to believe they were Brunello," and in 2006, in *The World of Fine Wine*, I wrote that "illicit blending with other grapes, to make Brunello's luminous ruby-garnet color unnaturally darker, is staunchly denied on all official fronts"; and again in *Wine News* in 2007, "Doubts can only remain in the face of some of the darker, impenetrable Brunellos sometimes seen." Eric Asimov, the *New York Times* wine critic, brought up the blending issue in 2006, writing that Montalcino's traditionally minded producers "insist that some producers are already adding wine made from grapes other than sangiovese to darken the color and to make the wine easier to drink at an early age."[1]

As a new breed of wine writers and increasingly better-educated wine lovers began to question the reasons behind these unnaturally darker Brunellos invading Montalcino, most could not help but notice the tempting vicinity, often in vineyards right next to hallowed Brunello vines, of the over 800 hectares (roughly 2,000 acres) of Cabernet, Merlot, and Syrah planted all over Montalcino under Sant'Antimo DOC and IGT, with the latter designation planted mostly in the south and southwest where in 2008 Banfi alone had 322 hectares (796 acres) of registered IGT vines along with 242 hectares (598 acres) of Sant'Antimo as reported in the Consorzio's *Brunello: I produttori* published that same year. However, over the years there have also been whispers of wines arriving in Montalcino in large tankers under the cover of night; Nero d'Avola was the alleged culprit one year, imported bulk Spanish wine the next, although none of these reports have ever been confirmed.

The widespread rumors and suppositions had been building for some time. At Montalcino's annual Benvenuto Brunello press tasting in February 2008, rumors were rampant that at least one major producer was under criminal investigation for illicitly blending other grapes with Sangiovese to make the firm's award-winning Brunello. So it was no great shocker when the blending scandal, almost immediately dubbed "Brunellogate" by the international press (and known as Brunellopoli in Italy) broke wide open in late March 2008, after Italian wine writer Franco Ziliani confronted the situation on his blog. In his March 21 post, "Rumors from Montalcino," Ziliani wrote about the insistent rumors filtering out of Montalcino that authorities had confiscated large amounts of Brunello at several famous Montalcino cellars because it did not adhere to the wine's production code. Later that same day the *Wine Spectator*'s then European bureau chief based in Tuscany, James Suckling, many of whose top-scoring Brunellos were made by producers known to be involved in the scandal, wrote, "I was shocked to say the least" over the blending rumors, adding that it was "hearsay" and, that although there was an investigation underway, he didn't "think is [*sic*] going to be a big deal. The vines can be changed over to Sangiovese."[2] Despite the latter's prediction, the story took off and hit its frenzied pitch a few weeks later at Vinitaly, the most important trade show for Italian wine.

While blending with other grapes may not seem like a big deal to the many wine lovers around the world who enjoy wines made under the more relaxed regulations adopted in other countries, namely the comparatively unrestricted New World appellations, in Italy breaking the *disciplinare* or production code is considered fraud, a serious crime punishable by either fines, jail time, or both.

According to the initial reports of the *scandalo*, Siena's prosecutor had confiscated nearly a million bottles of Brunello 2003, at the time the current release, from several leading producers. It was widely reported and later confirmed by the firms themselves that four large companies—Antinori,

Argiano, Banfi, and Frescobaldi—the latter two being the number one and number two volume players in the denomination, were not only under investigation for commercial fraud but that the magistrate of Siena at the time had indeed blocked the sales of their 2003 Brunellos, while the fate of vintages from 2004 to 2007, all in different phases of the mandatory aging period, was also in question. Even though the four above-mentioned wineries publicly took the heat for the whole denomination, unconfirmed reports claimed that far more wineries had had their Brunello sequestered and that as many as ninety-three firms were being investigated.

It should be noted that Italy's extremely tight privacy laws mean that authorities have withheld names and initially even precise quantities and other details from the public. These same laws proved extremely convenient for those involved. Citing the privacy laws and the sensitivity of the then ongoing investigation, the Brunello Consorzio, at the time still legally responsible for monitoring all aspects of production under the 2004 erga omnes decree, which empowered *consorzi* across the country with total authority over the denomination, remained tight-lipped and hired a PR firm to generate vague and insipid press releases. Most producers refused to go on record. The above four firms eventually opened up, however, shortly after their names and involvement appeared in online news sites, and in newspapers and magazines. "We came under investigation at the end of February, but were convinced that the whole thing would blow over once on-site inspections were completed. Instead, the magistrate impounded our Brunello 2003, and sequestered about 20 hectares of our vineyards," Tiziana Frescobaldi told me during an exclusive interview in the wake of the scandal in 2008. According to Frescobaldi, the prosecutor investigated to see if the firm might have used grapes other than Sangiovese to make Montalcino's foremost wine. "Of our 150 hectares of vines registered to Brunello production, about twenty hectares are planted with Merlot. We do not use these grapes for our Brunello but for Lamaione, our pure Merlot, and Luce, our Super Tuscan. We have always declared the presence of these vines to the Consorzio, along with the fact that these grapes do not go into Brunello, and until now it was never an issue," recounted Tiziana.

Antinori was also under investigation. "We voluntarily blocked our 2003 Brunello before any of it was shipped when we saw what was happening in Montalcino," confirmed Renzo Cotarella, head winemaker and managing director for Antinori. The firm's Pian delle Vigne Brunello 2003 was impounded while awaiting analysis to see if any other varieties had been added. "We have 60 hectares at our Montalcino estate, half of which are

Sangiovese registered to Brunello. We also have another twenty hectares of Sangiovese, and 10 hectares of other varieties such as Merlot and Petit Verdot, all of which go into our Villa Antinori IGT. Because of these other varieties, which are grown on the estate but are not registered to Brunello, the magistrate decided to investigate further," explained Cotarella in an interview with me in 2008. He added that confiscating the wines might have sent the wrong message to consumers. "Confiscating Brunello may have given consumers the idea that the wines were harmful, which was most certainly not the case," clarified Cotarella. "Our Brunello is made entirely with Sangiovese, and we want to prove it," continued the enologist. He went on to say that Antinori at the time hoped it would not have to declassify its Brunello to IGT, but that this decision depended on how long the situation dragged on.

Faced with the same dilemma of stockpiling the entire 2003 vintage while the Brunello 2004, a far superior vintage, waited in the cellar for its scheduled 2009 release, Argiano had already decided by spring of 2008 to declassify its blocked Brunellos. "It's not because we added any other grapes, but because we simply cannot afford to leave our wine blocked in the cellar for a prolonged period," reported Stephane Schaeffer, Argiano's sales director at the time. The declassified wine was promptly renamed "Il Duemilatre di Argiano" (Argiano 2003), an IGT designation, and was sold for about 15 to 20 percent less than its original Brunello price tag.

According to Banfi's vice-president Lars Leicht during an interview with me in 2008, the firm's six hundred thousand bottles of Brunello 2003 had been impounded on suspicions of overcropping, after investigators had found discrepancies between vineyard yields. "According to Brunello's production code, vineyard yields must be a maximum of 80 quintals per hectare. Some of our Brunello vineyards yield 75 quintals per hectare, while others yield 85 per hectare, with the average being the stipulated 80 quintals per hectare. These are vineyards, not machines, and as long as our overall yield was within the stipulated limits, we felt that we were abiding by the production code."

In reaction to all the press generated by the situation, the U.S Alcohol Tobacco Tax and Trade Bureau (TTB) even demanded that all imports of Brunello be accompanied by certification from the Italian government declaring that the wine had been made in full compliance with its regulations. This unorthodox and time-consuming requirement, coming as it did from Brunello's biggest market, where one in every four bottles of Brunello is destined, clearly demonstrated that the problem was not going to simply go away as had been originally hoped by Montalcino's producers.

TO BE BRUNELLO OR NOT BE BRUNELLO

The blending scandal drove home an issue that had been simmering in the denomination for years: the controversial question of changing the production code to legally allow different grapes into Brunello. Although those in favor saw modifying the regulations as "updating" Brunello and satisfying the market that supposedly demanded a little Merlot or Cabernet in all wines, those against the idea saw it as a question of making Brunello versus making just another one of Tuscany's countless, mainstream Sangiovese-based wines. Those in favor of keeping the production code as 100 percent Sangiovese also pointed out a simple fact: no one is forced to make Brunello di Montalcino, and estates wanting to make wines in Montalcino with grapes other than Sangiovese can do so under the Sant'Antimo DOC or Toscana IGT. However, producers under the latter designations, don't have the name recognition of either Brunello or Montalcino. Nor are they able to sell the wines at the same elevated prices as Brunello.

To settle the matter the Consorzio members called for a general assembly to vote on whether or not to change the production code. The announcement of the impending assembly, which was eventually held in late October 2008, was followed by a war of words that broke out in Montalcino among the producers in the months and weeks leading up to the vote, at a time when the denomination was under the media's intense scrutiny. In September, Ezio Rivella, Castello Banfi's retired manager and winemaker, spoke out to the Italian media, emphatically declaring that Brunello's production code should be changed. As he told Italian website www.winenews.it, "The modification to adopt is very simple: make Brunello using a minimum of 85% Sangiovese. Complementary grapes would have to be from Montalcino, and the same should apply to Rosso di Montalcino."[3] It should be noted that Ezio Rivella, who in September 2010, after nearly ten years of retirement from Banfi, was voted in as president of the Consorzio in a shocking albeit narrow victory, had been publicly airing his views since the scandal broke. In April, Rivella, who is apparently not a fan of Burgundy, nor it would seem (at the time anyway) of Brunello, declared, "Brunello's production code is too rigid. None of the great Bordeaux appellations or French wines in general stipulate the exact percentage of grapes that should be used.... The most important thing is quality and origin, the rest should be up to the producer."[4]

Rivella was not alone. In late August producer Angelo Gaja, who had previously shied away from taking a stand or even making any significant comments on subzoning both in his native Barbaresco and in Montalcino, told the *Corriere della Sera,* "Great expansion of Sangiovese cultivation in less than suitable areas requires that the production code should be changed."[5] Gaja then sent an open letter with his in-depth take on the situation to journalists, magazines, and websites in both English and Italian. In the statement Gaja wrote, "In Montalcino ... there is a minority of producers who enjoy a double privilege: that of owning vineyards officially registered for the production of Brunello di Montalcino and, in addition, of possessing vineyards capable of producing wines of true excellence," while "the majority of producers own vineyards that are simply registered for the production of Brunello but are not necessarily capable of producing transcendent wines."[6]

The latter group, according to Gaja, felt that Brunello's production code is too restrictive to insist upon 100 percent Sangiovese, given that Sangiovese did not excel in their vineyards. Gaja's letter then surmised that if the "current investigation should find that the use of other varieties different from Sangiovese" had been used for Brunello, then it was time to change the regulations and "remove the iron rule of 100 percent Sangiovese," thereby permitting other varieties for the "majority of Brunello producers with marginal vineyards" that were the result of "enormous expansion." Gaja also stated that "volume producers" should be "allowed to operate with greater flexibility."

Reaction was swift, as other Brunello estates angrily criticized Gaja and other colleagues who publicly advocated changing the production code, rightly feeling that such pronouncements sent a damaging message of, essentially, "We broke the law, so let's fix it by changing the law." Owner of Col d'Orcia and former Consorzio president Francesco Marone Cinzano told me at the time, "It's high time to stop these declarations that propose changing Brunello's production code to allow grapes other than Sangiovese," adding that the "vast majority of producers" wanted to "keep Brunello just as it is." Franco Biondi Santi, who agreed with Gaja that "Sangiovese excels in some areas but in other areas it simply does not," was firmly opposed to changing Brunello's regulations. However, the veteran producer, backed up by several producers including Marone Cinzano, advocated changes to Montalcino's second wine instead. "Rather than changing Brunello's production code, which should be left as is, we should think about allowing other grapes into Rosso di Montalcino, which would safeguard Brunello while allowing producers to use other grapes in a wine that still carries Montalcino on the label." Lovers of both Brunello and Rosso di Montalcino, myself included, disagreed with Biondi Santi's idea. Not only would allowing other grapes into Rosso turn it into just another of the myriad bland and boring Sangiovese blends made in Tuscany; it would also set a dangerous precedent that could eventually allow the same changes for Brunello.

Late on October 27, 2008, Montalcino's producers voted to keep Brunello's production code as well as that of Rosso di Montalcino as 100 percent Sangiovese. The minority of producers advocating for change got buried in the landslide victory, with 96 percent of the Consorzio's members voting to keep the production code for both wines unaltered against a mere 4 percent voting to change the regulations. However, in September 2011, just as this book was heading into print, the Brunello Consorzio's board of directors once again called for a vote to change Rosso di Montalcino's regulations. By then Biondi Santi and Marone Cinzano strongly opposed any change to Rosso, as will be explained in chapter 14. Thankfully, Montalcino's producers once again threw out any changes, endorsing the 100 percent Sangiovese rule for Rosso di Montalcino.

INCONCLUSIVE CONCLUSIONS

By the fall of 2008 most of the firms under investigation had had their Brunellos released by authorities after a good amount of declassification. Even so, the media still kept close watch over the denomination, and the large amount of unconfirmed data on the Internet and in the traditional press prompted Siena's prosecutor to take the unusual step of releasing a press release to set matters straight. The October 22, 2008, prepared statement, just days before the assembly voted on the respective production codes, declared that the investigation had started in September 2007. It went on to say that besides raiding wineries, seizing documents, and even inspecting the homes of many of the winery owners and estate managers, authorities had also inspected vineyards on foot and by examining aerial photographs. According to then Prosecutor Nino Calabrese, the results of the first phase of the investigation proved that many firms had violated the production code, leading authorities to impound 6.5 million liters of suspect Brunello and 700,000 liters of suspect Rosso di Montalcino, far more wine than had been estimated by the press and pundits.

The press release further stated that 1.1 million liters of Brunello and

450,000 liters of Rosso had been declassified to IGT, while about 1 million liters had been released after laboratory analysis could not detect the presence of other wines. The release further stated that 4.4 million liters of Brunello remained confiscated. Calabrese also confirmed that other recent vintages from 2004, 2005, 2006, and 2007 had also been impounded. According to the press release two firms were cleared and had had no wines sequestered because their wines were in full compliance with the production codes since investigators found no evidence of blending. It was later revealed by the firms themselves that the two cleared producers were Col d'Orcia and Franco Biondi Santi. Biondi Santi openly admits that investigators came and combed through documents and registers and inspected the vineyards, and were immediately satisfied that the very few vines of Canaiolo that the Consorzio's vineyard controls had discovered a few years earlier within registered Brunello vines had long been ripped up.

In July 2009, the Guardia di Finanza (Italy's police, part of the military corps, that investigates tax and financial crimes) announced the conclusion of the preliminary investigation that in the end impounded a total 6.7 million liters of Brunello of which 20 percent (1,300,000 liters) was declassified to IGT Toscana while 500,000 liters of Rosso were also declassified. The Guardia di Finanza also stated that during the investigation authorities had sequestered more than 400 hectares of vineyards planted with grapes that were not in compliance with Brunello's production code. After the various declassifications, the rest of the confiscated wine was later unblocked and approved for commercial sale and 350 hectares (865 acres) were "regularized" to comply with the law. The Guardia di Finanza's statement, widely available upon its release over the Internet, concluded that seven firms were involved in commercial fraud, and seventeen people, among them winery owners, enologists, and estate managers, and even a few of the higher-ups in the Consorzio and certification committee, faced indictment. At the time, eight of the indicted had already plea-bargained while the others were evidently waiting for their day in court.

Satisfied with the results of the investigation, in March 2010 the U.S. TTB dropped its requirement that all Brunello imported into the country be accompanied by a certificate that guaranteed the product complied with its production requirement. The document also specified that "Banfi srl; Antinori Società Agricola; Pian delle Vigne di Montalcino srl; Agricola Centolani srl di Montalcino; and Azienda Agricola Casanova di Neri Giacomo di Montalcino—have resolved their cases with the judicial authorities," and that "two additional wineries—Argiano srl di Montalcino and Tenuta CastelGiocondo and Luce della Vite srl di Montalcino—are still in the process of resolving their judicial cases."[7]

In October 2010, a report published by the Florence edition of *La Repubblica,* a leading Italian daily newspaper, reported that of the seventeen individuals who had been indicted, most had already resolved their cases. Although *La Repubblica* cited names, in observance with Italy's strict and rather confusing privacy laws, I have left them out. According to the newspaper, two individuals had plea-bargained and received sentences of sixteen and twelve months, respectively, for falsifying public documents, while a leading producer and his enologist were charged with selling fraudulent goods. The latter two plea-bargained and had their sentences reduced to fines. The report also declared that the former winemaker of a very large firm, who had been accused of making false statements to a public prosecutor, was exonerated while the manager of another winery was due to go in front of a judge in March 2011, although I have not been able to find updates on the latter individual. It should be noted that while other media outlets quickly cited the article in *La Repubblica* and also named the individuals implicated, Italian authorities have never officially released any names. As a result, all of the wineries and individuals involved have been allowed to carry on as if nothing had ever happened, although there were apparently undisclosed fines paid.

AFTER BRUNELLOGATE

As of October 2010, the case is considered closed. And while there will always be those producers still tempted to blend Merlot with Sangiovese and call it Brunello, the scandal (despite the lax sentences) and ever-improving testing methods have made this harder to do. The DOCG tasting commission responsible for analyzing Brunello and deciding if the wines meet all of the production code's stipulations has come under intense fire for passing the many unnaturally dark Brunellos. It has also been blamed for reportedly blocking a number of lighter-colored Brunellos, in what many feel were obvious attempts at trying to legitimize a particular style, especially because several regular tasters on the DOCG tasting panel are winemakers and enologists themselves and adhere to the more internationally styled and impenetrably hued wines.

The Brunello Consorzio was admittedly under tremendous pressure from the scandal because from 2004 until shortly after the scandal broke, it had been responsible for regulating and controlling all aspects of the wine's production. Brunello's Consorzio was actually one of the first consorzi in Italy to be invested with such powers under a pilot program of the much-touted erga omnes decree, which in the end may have been what eventually triggered the scandal. Under erga omnes, the Brunello Consorzio was obliged to inspect every vineyard in the denomination, a process which took years. Upon finding irregularities, the Consorzio presumably asked those producers involved to grub up the vines, but apparently they did not report the names of these producers to Italy's fraud squad, perhaps preferring to give the estates some time to conform. Press statements issued by the Consorzio in the wake of the debacle stated that after inspecting over 1,667 hectares (4,145 acres) of Brunello vineyards between 2004 and 2007, the Consorzio had found only 17 hectares (42 acres), or about 1 percent, that were not in compliance. According to informed sources in Montalcino, a call to authorities from an infuriated producer who had had enough of the black and the inky Brunellos set the whole thing in motion, but again, this has never been confirmed.

The Brunello scandal's fallout was felt all over Italy. After Italian authorities initially launched erga omnes in just a few leading consorzi in 2004, over the years the law was extended to major consorzi across Italy. The decree gave these growers' unions complete authority over regulating their respective wines, and they were supposed to ensure that producers abide by production codes. But the scandal drove home the fact that there was simply too much of a conflict of interest in having a consorzio (made up of members of the denomination who are the producers and growers) be responsible for regulating and overseeing all aspects of their own production. In the immediate aftermath of Brunellogate, the Brunello Consorzio hired a former director of the food-fraud repression office to oversee the checks and controls of the Brunello production code who would also help them create a new structure to guarantee that producers adhere to protocol.

By 2009, wine consorzi all over Italy had hired outside companies such as Valoritalia and CCIAA to oversee and enforce production regulations while the consorzi concentrated instead on promotion, marketing, and administrative duties. While the official word is that these developments were all part of changes mandated by the in-coming European reforms to the wine sector, most other wine consorzi in Italy say off-record that pressure and criticism generated from Brunellogate were the real deciding factors in hiring third-party overseers. In classic Italian politicking—which excels at recycling the same people by simply giving them new titles—in most cases the new quality-control companies recruited their employees from among those working at the local consorzi and who basically do the same job but now for another entity.

While many producers feared bad publicity generated from Brunellogate, according to leading American importer and Italian wine specialist Neil Empson, most of the reaction has actually been positive. "If anything, the little customer feedback we've had on the Brunello blending issues demonstrates that consumers actually feel reassured, because it seems that the Italian system of checks and controls works," says Empson. However, in terms of wine news, the scandal generated nearly unprecedented feedback on the Internet. Impassioned Brunello lovers vented their feelings on the numerous blogs and websites that covered the scandal in real time, and almost without exception, these readers overwhelmingly supported the 100 percent Sangiovese rule for Brunello. In the end, Montalcino's blending debacle drove home a crucial message: Brunello makers wanting to add other grapes should make a different wine rather than Brunello, and that those consumers who don't like 100 percent Sangiovese should simply drink something else.

SEVEN

Brunello Today and Tomorrow

THE RETURN TO *TIPICITÀ*, OR BUSINESS AS USUAL?

In the immediate aftermath of the scandal, a number of Brunello producers believed that Brunellogate would give the denomination a much-needed wake-up call by forcing Montalcino's producers to adhere to the rules and focus on Sangiovese. Many pundits felt the investigation happened at just the right time, given fundamental changes that have occurred both in the world wine markets and within the denomination itself during the first decade of the new century. The first few vintages released after the scandal, the 2004 and 2005 that were released in 2009 and 2010, respectively, seemed to confirm this view. At the annual Benvenuto Brunello press tastings held in Montalcino every February, most wine writers who were covering the first two editions after the scandal broke (2009 and 2010) seemed to agree that there was a noticeable return to Sangiovese. Many estates that were known for making inky black and dense Brunellos were suddenly producing a more restrained style that championed Sangiovese's hallmark color, aromas, and flavors, and while the timing seemed coincidental, it also seemed plausible that these savvy estates had noticed the consumer trend toward more authentic Brunello styles when the wines were being vinified four and five years before their release.

Yet the 2006 vintage, released in 2011, demonstrated what appears to be an abrupt turnaround for many of these same firms, who were suddenly back to the jammy, high-alcohol, and oak-driven wines they favored before the scandal hit. Such extreme differences cannot be explained solely on vintage variation. This about-face in wine styles from one year to the next, especially given Brunello's lengthy aging requirements, has helped give credence to the abundant rumors and speculations that many of the firms under intense scrutiny in the wake of the scandal had replaced their own 2004 and 2005 bottlings with Brunello they acquired directly from the denomination's more traditionally minded producers. Given the dismal slide in sales after the global economic crisis, prices and demand for Brunello, as for all high-end wines, fell sharply, making such an operation less costly than one would imagine. A number of 2006 Brunellos (the first vintage to be released after the official close of the blending case) from several high-profile firms have sent a message of "back to business as usual." However, one cannot help but think that those producers who have suddenly reverted to their former heavy-handed style, producing high-alcohol and wood-driven Brunellos, are behind the times, even though some of these undrinkable powerhouses have reaped top awards from those same wine critics who have long promoted this style.

Consumer tastes and preferences have evolved, even though those of many established wine critics obviously haven't. An increasing number of wine drinkers who used to crave Italy's internationally styled wines—ones that boasted Merlot's plummy softness and Cabernet's familiar sensations of black currant and bell pepper, and the recognizable and comforting nuances of vanilla, coffee, and chocolate of new oak (the latter sensations can also come from a number of synthetic flavor additives mixed into the wine though no one will broach this taboo subject, but such flavors and aromas do not come from grapes)—are now bored with these once seemingly innovative wines. It should also be noted that even though French grapes excel in their original environment, when grown in the heat of Tuscany most of these same varieties produce cooked, jammy wines with high alcohol but little refreshing acidity or bouquet. Drinking more than a glass at a time can be downright demanding.

The recent emphasis on food and wine pairing among enophiles around the world underscores how difficult it is to pair food with bombastic wines, further adding to their demise. Besides palate fatigue and sheer monotony, retail price is also a crucial issue: well-priced, high-quality Merlot, Cabernet, and Syrah from the New World now jostle for space on crowded wine-store shelves in key export markets. Similar offerings from Italy's top denominations cannot compete in terms of price thanks to the country's soaring labor costs compounded by the steep terrain in top appellations such as the best areas of Montalcino, which necessitate manual labor.

The collective boredom of high-octane wines made from international grapes produced around the world means that more wine lovers than ever are looking for out-of-the-ordinary bottlings, and are turning a keen eye to Italy's wines made from native vines, like select Brunellos that boast quintessential

Sangiovese in all its floral, vibrant, earthy, cherry-berry, and mineral glory. Although many of the denomination's cult estates and historic Brunello houses have long enjoyed a loyal following of domestic and international connoisseurs, and have always strongly opposed adding other grapes to Brunello, they are joined today by a growing number of Brunello estates, most of which are very small in size. Even those producers who told me off-record before the October 2008 vote that they believed grape restrictions should be relaxed, now admit that doing so would signal the wine's death knell because it would allow Brunello to become just another one of Tuscany's many Sangiovese blends.

Sales of certain Tuscan wines that seem to have little to do with Italy or the region, once leaders in the sector, have tanked in the last few years. "Super Tuscan sales have collapsed, and their winemakers can't even give them away," says outspoken producer Giulio Salvioni, whose tiny production of Brunello has won him diehard fans across the globe. "People in Montalcino have noticed and want to differentiate their wines from those that can be made anywhere else in the world, by focusing solely on Sangiovese and making genuine Brunello, a wine that can't be copied anywhere else on the planet but can only be made in Montalcino," adds Salvioni. Andrea Costanti, from the historic Colle al Matrichese estate, agrees. "Consumers, especially of fine wine, are looking to Italy for our unique wines, not Australian imitations. And here in Montalcino, we're incredibly fortunate because we have all the right conditions to make a unique, world-class wine. Even though international varieties do well all over the world and are planted everywhere, great Sangiovese is very much a consequence of its terroir, and does especially well at the higher altitudes here in Montalcino," says Costanti.

Although classically crafted Brunellos, just like classic Burgundies and Barolos, may not be for everyone, this doesn't mean that winemakers should change their wines to suit global palates by employing methods that mask the unparalleled beauty and authenticity of these wines. Thankfully, more and more of Montalcino's producers are realizing the importance of making Brunellos that stand out from among the many similar wines in the world, and a number of estates throughout Montalcino are taking a step back from new French oak and intrusive cellar practices, reflecting a trend that has occurred across Italy. However, with over four years of mandatory cellar aging for Brunello, trends take longer to materialize in Montalcino.

If just a few years ago many Brunello makers sought lower acidity and overripeness, the best firms are going back to a brighter style, perfect for both food pairing and longer cellaring. In short, while the finest Brunellos have always expressed the wine's *tipicità,* a number of estates are returning to the wine's quintessential expression, that first made it famous among collectors and aficionados. It should also be pointed out that greatly improved vinification methods, cooling equipment, and cellar hygiene now mean there are very few of the rustic or defective wines that could be found in the days of yore. However, this unfettered, hands-off style demands perfect growing conditions that many firms in the denomination simply don't have.

TWENTY-FIRST-CENTURY CHALLENGES

Although Brunello has undoubtedly benefited from the interest in Italy's traditional wines made from native grapes, and in wines from select growing areas that beautifully express these grapes, the beginning of the second decade of the new century remains a challenging time for the denomination. Huge increases in plantings and production means that an awareness of the various subzones and of the best producers is crucial for understanding and appreciating modern-day Brunello. Even if the economic downturn of 2008 and 2009 slowed global sales of the most expensive and esteemed Bordeaux, Burgundies, Barolos, and Brunellos, the global crisis could not have come at a worse time for Brunello. Just when more Brunello than ever had begun hitting the market as a result of unchecked vineyard expansion, the market for fine wine staggered, especially at the restaurant level. Interestingly, importers in both the United States and the United Kingdom are quick to point out that Brunello sales have not slowed down more than sales of other fine wines, leading them to believe that the blending scandal had little if any economic impact.

Yet for the first time there is more product than demand in Montalcino. Prices for Brunellos made by numerous little-known estates have fallen dramatically, while established producers have kept their relatively high prices stable, creating tension among estates and disorientation among consumers. Vineyard land in Montalcino, at an all-time high of €350,000 per hectare in 2007, fell between 30 and 40 percent by early 2010, causing further stress on producers. Although the denomination currently has enough registered Brunello vines to produce 12 million bottles a year, producers and the Consorzio have wisely been keeping production in check. Estates are declassifying more Brunello to Rosso and the Consorzio has implemented a management measure to force producers to keep yields lower by one ton per hectare in recent harvests. Thanks to these measures, producers are keeping overall Brunello production to around 8 million bottles annually. Yet a number of new producers, desperate to start getting a return on their expensive Brunello-making investment, or to at least cover some of the costs incurred, are selling their Brunello to large wholesalers and merchants in other parts of Italy who in turn put their own labels on the bottles, further increasing consumer confusion. It also goes without saying that most of these Brunellos sold off to large wholesalers are not of the greatest quality.

Signs of recovery are spreading seeds of optimism, however. In August 2010 the Italian Wine and Food Institute, based in New York City, released some promising statistics for the first half of the year regarding the crucial U.S. market, which saw an overall decrease in quantity of imports compared to 2009 but at the same time an increase in overall value. The same statistics confirm that not only did Italy maintain its role as the leading exporter to the United States, but 2010 marked a 12.5 percent increase in the exports of bottled wine to the United States, indicating that recovery is coming, albeit slowly for high-end wines.

Given that what was long deemed Italy's golden denomination is facing obstacles for the first time since it became DOC in 1966, local politics are increasingly another point of contention in Montalcino. Under EU laws regulating *consorzi*, the biggest members in terms of volume, production, and sales pay higher dues and also have the most power within the Consorzio. This means that the 66 percent of Montalcino's 250 growers (200 of whom are also bottlers) who have 5 hectares (12 acres) or under have less power than the minority of mid-sized and large wineries. Although only 9 percent of Montalcino estates have between 15 and 100 hectares (23 and 247 acres), and a mere 1 percent have more than 100 hectares, this powerful minority usually gets its way in key votes. To put it in straight numerical terms, small wineries with 5 hectares and less have an average of three votes each, while the largest Brunello firm, Banfi, has approximately sixty votes, depending on the vintage.

This political power play was made exceptionally clear in June 2010, when Ezio Rivella, Banfi's long-retired winemaker and estate manager, was voted president of the Consorzio, a shock to the majority of small and mid-sized producers who didn't think he had a chance. According to those close to the situation, Donatella Cinelli Colombini had been the clear favorite, and won the most votes by far in the first election for the new board of directors, usually a precursor to the final results of the presidential vote held a few weeks later by the newly elected fifteen board members. Rivella also made it onto the board of directors, although other members have told me he got in with the bare minimum of votes. In a surprising turnaround on the morning of the election for president, Cinelli Colombini bowed out, and Rivella was voted in. Given Rivella's very public declarations on the necessity of allowing other grapes into Brunello, this was a shocking turn of events. As Fabrizio Bindocci of Il Poggione, one of the board members who had backed Cinelli Colombini and who had even tried to step in at the very last minute as a candidate for the presidency, told me shortly after the election, "The president of the Consorzio has to work for the members, and since the members voted to keep Brunello as 100 percent Sangiovese, no one can change this." And as Rivella himself told me after he was elected, despite his own preferences, as president he "would bow down to the will of the producers who had voted to keep Brunello and Rosso 100 percent Sangiovese. For now any changes are not on the table."

This very diplomatic declaration is, however, a far cry from what Ezio Rivella told Italian journalist Carlo Macchi in July 2010. In a videotaped interview, Rivella casually told Macchi that, at least up until the scandal broke, "80 percent of Brunello was not pure Sangiovese" and that the practice of "adding up to 3 percent or 5 percent other grapes was common."[1] At one point in the video, responding to a question about changing the production code, Rivella states that in 2010, still in the aftermath of the scandal, it wasn't the best time to discuss changing Brunello's production code, but that certainly "it would be discussed again," and that in the meantime it "is necessary" to change Rosso's regulations. Based on this, I can't help but feel that Rivella's presidency is not good news for Brunello and Sangiovese purists.

Besides the power play in local affairs that gives most control to the minority of high-volume producers, the majority of Montalcino's small family-run estates have equally small marketing budgets and an even smaller staff. It is no wonder that they get very little press coverage when compared to the large estates, which usually have a full-time PR person or consultant and regularly buy ad space in popular wine and food magazines. These large estates also frequently organize press visits to their wineries, as well as hold tasting events and dinners for journalists in Montalcino and key export markets. Since the vast majority of Brunello estates have very little means for promotion, all but a few cult properties remain little known even among diehard Brunello fans, although nearly all of them export to key markets albeit in tiny quantities.

Although several of Montalcino's largest firms purposely promote a distinctly grand Bordeaux châteaux image, most of Montalcino's estates have more in common with their counterparts in Barolo and in Burgundy's Côte d'Or. Wines from Montalcino, Barolo, and Côte d'Or, often considered the greatest wines in the world, come from three distinct places and are made exclusively from the best expression of single grapes. While Burgundy is neatly divided into Grand Cru, Premier Cru, and Village designations, and Barolo has finally delimited its own growing zone into specified geographical areas that may eventually lead to more serious zoning, with the exception of banning vines over 600 meters (1,968 feet), Brunello remains totally unregulated in terms of where vines can be planted in the denomination—unfathomable given the status of the wine and the indisputable complexity of both the growing zone and Sangiovese. The only obvious explanation as to why the denomination remains unzoned is political if not to say commercial. Many of the biggest firms, with the highest volumes and sales figures, are located in areas where Sangiovese does not excel.

THE FUTURE AND THE NEED FOR SUBZONES

Thanks to unchecked expansion in unfit parts of the denomination, the subsequent explosion in production, and a plethora of Brunello styles, buying Brunello has become a complicated undertaking, as finding the right style is more difficult than ever for consumers. Dividing the growing area into subzones is a crucial first step to getting a handle on Brunello. Yet because no official attempt has been made at zoning the denomination, even many of the wine writers who descend on Montalcino every February at the annual Benvenuto Brunello press tastings are overwhelmed by the different styles and are unaware of the vast differences within the large growing area.

The tasting itself, while one of the most important tasting events in Italy, and in many respects one of the best organized, has a crucial flaw in the way it is set up. While Benvenuto highlights the new vintages, it does not guide journalists through the intricacies of the denomination, and many writers leave the event disorientated, convinced that Brunello has a serious identity crisis. Rather than the current system of arranging the producers' stands alphabetically or relying on the essentially random tasting order applied at the serviced tables, Brunellos at the Benvenuto tasting should be grouped into specific geographical areas. Dividing the tasting by the names of the hamlets and villages closest to the vineyard areas would greatly add to the overall appreciation and understanding of Brunello. Even if today a number of Brunellos are a blend of Sangiovese from different areas within the production zone, this would at least be a step in the right direction as opposed to the current erratic and incoherent system of tasting the wines in any order at all. This lack of any guidance in the tasting order results in attendees often trying many of the more immediate, powerful, and high-alcohol Brunellos before the more elegant and subtle offerings, which severely penalizes the latter wines with their more delicate sensations that are easily overwhelmed by the more in-your-face aromas and flavors of brawnier Brunellos.

While it is true that aggressive cellar techniques and radically lower vineyard yields can obliterate both the subtle and less-than-subtle expressions of terroir, in Montalcino as a general rule different winemaking styles often depend on the subzones, although of course there are exceptions to this rule. Generally speaking, however, many if not most estates in the higher altitudes of original growing areas around Montalcino, where Sangiovese yields highly perfumed Brunellos of strength and light, and in the mid- to high altitudes where Sangiovese boasts ripeness and complexity, tend to use more Sangiovese-friendly methods that often include botti of medium and large capacities, or *tonneaux* (500-liter French oak barrels), and rely overall on less intervention in the cellar—factors that exalt Sangiovese's quintessential aromas and flavors. In the extreme northern areas, where producers sometimes try to add structure, and in low-altitude vineyards such as those in the far southwestern and southern areas of the denomination where Brunellos have naturally more weight and higher alcohol, producers tend to use increased intervention in the cellar, including more extreme extraction methods. Compared to producers with mid- and high-altitude vineyards, more producers in these areas age their Brunello in new barriques, at least in part, to speed up aging and to impart greater tannins. Even though many producers of the rounder, full-bodied Brunellos hailing from the southwest claim that their Brunellos can easily support aging in small oak because of their naturally bigger structures, critics claim that the new barrels are instead employed to give intense wood-driven aromas and flavors as well as added tannins to wines that lack the violet, earth, and underbrush aromas as well as succulent cherry-berry and mineral flavors of quintessential Brunello.

Despite the obvious differences in growing conditions within the denomination, which in turn often impact winemaking styles, in the recent past few of Montalcino's producers have advocated subzoning and even fewer would dare concede on record that many Brunello vineyards were planted in insufficient areas. Both wanton planting as well as the grape-blending scandal have changed the locals' attitude of "what goes on in Montalcino stays in Montalcino." For the first time a number of producers are publicly admitting that there are areas in the growing zone where Sangiovese does not excel, hitherto a forbidden topic in Montalcino. While some, like Gaja, have proposed allowing other grapes besides Sangiovese into Brunello to elevate the quality of mediocre wines from inferior vineyards, other producers and enologists instead say it is high time that Brunello makers reevaluate their growing zone and the current situation, to "wake up and smell the Brunello" so to speak.

Famed consulting enologist Carlo Ferrini is one of these newly proclaimed advocates of Brunello zoning. One of Italy's most successful and most affable consultant enologists, I hadn't expected Ferrini to be in favor of subzoning in Montalcino, given that his wines, rippling with muscle and opulence, have never struck me as being particularly terroir-driven. Since the early 1990s Ferrini has been behind some of Italy's most celebrated wines, among them a number of impenetrably dark and exceedingly rich Super Tuscans, Chianti Classicos, and Brunellos. Keeping up with new market demands, even Ferrini has lately traded in his signature all-new barriques for larger tonneaux because they do not impart as much vanilla and toast, which can smother the more subtle nuances of many of Italy's native grapes, especially Sangiovese. Ferrini admits, however, that he still prefers a highly concentrated, dense style of wine.

During an interview in early 2010, I asked Ferrini if he agreed with another winemaker who had recently proclaimed to the international press that "Sangiovese can make good to excellent wines, but never exceptional." Ferrini's answer surprised me, given that he works quite a bit with international varieties in Tuscany and across Italy. "I strongly disagree. Sangiovese can absolutely produce exceptional wines. The problem is that Sangiovese isn't easy; the grape needs to be pampered in both the vineyards and in the cellar," he asserted. Encouraged, I popped the million-dollar question at a time when Italy's high-profile wine figures were ducking any public declarations on Brunello. Did Ferrini think that Brunello producers should change their production code and allow international grapes into the wine? His response was succinct and fierce. "No, I don't see it that way. But it is time Brunello producers took a long, hard look at the situation and decide what they really want. If they want to make great Brunello from only 100 percent Sangiovese, then they have to get serious about zoning. This is a grape that performs exceptionally only in select parts of Montalcino, but producers pretend it's going to be great everywhere, and as a result they've planted the grape in every corner of Montalcino, from river banks to compact clay," argued Ferrini. "If, on the other hand, producers want to make great wine everywhere in Montalcino, even where Sangiovese doesn't yield exceptional results, then adding other grapes to compensate is necessary," continued the enologist.

BREAKING IT DOWN

Despite the mounting evidence and growing sentiment that subzones are crucial to the future of Brunello, realistically the denomination won't be petitioning Italy's minister of agriculture for zoning the area very soon, if ever. While other denominations, such as Barolo and Barbaresco, have made real efforts to limit uncontrolled expansion and to prohibit planting in blatantly inadequate areas and incorporating these changes into their production regulations, the official line from the powers that be in Montalcino is that subzones are not only unnecessary but that they would further complicate things. "It's not that we feel subzones don't exist, but because there are too many and recognizing them all would only create more confusion," said Consorzio director Stefano Campatelli in an interview with me in 2006.

It should be noted that this is one of the best-organized and hardest-working consorzi in Italy, and that it is not taking the issue lightly. No one can underestimate what a difficult endeavor zoning would be at this late date, given that it would greatly affect established firms and enormous commercial interests in Montalcino. But zoning would not necessarily mean a classification on the order of Grand Cru or Premier Cru; it could be divided geographically, at least at first. The primary areas and their pros and cons should be identified because consumers need guidance, or the whole denomination could suffer given the number and ambiguity of Brunello styles available on the market today. Global warming, which has raised average temperatures by one degree Celsius in Montalcino in the last thirty years and reduced annual rainfall for this same period, has further exaggerated the differences between subzones, with ripening improving in the higher reaches and overripening and very evident alcohol becoming increasing problems in the hottest areas of the denomination—further testament to the urgent need for zoning.

As Brunellos of different types and varying quality continue to reach the market, the best strategy for consumers is to seek out estates with a proven history of excellence and to keep an open mind when trying new labels. However, the denomination really must distinguish the best Brunellos—world-class wines handcrafted from magnificent terroirs that will allow them to age for decades—from those Brunellos being mass-produced in less suitable terrains or with cellar practices that mask Brunello's unique allure. In neighboring European wine countries, namely France, prime growing areas are protected and cherished, and one can only hope that some measures will be taken in Montalcino to single out and preserve the best areas. Otherwise the entire denomination risks being stigmatized by overproduction and a roller coaster of Brunello styles.

The following subzones, while unofficial, are widely agreed upon by Montalcino's producers and by academics that have researched the growing zone. For each subzone, I have included all the relevant information made available to me by producers, the Consorzio, historians, and university academics. Some areas have a wealth of information to choose from; other areas have less information available. Since the number of producers in each growing zone varies greatly, the number of producers profiled varies accordingly, with a greater number profiled in the Montalcino subzone given that the majority of Montalcino's producers are clustered in this area. For each subzone, I profile what I feel are the best estates whose Brunellos express their respective growing areas.

In brief, I have divided Montalcino into seven subzones: Montalcino (discussed in chapter 8), Bosco and Torrenieri (chapter 9), Tavernelle (chapter 10), Camigliano (chapter 11), Sant'Angelo (chapter 12), and Castelnuovo dell'Abate (chapter 13). The Montalcino growing area, which lies directly to the north and south of the town of Montalcino, has the highest altitudes and the oldest soil, which according to academics restrains Sangiovese's natural vigor. Brunellos from Montalcino tend to be among the most elegant, complex, and long-lived, and among the most highly perfumed. There are only two wineries in the subzone I have named Bosco in the northwest, an area often subject to spring frosts. Better clones, rigorous vineyard management, and careful grape selection are key to this area. In Torrenieri in the northeast, thick clay, frost, and fog make for less than ideal conditions in most of this subzone . This is perhaps the most disputed Brunello production area, and home to many start-up producers who only recently have converted their farms over to winemaking.

Heading south and west of Montalcino, Tavernelle is a fascinating area, making ripe Brunellos of great depth at what is often considered the ideal altitude for Sangiovese. Further southwest, Brunellos from the subzone spreading around the hamlet of Camigliano rely more on raw muscle and dense concentration than on complexity due to the lower altitudes and soil composition. Sant'Angelo in the deep south is divided into two distinct sections: Sant'Angelo in Colle and Sant'Angelo Scalo. Thanks to their high altitude and ideal exposure, Brunellos made from vineyards beneath the hamlet of Sant'Angelo possess an enticing combination of power and finesse, with ripe fruit and fine but bracing tannins. Many Brunellos from the best vineyards in Sant'Angelo in Colle boast surprising longevity and complexity. However, vineyards in the flatlands of Sant'Angelo Scalo, situated at very low altitudes in the youngest soils, suffer from scorching summertime temperatures. The results are Brunellos with little complexity or elegance, and often very high alcohol and massive tannins. Finally, the subzone of Castelnuovo dell'Abate, in the far southeast, is turning out some of the most exciting, well-balanced, and intriguing Brunellos in the entire denomination.

PART TWO

Leading Producers by Subzones

EIGHT

Montalcino

Directly to the north and south of Montalcino lies what is Brunello's original growing area, where the wine was first created and where, in the latter half of the nineteenth century and the early part of the twentieth, nearly all of the denomination's first pioneers chose vineyard sites. Today the majority of Brunello's 250 growers and bottling estates—almost without exception decidedly small-scale, family-run wineries—are clustered in this hilly terrain spreading outside the town gates. For many years the land around the town was the only Brunello-producing area. Unsurprisingly, this subzone is home to many of the oldest and most recognized names for Brunello, including Biondi Santi, Costanti, Fattoria dei Barbi, Canalicchio, Altesino, and Fuligni, as well as a large number of local farmers and growers-turned-winemakers.

Average vineyard altitudes range from 350 to 500 meters (1,148 to 1,640 feet) above sea level, giving these Brunellos an intricate range of aromas and impressive depth that Sangiovese grown in low altitudes simply cannot achieve. The very steep terrain along the ridges around the town necessitates manual vineyard maintenance and harvesting, which also benefit this difficult variety. The complex soil in this subzone is a key factor to the overall high and very high quality of wines from the classic growing area. According to Professor Costantini's excellent map on soil aptitude for Sangiovese vines, the Montalcino growing area, both to the north and the south of the town, possesses highly suitable soil for Sangiovese, with large areas that are defined as having both "high and moderate frequency of highly suitable soil" for this temperamental vine. Since the areas to the north and the south do have some differences in terms of climate, pedology, and geology, I have divided Montalcino between the north and the south, starting with the area just south of town, the official birthplace of Brunello.

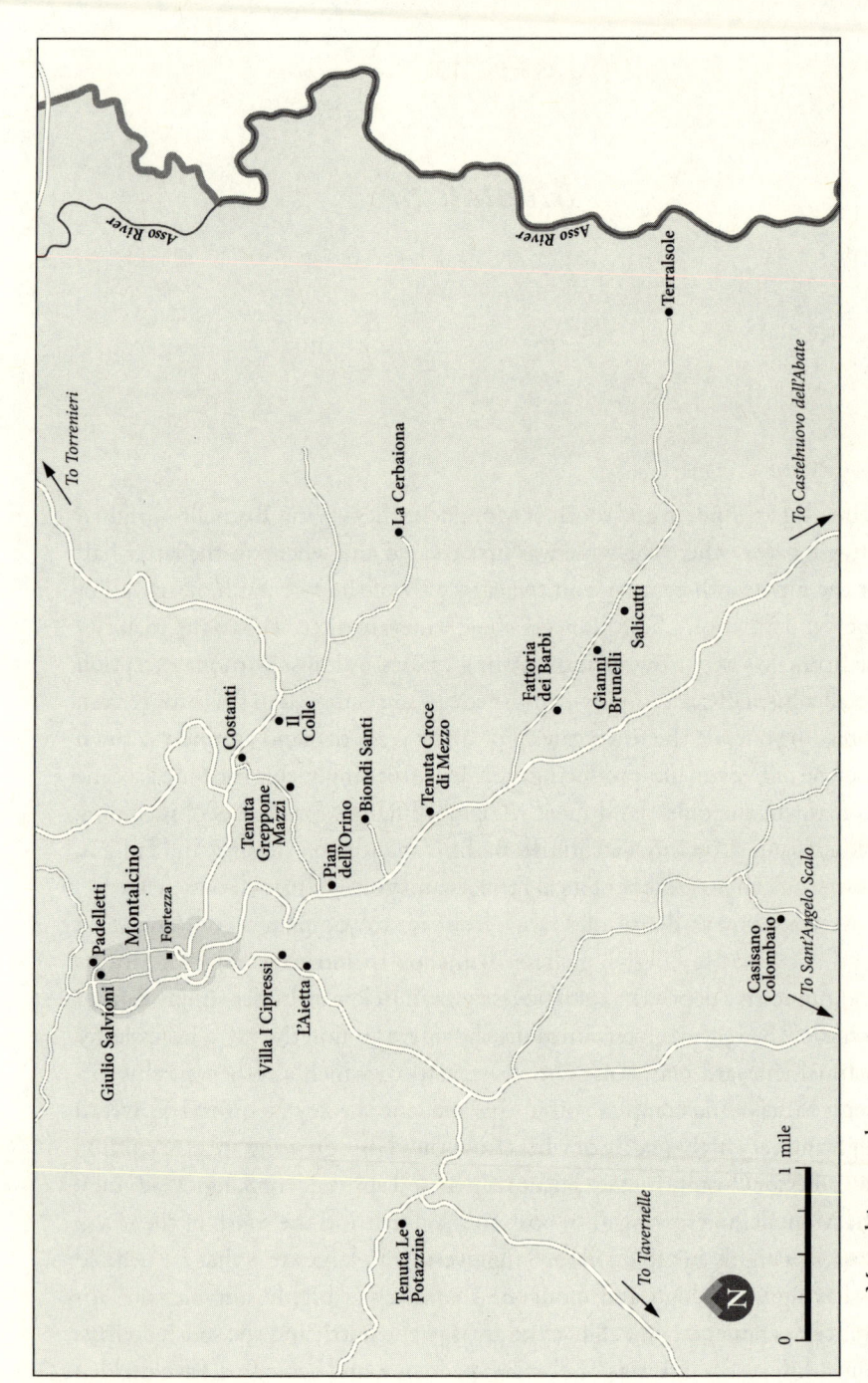

MAP 2. Montalcino, south

Soil structure in this zone is among the most ancient, dating from the Cretaceous period to the Eocene epoch when these higher altitudes emerged before the rest of the area from the oceans once covering the earth. This thin but well-draining soil, perfect for Sangiovese, is mainly calcareous and sandy limestone, though mineral-rich shale and sandstone formations as well as a flaky, marly limestone, commonly called *galestro* (though most geologists say that this is technically not an exact term for the friable rock in Montalcino), are also present in some of the best vineyards, including those at Biondi Santi's Greppo estate and Costanti's Colle al Matrichese property. According to Professor Costantini, "The highest reaches in the denomination contain ancient soils, or paleosoils, but unlike many other areas around the world with soil this old, the soils in the highest parts of Montalcino boast an extremely high mineral content. So while infertile, this soil has not been impoverished."

Here among the vertiginous reaches of the production zone, the most elegant and long-lived Brunellos are produced, complex and beautifully balanced with rich aromas that develop over time. Yet soil alone is not the only factor, and according to producers in this area, altitude plays a major role in Brunellos hailing from vineyards just south of Montalcino. The elevated vineyards generate great differences between day and night temperatures, especially during crucial ripening months when early-morning sun shines on south- and southeastern-facing vines, quickly heating up the grapes from the area's cool evening temperatures. These temperature variations cause slow-ripening grapes that are essential for developing the wine's perfume. The high altitude also imparts a relatively high acidity, which is the main element responsible for classic Brunello's marathon aging.

This is not to say that this area is perfect—no area ever is. In cool or wet years, grapes cultivated at these altitudes can have difficulty reaching ideal ripening. The Montalcino subzone as a whole suffered the most during the disastrous 2002 vintage, when torrential rain essentially rotted grapes on the vine just before harvest time. While the high altitude keeps the vines safely above harmful fog and constant breezes can quickly dry humidity, late spring frosts can cause a serious reduction in crops. However, in very hot and dry years, like the torrid 2003 vintage, these cooler, high-altitude temperatures can yield the freshest Brunellos in the denomination, not only because of the naturally higher acidity in the grapes, but also because, unlike the hotter, drier areas where heat and water stress can shut down ripening as happened in 2003, grapes grown in this subzone can actually attain better all-around maturation.

Franco Biondi Santi

Tenuta Greppo
53024 Montalcino (SI)
Tel. +39 0577 848087
www.biondisanti.it
biondisanti@biondisanti.it

For decades, Biondi Santi was synonymous with Brunello di Montalcino, and today the perennially dapper and dignified Franco Biondi Santi, eighty-nine as this book goes to print, remains Montalcino's iconic winemaker. Although I have already written about the family's crucial role in the history of Brunello (in chapters 3 and 4), at the risk of repeating, it is worth mentioning that it was at the family's splendid Greppo estate two miles south of Montalcino, the undisputed birthplace of Brunello, that Franco's grandfather Ferruccio Biondi Santi in the late nineteenth century created the wine from select Sangiovese plants and bottled and labeled it Brunello. Even though a few other gentlemen farmers in Montalcino began producing Brunello around the same time, most stopped in the early decades of the twentieth century. Only the Biondi Santis have carried on producing Brunello uninterrupted since the mid-nineteenth century.

The finesse, depth, and longevity of Ferruccio's wines shocked his contemporaries. Even today, Ferruccio's 1888 and 1891 vintages, jealously guarded under lock and key at the estate, remain intact. These spry centenarians dazzled tasters when they were last opened for the press in 1994. Ferruccio's son Tancredi, one of the greatest Italian enologists of the twentieth century, inherited the magnificent property in 1917 and imposed even more rigid production standards. He also had the shrewd foresight to create a library of old vintages to demonstrate the wine's nearly mythical longevity, and in 1944, Tancredi had the presence of mind to hide the old 1888–1925 Riservas before German and then Allied soldiers reached Montalcino. He and Franco along with a trusted cellar hand worked all through the night to wall up the old bottles, because as Tancredi put it, the armies would "either drink them or steal them."[1]

After Tancredi's death in 1970 Franco took over the business, and although

FIGURE 5. Montalcino's iconic winemaker, Franco Biondi Santi, has run his family's celebrated Greppo estate since 1970. Photograph by Paolo Tenti.

unfounded rumors have often maintained that his son Jacopo is at the helm, Greppo remains firmly in Franco's capable hands while Jacopo is busy fulltime at his own Maremma estate, the imposing Castello di Montepò. In early 2011, however, father and son aligned to jointly distribute their products. Franco, despite his age, still oversees every aspect of the vineyards and winemaking. Rather than being an innovator like his grandfather and father, Franco proudly declares that his role "is to protect the traditions that created Brunello, and to defend the *tipicità* of this great wine from any winemaking practices that could change its quintessential character." Accordingly, Franco applies the same scrupulous techniques passed down from his father, including severe grape selection that keeps yields very low—3 to 5 tons per hectare, even if the limit imposed by the regulations is 8 tons per hectare. Franco has a healthy respect for old vines, and shuns both herbicides and pesticides in the vineyards that he says "would mutate the strain of indigenous yeasts that are necessary for natural fermentation." As can be imagined, then, Biondi Santi never uses selected yeasts for fermentation, which is carried out under controlled temperatures in resin-lined cement vats for both Brunello and Rosso, and in Slavonian oak vats for the Riserva. Aging takes place exclusively in 30- and 50-hectoliter botti, a few of which are very old but perfectly maintained.

While the Brunello Annata is also capable of aging for twenty to forty years depending on the quality of the harvest, the firm's grand Riserva is Biondi Santi's calling card. Franco continues the house tradition of laying down past bottlings and in the process has created the most complete wine library of old vintages in all of Italy. Biondi Santi is one of the few estates in the world to top up its old Riservas when wine has visibly evaporated in the bottle (a process that happens as corks age) with wine from the same vintage from the family's personal cellars, though needless to say the firm charges a hefty price for this unique service.

Biondi Santi's wines are exceedingly elegant, and more complex than powerful, with enticing floral aromas and wild-cherry, tobacco, and mineral flavors. Firm tannins and bracing acidity soften with the years as the wines take on tertiary aromas and flavors of leather, tealeaf, flint, *goudron*, and carob. In top vintages, Biondi Santi's Riservas, among the most expensive bottlings in Italy, demonstrate the impeccable balance and depth that hallmark Burgundy's best Grands Crus. Vineyard altitudes range from 360 meters to 500 meters (1,181 to 1,640 feet), and the latter are among the highest in the denomination. Ideal exposures play a fundamental role in the wine's finesse and bouquet, as they generate sharp differences between day and night temperatures during the grape maturation period that in turn create complex aromas. Sangiovese cultivated at these heights have naturally high acidity, meaning the firm's Brunellos need time to develop and the estate's legendary Riservas can last for decades—some vintages even a hundred years, as verticals have proven.

Biondi Santi's vineyards are dispersed between Greppo, where the altitude is the highest and the soil is lean marl with friable, rocky schist; and the bordering Pieri estate, owned by Franco's wife, Maria Floria Petri; and Biondi Santi's other historic estate vineyards north of Montalcino, Pievecchia and Scarnacuoia. All of these have mixed soils of clay and rock. Vineyard age plays a key role in determining the structure of Biondi Santi's Brunellos and Rosso. Riservas, produced only in the best years and in amounts rarely exceeding 15,000 bottles, are made from vines over twenty-five years old, with the oldest vines over seventy. Vines for Brunello Annata, on the other hand, are between ten and twenty-five years old, and the firm's Rosso, which in great vintages can have as much depth as many other estate's Brunellos, hails from vines under ten. To uphold the firm's strict quality standards, in poor harvests Biondi Santi declassifies Brunello to a special edition Rosso di Montalcino called Fascia Rossa, or Red Stripe. Over 50 percent of all the vineyards are planted with BBS 11, an estate clone chosen after years of research with the University of Florence, and the rest are a mix of other estate clones.

Biondi Santi Brunellos were ferociously attacked throughout the 1990s and until the middle of the first decade of the new century because they are the polar opposite of the inky, jammy, and oak-driven Brunellos so loved by certain wine critics. During the long maelstrom, Franco Biondi Santi dug in and resisted what he saw as a passing trend and continued to make classic wines using Sangiovese-friendly methods, hanging onto his Slavonian botti and refusing to employ barriques or change his rigorous winemaking methods. His stubbornness paid off: the latter half of the first decade of this century has seen a huge return to the estate's traditional Brunellos, which have won several prestigious awards for recent vintages from the same publications that had previously criticized them.

Production

Total surface area: 152 ha between Pieri and Greppo (375 acres)
Brunello: 23 ha (57 acres), 50,000–70,000 bottles
Riserva: 8,000–10,000 bottles when produced
Rosso: 2 ha (5 acres), 12,000 bottles

Brunello.   While the Riservas are Biondi Santi's pride and joy, Brunello constitutes the bulk of production. Although the firm's Brunellos do not have the fame or the same structure and longevity of the estate's celebrated Riservas, they are very focused, with exquisite floral and leather aromas accompanied by an extremely elegant palate. Austere in their youth thanks to racy acidity and bracing tannins, they are also impeccably balanced, and begin to bloom ten to fifteen years after release, but can age for twenty to thirty years and longer. Made from vines between ten and twenty-five years old, Greppo's Brunellos boast impressive depth, and the latest vintages show a remarkable range of fresh berry and mineral flavors. The 1997, one of the very best from the vintage, was just starting to come into its own in 2010 but still needs time, while the 1999 and 2001 will be best after 2015. The 2004, on the other hand, should reach maturity in about 2020, but will drink well throughout the 2040s. Those years when the Riserva is not made, as for example in 2000, 2003, and 2005, the estate's oldest grapes go into the straight Brunello, generating more complexity and concentration. While more approachable earlier than the Riservas, this too is a wine for patient people.

Brunello Riserva. Made with the estate's oldest vines, Biondi Santi's Riservas have an extra dimension than the straight Brunellos and are among the most sought-after and expensive bottlings from all of Italy. Over the years I have tasted nearly all of the estate's top Riservas, and since slow but continuous evolution and marathon aging are part of what first made Brunello famous, here are my top picks from Biondi Santi's impressive library of old Riservas. As tastings back to 1945 have proven, they are well deserving of their lofty reputation.

❧ *2004.* This is perhaps Franco Biondi Santi's true masterpiece, and is a monument to Brunello. Intense floral and earthy fragrance, with hint of spice and leather with layers of wild cherry, earth, and mineral, and a hint of tobacco. Impeccably balanced with compelling depth of flavors. Will age for decades thanks to vibrant acidity and elegant but bracing tannins. A stunning, gripping wine with Grace Kelly–like finesse and polish. Should drink best 2024–54.

2001. A signature Biondi Santi with firm acidity, mineral, and restrained but delicious cherry-berry and earthy sensations. Great breeding, finesse, and complexity. Best 2020–40.

1999. Delicate floral aromas with a hint of underbrush, and a mouthwatering palate of ripe, crushed cherry, and pastry cream perfectly balanced with fresh acidity and supple tannins. Tasted in 2009, this was still a teenager that needs time to develop fully. Will age for decades, and best after 2020.

1998. Although initially closed when first tasted in 2005, as each year passes this sleeper vintage opens up remarkably and was showing beautifully when last tasted in 2010, with bright berry and energizing mineral. Focused and compelling, with fantastic length. Best after 2015 and should drink well through 2025.

1997. When last tasted in 2009, this was still sorting itself out, but has all the makings of becoming one of the house's signature Riservas. Nose is still somewhat closed, but bracing tannins and still very firm acidity are balanced by a rich palate layered with ripe berry, earth, leather, tobacco, and carob. Mesmerizing complexity though this youngster still needs time. Best after 2025.

1985. Earthy but refined nose with dried rose petals and a whiff of *vin santo*–like aromas. Creamy-cherry and *zabaglione* flavors with a long mineral finish. Fantastic length and depth, and is remarkably fresh when tasted at twenty-five years old. Should drink well at least through 2025, perhaps longer.

1983. First vintage with temperature-controlled fermentation equipment. Intense floral nose with leather and tobacco. Rich, creamy cherry, and strawberry punctuated by an extraordinary mineral purity. Very focused and perfectly balanced by bright acidity and supple tannins. Extreme elegance and fantastic length. Still vibrant when last tried in 2011, can age for decades more.

❧ *1975.* When I first tasted this bottling, in 2005 for an article in *World of Fine Wine*, I gave it my first ever perfect score of twenty out of twenty. Between then and 2011, I've tried this wine three more times, and it is still magnificent, with an intense bouquet of spice, flint, pepper, and tobacco. Rich berry and fig flavors are balanced by still fresh acidity and supple, silky tannins. Incredibly youthful and focused. Will continue to age smoothly for decades. A gorgeous, glorious wine and so far my personal favorite of all the estate's Riservas.

1964. I've tasted this wine several times, and its youthful structure and cherry fruit never cease to amaze me. A wine of great breeding, finesse, and subtle power. Aging slowly and majestically, it has the structure and energy to maintain for decades.

1955. Well deserving of its lofty reputation. Rich and complex bouquet of tar, cedar, and pipe tobacco. Creamy cherry flavors with a hint of black tea and fig. Refined, velvety tannins, and long, lingering sweet tea and spice finish. Still evolving. Fascinating wine. When last tasted in 2011, it boasted impressive intensity of aromas and flavors.

1945. Although it has lost much of its color, this still shows surprising freshness when tried in 2005, with lingering acidity balanced by the smoothest tannins and delicate, creamy cherry fruit and tobacco. Captivating.

Rosso. Aged for two years in botti, in great years Biondi Santi Rossos have the depth and complexity one would expect from a Brunello. Although approachable upon release, Biondi Santi's Rossos, which boast the estate's hallmark balance and restraint, can age well, over ten years in top vintages. The 2006 is superb, with the flair, finesse, bright fruit, and minerality of fine Burgundy, an impressive effort for Rosso. Best through 2020.

Conti Costanti

Colle al Matrichese
53024 Montalcino (SI)
Tel. +39 0577 848195
www.costanti.it
info@costanti.it

Costanti is another historic name in Montalcino, with Brunello roots reaching back to the late nineteenth century. Today Andrea Costanti and his enologist, Vittorio Fiore, make sleek Brunellos with ripe fruit and round tannins that appeal to international palates but that still have Sangiovese's floral, earthy, wild-cherry charm. These Brunellos are renowned for their elegance and drinkability, effectively bridging the sometimes wide divide between the jammy, fruit-forward Brunellos and a more restrained style.

Andrea, who took over the estate in 1983 while still at university, descends from a noble Sienese family that fled the city in 1555 to take refuge in the Republic of Siena's last stronghold, the fortress of Montalcino, where they would spend the next four years. When the republic finally fell in 1559 to Florentine and Spanish soldiers, the Costanti family decided to remain in Montalcino, where they had obtained large holdings. Their lovely Colle al Matrichese estate, with its fifteenth-century stone palazzo, located just over a mile from the town center and surrounded by vineyards, has been in the Costanti family ever since. The family's Brunello roots stretch back to the wine's earliest pioneers; documents show that Tito Costanti presented a wine he called Brunello at a wine fair in the Province of Siena back in 1870. Production was tiny, however, and Costanti Brunello was made exclusively for the family and their lucky friends, until 1964, when Andrea's great-uncle Emilio began increasing production and became one of the first Montalcino producers to bottle and sell Brunello. The breeding and finesse of Costanti Brunellos soon made them a sensation among wine lovers, though demand quickly outstripped supply.

Production is still limited. Costanti makes between 30,000 and 35,000 bottles of Brunellos a year from 7 hectares of vineyards surrounding Colle al Matrichese, and between 10,000 and 20,000 bottles of Rosso from the same vineyards as well as from 1.3 hectares of the Calbello Alto vineyard, near Montosoli. In exceptional years, such as 1997, 2001, and 2004, Costanti also makes a small amount of Riserva from a selection of the best barrels during the aging process.

Vineyard altitudes for Costanti Brunello range between 400 and 450 meters above sea level, which lend their wine enough fresh acidity for cellaring while diurnal and nocturnal temperature changes generate complex aromas. Vineyards, many planted with the BBS 11 clone, range from five to twenty-five years old, with the oldest vines between twenty and twenty-five years old lending the wine its depth. Like all top Brunello producers, Costanti keeps yields far lower than required by the production regulations for both Brunello and his well-structured Rosso, to further enhance quality.

While Andrea respects traditional Brunello, he also likes to mix it up a bit in the cellar. His Rosso spends twelve months in 350-liter Allier barriques and 500-liter Allier tonneaux, 25 percent of them new. His Brunello, on the other hand, ages for eighteen months in new and used 350- and 500-liter Allier barriques/tonneaux and eighteen months in mid-sized 30-hectoliter Slavonian oak botti. Renowned for their floral, spicy bouquets, Costanti Brunellos are more approachable upon release than many more traditionally crafted Brunellos, thanks to softer tannins, though they develop more complexity with aging. Despite backing away from 225-liter barriques in recent years, in lesser vintages the wines can demonstrate evident oak sensations. In good and outstanding years, however, Andrea's Brunellos and Riservas are exceptional.

The longevity of Costanti Brunellos is indeed remarkable, and the older vintages in particular benefit from a slow evolution and have impressive staying power. I had the opportunity in 2010 of trying a series of older vintages at the estate, an experience that might be characterized by only one adjective: magnificent.

Production

Total surface area: 12 ha (30 acres)
Brunello: 7 ha (17 acres), 30,000–35,000 bottles
Rosso: 1.3 ha (3 acres), 10,000–20,000 bottles

Brunello. This is the focal point of the estate's small production, and Andrea prefers to make Brunello with the best grapes on the estate, making just a miniscule amount of Riserva and only in truly superlative vintages. Costanti Brunellos are highly perfumed with nuances of incense, sandalwood, and spice, all of which carry over onto the palate, along with ripe black- and red-berry flavors, and a whisper of oak. Gripping but elegant tannins boast impressive structure. Costanti's Brunellos are best at the ten- to fifteen-year mark, but in top vintages they can age very well. The 2001 is both subtle and stunning.

Riserva. Andrea feels that Riserva, which is selected in the cellars, should be made exclusively in exceptional vintages, and even then just in small amounts. "To make Riserva in most years, or even in every good year, you risk harming the straight Brunello, because all the best grapes go into the Riservas," explains Costanti. However, in extraordinary vintages, Andrea does choose a small amount of the most structured Brunello and produces a wonderful Riserva destined for lengthy aging.

2004. Still rather closed nose. Very ripe black-fruit flavors, with hint of oak. Needs time to develop, and while very fruit-forward and concentrated, still has great finesse and flair. Best after 2015.

2001. Gorgeous. Complex aromas of sandalwood, incense, and spice. Restrained but ripe berry flavors with energizing minerality. Beautifully balanced and great length. Will age for decades. Best 2011–25.

1997. Costanti's quintessential incense and spice aromas, with lush fruit and velvety tannins. Still very fresh with great length. One of the best examples from what was an extremely overrated vintage. Best through 2017.

1995. All incense, leather, and spice with rich berry-cherry fruit. Elegant and bright, this is a breathtaking Brunello. Very young but with great depth and complexity. Will age wonderfully for years. Best through 2020.

1988. More upfront than 1985, not as vibrant or complex. But has big ripe black-cherry and spice flavors. Delicious, round, and ready. Will not age as well as 1985, 1977, or 1967, but is a lovely twenty-two-year-old when tasted in 2010.

1985. Initially closed then nose opens up to reveal incense and spice. Palate is bright and fresh with ripe, rich cherry-berry and carob flavors and a clean mineral purity. Very elegant and complex.

1977.   The first Brunello bottled by Andrea after he took over the estate. Tar and mineral nose with hint of graphite. Creamy strawberry-berry fruit and lively acidity, firm tannins. Impeccable balance and depth. Fantastic wine with years to go.

★ *1967.*   Gorgeous wine. Incredibly youthful, with complex aromas of spice, earth, and dried fruit. Remarkably rich cherry and spice flavors demonstrate ripe cherry with big spicy notes. Extraordinarily bright, and well balanced with vibrant acidity and firm tannins. Remarkable length. Can still age for years.

Brunello 1965.   While this was not a stellar year in Montalcino, this straight Brunello was still standing, and gracefully at that, when tried in 2010. Animal and goudron aromas are intense but evolved; the palate retains delicate fruit flavors with tealeaf and mineral notes. Still lingering acidity, but on its slow decline.

Rosso.   While I have had many fine Rossos from the estate in the past, I must admit that new oak in recent vintages, such as the 2007, muffled the underlying vibrant fruit and mineral.

Il Colle

Località Il Colle 102B
53024 Montalcino (SI)
Tel. +39 0577 848295
ilcolledicarli@libero.it

Il Colle is one of the many small jewels in Montalcino's original growing area. Despite its tiny production, over the last decade Il Colle's graceful yet structured Brunellos have garnered well-deserved attention from both critics and connoisseurs who love the firm's pure, unfettered expression of Sangiovese. Situated just outside of town, Il Colle was once part of Conti Costanti's Colle al Matrichese property, but family inheritances and divisions split the original property back in the eighteenth century. Many of Il Colle's vineyards border directly on Costanti's, and the two wineries are actually housed in separate sections of the same large fifteenth-century palazzo that once belonged solely to the Costanti family. Alberto Carli, a notary from Siena, and his wife, Ernesta Giannelli, purchased the property in 1972 and immediately planted their first vineyards, with their debut Brunello hailing from the 1978 harvest.

Il Colle has always been staunchly traditional, and has employed the much sought-after consulting services of Sangiovese purist Giulio Gambelli since 1981. After Alberto Carli passed away in 2001, his daughter Caterina took over and still relies on the advice of Gambelli, though she is very much in charge of day-to-day operations. Caterina has lovingly held on to her father's "Gambellian" winemaking methods, which include steering clear of selected yeasts for fermentation, which takes place with no temperature control, and preferring rather long maceration on the skins. Aging takes place in Slavonian botti for up to four years for Brunello, though Caterina also has two large Allier botti that are now over twenty years old. Like her father, Caterina also forgoes filtering.

Il Colle's Brunellos and Rossos have always been extremely elegant, at times almost ethereal, no doubt thanks at least in part to the high vineyard altitude of between 400 and 450 meters (1,312 and 1,476 feet), where grapes yield more delicate wines and may not always attain perfect ripeness in difficult years. To add more structure to their graceful and understated wines, and to split the risk of having grapes from a single subzone that could suffer more than other areas in certain vintages, the Carlis decided to invest in one of the denomination's warmer areas where they could cultivate grapes that would be blended with those from Il Colle. In 1998 the family purchased land at 220 meters (720 feet) above sea level, in Castelnuovo dell'Abate, which they planted that same year. These more southern grapes are harvested on average ten days earlier than those at Il Colle and have lent body and ripe fruit to the exquisite aromas and finesse of Il Colle Brunellos ever since the two estates were first blended together with the excellent 2001 harvest.

Production

Total surface area: 20 ha (49 acres)
Brunello: 4.75 ha (12 acres), 20,000 bottles
Rosso: 1.5 ha (3.7 acres), 8,000 bottles

Brunello. This is the hallmark wine for Il Colle, especially since the estate rarely makes a Riserva and only then in truly exceptional vintages, the last one being produced in 1990. Brightly colored, Il Colle Brunellos are supple and refined with quintessential aromas and flavors of Sangiovese: earth, tea-leaf, wild cherry, and hints of leather, and a seducing mineral purity in place of raw power. This is not to say, however, that these are lightweights, as their firm acidity and noticeable tannins demonstrate.

Rosso. Most of the estate's Rosso is declassed from Brunello vines, and are vibrant, delicious, and very food-friendly wines that are perfect to enjoy while young. Very earthy with bright cherry, and made entirely without pretension, these Rossos never aspire to be "Baby Brunellos." Pure pleasure.

Pian dell'Orino

Località Pian dell'Orino 189
53024 Montalcino (SI)
Tel. +39 0577 849301
www.piandellorino.it
info@piandellorino.it

When Caroline Pobitzer left South Tyrol and her family's Castel Katzenzungen winery, famous for its six-hundred-year-old, 350-square-meter vine, arguably the oldest and undoubtedly the largest grapevine in the world, for Montalcino, she knew she wanted to make Brunello, but had no idea that in doing so she would also find her future husband. In 1996 Caroline purchased the Pian dell'Orino winery situated right next to Biondi Santi's Greppo estate, and shortly afterward enlisted German-born Jan Hendrik Erbach as her consultant winemaker and the pair married just a few years later.

The original acquisition included nearly one hectare of vines around the villa, on the border with Greppo, and Caroline and Jan have since invested in other vineyards further southeast in and around Castelnuovo dell'Abate. Caroline and Jan are firm believers in Sangiovese, and together with Francesco Leanza from Podere Salicutti and Stella di Campalto, have started the long process of officially separating from the Brunello Consorzio and have founded "Sangiovese per Amico," an association to study and promote both the variety and Montalcino's diversity. "We don't feel that the Consorzio has the best interests of the small producers in mind, even if we make up the majority of the denomination," argues Jan.

The dynamic young couple has some rather unconventional ideas, to say the least. As Caroline says, their goal "is to create and sustain the maximum harmony possible between vineyard, climate, soil, and mankind." Needless to say after that declaration, Pian dell'Orino is certified organic: Caroline and Jan have never used herbicides, chemical pesticides, insecticides, or chemical fertilizers in their vineyards. Instead they resort to natural remedies to reinforce their vines, including infusions made from nettles, yarrow, and other biodynamic elixirs, and administer propolis to ward off infections caused by fungus or bacteria. They also plant an array of flowers, clove, and grass between the vines to maintain a vital ecosystem of predator insects. Caroline and Jan have studied every aspect of their separate vineyards, and each is coddled and pampered according to its own needs. While the Pian dell'Orino vineyard, situated at 470 meters (1,542 feet) above sea level, is predominantly clay and sand, their Pian Bossolino vineyard, 390 meters (1,280 feet) above sea level, is a mix of clay, sand, silt, and limestone. Their third Brunello vineyard, Cancello Rosso, in Castelnuovo dell'Abate, 310 meters (1,017 feet), contains silt and limestone as well as mineral-rich red rocks. Caroline and Jan have some BBS 11 clones, but have also replanted using many of the newer clones, including Tin 10 and 50, Janus 10 and 20, and BF 10, which give their Brunellos a much darker color.

Grape selection is key to the estate's richly structured and fruit-forward wines. Besides rigorous, almost ruthless, thinning out of the grapes, the firm also selects prime berries on a sorting table at harvest time. The almost maniacal attention to quality and detail carries over to the winemaking, starting with the firm's unique, round cellar, which was designed to imitate a cradle, and made from what Caroline calls breathable material; clay, wood, lime, and stone, all sourced from their vineyards. Jan relies only on wild yeasts and spontaneous fermentation, with no temperature control for Brunello, which takes place in wooden vats, with each vineyard vinified separately, followed by thirty to forty months aging in Slavonian oak. Rosso is vinified in steel, under temperature control, and is aged for over a year, partly in botti and partly in French tonneaux. These ripe, muscle-flexing Brunellos and Rossos are not for the faint-of-heart.

Production

Total surface area: 10 ha (25 acres)
Brunello: 3.5 ha (8.6 acres), 6,000–12,000 bottles
Rosso: 1 ha (2.47 acres), 6,000–12,000 bottles

Brunello.   Pian dell'Orino's Brunellos are richly concentrated, with a big, powerful structure, and gorgeous, succulent fruit. However, perhaps because of the almost obsessive bunch thinning and selection, the wines can sometimes lack vibrancy, a key element to Brunello, and can also display very evident alcohol sensations.

Rosso.   Very bright, cherry fruit, with well-integrated oak. Again, I would prefer less noticeable alcohol, but this is still a very friendly wine.

Fattoria dei Barbi

Località Podernovi 170
53024 Montalcino (SI)
Tel. +39 0577 841111
www.fattoriadeibarbi.it
info@fattoriadeibarbi.it

Fattoria dei Barbi is another one of those historic Montalcino names, as is the surname of the estate's owners, Colombini. The family has had extensive holdings throughout Montalcino since the fourteenth century, and today owns 450 hectares (1,112 acres) dispersed between Montalcino, Chianti, and Scansano, but their Barbi property in Montalcino, acquired in 1790, is the family's headquarters and most acclaimed property. Fattoria dei Barbi, located along the road from Montalcino to Sant'Antimo in an area known as Podernovi, is one of the largest estates in Brunello, in terms of acres under vine and volume. Despite its size, Fattoria dei Barbi remains a family affair and today Stefano Cinelli Colombini runs the business, although his mother, Francesca, who inherited the estate from her father, still has a strong presence in the firm where she has worked for decades. In the late 1990s, the family's vast holdings were divided between Stefano and his sister, Donatella Cinelli Colombini, who left in 1998 to set up her own eponymous winery after decades of working alongside her mother and brother.

Stefano is quick to point out his family's role in Montalcino's rich history as part of the privileged class of landed gentry, and above all as Brunello pioneers. The estate's first Brunello was the 1892 vintage, and according to Stefano, Barbi was also "the first to export the wine to Europe, America, and Asia." Fattoria dei Barbi also presented Brunello at Siena's early wine fairs in 1933 and 1935, but it was not until Stefano's grandfather Giovanni Colombini, one of the founders of the Consorzio, started bottling Brunello in the late 1950s that the firm began consistently producing the town's flagship wine.

The estate's vineyards stretch along undulating hills around the winery from Podernovi down a few miles to the tiny hamlet of Barbi en route to Sant'Antimo, and enjoy a wide array of altitudes, soils, and exposures. Roughly speaking, vines average 350 to 400 meters (1,150 to 1,312 feet) above sea level and are planted in a combination soil of marl, lime, and clay, at average densities of 5,000 plants per hectare, with a wide variety of clones, including estate clones as well as M 42 and R 24.

Although in the past I sometimes found Barbi's Brunello Annata, the straight Brunello, a bit lackluster, recent vintages have demonstrated a firm commitment to raising quality. In 2001 Stefano began experimenting with pre-fermentation cryomaceration, a process that freezes the grape skins for forty-eight hours, during which time cells within the grape explode but don't damage the skins or seeds. Cryomaceration helps extract color and soften tannins, while increasing complexity. Perhaps the most fundamental change came when Paolo Salvi joined the firm in 2003 as in-house enologist. Salvi has noticeably improved quality, especially for the straightforward Brunello, thanks to scrupulously vinifying every vineyard separately and insisting on careful selection before deciding on the final assembly for Brunello. In the past this painstaking and time-consuming process was performed only for the firm's Riservas and of course for its single-vineyard Brunello Vigna del Fiore, both of which are made in small amounts in top years and which are consistently very good to downright excellent.

Even though Brunello production is the estate's priority, Barbi has remained a working farm and grows other crops as well as raises livestock. Their products, along with herbs from their well-stocked garden, are the staple for the authentic local dishes served at their on-site tavern, while the estate's gourmet shop sells the firm's own cheese, salami, and olive oil. Stefano also founded the Museo del Brunello next door to the estate, a must-see for Brunellophiles. It is filled with photos of Montalcino's pioneers along with antique winemaking artifacts and documents that chronicle Brunello's and Montalcino's history.

Production

Total surface area: 338 ha (835 acres)
Brunello: 42 ha (104 acres), 250,000 bottles
Rosso: 15 ha (37 acres), 100,000 bottles

Brunello. If in the past these wines suffered from being made in high quantities, the most recent vintages show great improvement, once again thanks to better grape selection and improved cellar methods. Aged for two years in botti, the 2005 is an archetypical Brunello, and not just for the vintage. Very approachable and enjoyable, boasting delicious berry and mineral. Best through 2015.

Riserva. Barbi only makes about 12,000 to 20,000 bottles of Riserva, exclusively in top vintages and from a selection of the best grapes. Aged for three years in various-sized botti ranging from 5 to 80 hectoliters, Barbi's Riservas display all the quintessential leather and tobacco sensations accompanied by restrained but ripe fruit and the depth one would expect from Brunellos from Montalcino's classic growing area. These usually age well for at least twenty years, longer in exceptional years.

Vigna del Fiore. In outstanding vintages Barbi also produces a single-vineyard Brunello, Vigna del Fiore, from a 5.7 hectare (14 acres) parcel located in the estate's most southern vineyards. Loaded with floral and spicy sandalwood aromas and chock-full of black berry, cherry, and mineral, this Brunello combines muscle, finesse, and complexity. The 2005 was already enjoyable in 2010, but this will be at its top in 2015 and will drink well through 2020.

Rosso. The firm's Rosso has noticeably improved, thanks to better selection. While the farm has some registered Rosso vineyards, it also declassifies a good amount of Brunello. Barbi's friendly Rosso is earthy, bright, and very drinkable, with a little more structure and balance in recent vintages.

Tenuta Crocedimezzo

Località La Croce
Montalcino (SI)
Tel. +39 0577 848007
www.crocedimezzo.com
crocedimezzo@crocedimezzo.com

Crocedimezzo is another one of Montalcino's little-known treasures, and the firm's Brunellos are a refreshing and exemplary expression of Sangiovese from Montalcino. Exquisitely perfumed and extremely elegant yet well structured, the wine from this boutique winery is a must for lovers of classic Brunellos and for those who enjoy the charms of fine Burgundy.

The lovely family-run estate just a few miles south of Montalcino is located between Biondi Santi's Greppo and Cinelli Colombini's Fattoria dei Barbi. "Crocedimezzo's location is Montalcino's version of an island paradise, being right in the middle of the denomination's most historic estates, Biondi Santi's Greppo and Fattoria dei Barbi," declares Barbara Nannetti. Barbara and her brother Roberto have run the winery, founded in 1971, since 1998, though her mother, Fiorella Vannoni, is still active at the winery and its on-site country hotel.

Named after the nearby fourteenth-century parish church La Croce, which according to Nannetti would have been one of the stops for religious pilgrims traveling to Rome on the Via Francigena, the estate is a prime location for Brunello production, and the family's first Brunello came out with the excellent 1985 vintage. Vineyards average 480 meters (1,575 feet) above sea level and enjoy east, southeast, and northeast exposures, while the infertile soil is a mixture of clay and sand with a strong presence of stone. Here in the heart of the original production area Sangiovese yields full-bodied, classic Brunellos with restrained but succulent, bright fruit, and are more reserved than forward. Roberto Nannetti, who enlists the help of consultant Paolo Vagaggini, ferments in temperature-controlled steel tanks in the firm's spacious underground cellars, and ages Brunello for one and a half years in Slavonian botti, and one and a half years in Allier botti. Rosso, on the other hand, is aged for nine months in the same kind of casks as Brunello.

Production

Total surface area: 47 ha (113 acres)
Brunello: 9.7 ha (24 acres), 30,000 bottles
Riserva: 2,000 bottles
Rosso: 0.75 ha (1.8 acres), 30,000 bottles

Brunello. These Brunellos offer all the benchmark Sangiovese sensations of cherry-berry, earth, and mineral with an invigorating whiff of spice. The 2004 is gorgeous, with candied cherry flavors with a succulent creamy texture, all buoyed by energizing minerality, firm acidity, and supple tannins. A polished Brunello with striking depth that will be best after the ten-year mark. The 2005, not a great vintage overall for Montalcino, is also exquisite, with floral aromas and a whiff of sandalwood. With its vibrant cherry and mineral palate and smooth, refined tannins, this was already drinking well in 2010 and should continue to maintain until 2015–20.

Riserva.   Produced exclusively in superb years, such as 1997, 1999, and 2004, Crocedimezzo chooses the best grapes from its Poggio vineyard to make a Riserva that boasts more depth and power than the Annata, with bracing but refined tannins. While the Riservas need more time to soften, they will age wonderfully. The 2004 is superb, with leather, fennel, and earth aromas accompanied by earthy flavors of succulent wild cherry, clove, and mineral balanced with ripe, chewy tannins and lovely acidity. Best after 2015 but will drink beautifully through the 2030s.

Rosso.   Floral berry aromas and bright, mouthwatering fruit flavors. Very friendly and exhilarating, this delicious wine will pair beautifully with dishes from humble *pasta pomodoro* to chicken to steak.

Gianni Brunelli—Le Chiuse di Sotto

Località Podernovone 157
53024 Montalcino (SI)
Tel. +39 0577 849337
www.giannibrunelli.it
laura.brunelli@giannibrunelli.it

With a last name like Brunelli, it would seem that destiny had long ago guaranteed the late Gianni Brunelli's future as a top Brunello producer. Gianni's Brunello-making adventure was not a quick or easy ride to the top, but an adventure it was, filled with passion and joy that his friends and Brunello admirers can see mirrored in his vibrant, full-bodied yet graceful Brunellos.

Gianni was born in Montalcino, where his father had a small vineyard and farm at Le Chiuse di Sotto just north of Montalcino. When Gianni was very young his parents reluctantly sold the farm and moved the family to Siena in the hopes of finding work during what were some of the darkest years for Montalcino, when the town was the poorest in the entire Province of Siena and one of the poorest in all of Tuscany. Gianni's mother, widowed shortly after moving to Siena, always wished they could have hung on to the family farm, something Gianni never forgot.

FIGURE 6. Gianni Brunelli's beautiful Olmo vineyard. The estate never uses harsh chemicals or herbicides and makes structured but graceful wines with mineral complexity. Photograph by Paolo Tenti.

In the late 1960s, Gianni became a young but adamant protester during Italy's turbulent period of social reform before he eventually met Laura, his future wife and life-partner in every sense of the word. They later established one of the city's most successful restaurants, Le Logge, near the Piazza del Campo, where Gianni and Laura insisted not only on using the freshest ingredients available but also added their own personal flair to revamp traditional dishes. Gianni's warm and gregarious personality and Laura's easy-going manner and sharp wit have always made patrons feel more like visiting relatives, and it is no wonder locals keep Le Logge one of the city's most jealously guarded secrets from the throng of tourists that descend on Siena every year.

Gianni soon decided to make his own wine and olive oil for the restaurant and for friends, and he duly combined his own ambition with his mother's dream of reclaiming the family's Montalcino farm. In 1987, he achieved his goal and proudly acquired their original 2-hectare (5-acre) vineyard just north of town, where he began making both Brunello and olive oil. In 1997, Gianni and Laura bought a splendid property with 4.5 hectares (11 acres) of south-facing vineyards at Podernovone, just next door to Fattoria dei Barbi, with a stunning view of Monte Amiata. As Gianni told me back in 2005, he wanted to blend Sangiovese from the two properties to naturally create perfect balance: "Wines made from Le Chiuse di Sotto grapes have the most beautiful, expressive bouquets, while Podernovone's grapes give the wine more structure and depth, which I wanted for my Brunello. I would never try to create this balance with various cellar practices, but achieve it instead by blending Sangiovese from the two vineyards."

After Gianni's premature death in 2008, Laura has carried on his legacy, and her dedication to their dreams means that she continues the high standards that allowed her and Gianni to create stunning Brunellos that boast quintessential Sangiovese sensations of wild cherry fruit and mineral complexity. Laura and her agronomist, Laura Bernini, keep treatments against vine diseases to the bare minimum and forgo herbicides and pesticides. The vineyards at Podernovone are particularly beautiful not only because of the breathtaking panorama of the valley of Castelnuovo dell'Abate below, but also thanks to Laura Brunelli's penchant for rare antique roses and shrubs, which she has planted alongside her manicured vineyards. In the cellars, tradition prevails, and the estate, advised by consultant enologist Paolo Vagaggini, uses only native yeast for fermentation and ages its Brunellos in medium-sized Slavonian casks. These are simply gorgeous, delicious Brunellos made with careful attention and the utmost respect for nature that require not only full-time dedication and supervision, but, to use another one of the most abused words in winespeak, passion.

Production

Total surface area: 15 ha (37 acres)
Brunello: 4 ha, 25,000 bottles
Rosso: 1.5 ha, 13,000 bottles

Brunello. The estate's flagship wine. These are hallmark Brunellos with floral, leather, and tobacco aromas accompanied by ripe, wild-cherry, and mineral flavors. Vertical tastings over the years have demonstrated that the estate can make compelling wines even in lesser vintages, as the 1996 tasted in 2011 amply demonstrated.

🅰 *Riserva.* In top years, the boutique estate also makes a superb Riserva. The 2001, the first year that Sangiovese from both Montalcino estates were blended, owes its gorgeous floral aromas to Le Chiuse di Sotto and muscle to Podernovone. This has the essential structure to age beautifully for at least another decade and longer. Best through 2025. The 2004 is exceptional and is a must-have Brunello for collectors and connoisseurs alike. Intense and earthy with beguiling aromas and remarkable depth. Best 2014 to 2030. This Riserva is to Brunello di Montalcino what Robert Johnson is to the blues: a benchmark.

Rosso. Bright and structured yet so drinkable, this is everything a Rosso should be, and more.

Salicutti

Località Salicutti 174
53024 Montalcino (SI)
Tel. +39 0577 847003
www.poderesalicutti.it
leanza@poderesalicutti.it

If you appreciate the subtle elegance and complexity of great Burgundy, this is your Brunello: luminous and garnet-colored with earthy flavors and a silky palate. Proprietor Francesco Leanza makes his graceful Brunellos with organic farming methods, wild yeasts, and as little intervention as possible in the cellar.

Given that Leanza spent twenty years as a chemist in Rome before starting a new life in Montalcino, his hands-off attitude in the cellar is somewhat surprising, as is his rather unscientific belief in the existence of terroir. "I accompany the wine, but I never force it or change its natural course," says Leanza, who adds that it is the estate's unique growing conditions that make distinct wines. Leanza, a brooding perfectionist with an infrequent but stunning smile, concedes that he is rarely satisfied, always thinking he could do better. "I do what I can, but at some point, I just accept the wine for what it is any given year," according to Leanza.

Fortunately for Leanza and for Brunello fans, the ex-chemist ended up choosing an ideal location that has allowed him such great fruit that it need only be guided rather than forced, though originally his choice was not Brunello-based at all. After vacationing several times in Montalcino in the late 1980s, Leanza decided he would like to buy a home there, and after a lengthy search found the 11-hectare property known as Salicutti. "When I acquired the property back in 1990, the Brunello vineyard register was closed, so I could only make Chianti Colli Sienese here, which didn't appeal to me," explains Leanza. A few years after buying the property, in 1994, Leanza planted a vineyard anyway, having caught the wine bug that is in the air around Montalcino, and then bought a small Brunello plot in Sant'Angelo, which he pulled up, transferring the planting rights to his Salicutti vineyard. When the Brunello registers unexpectedly reopened in 1997, Leanza was able to enroll his 3.5 hectares (8.6 acres) of Salicutti vines into the Brunello books. By then he had already left Rome and moved definitively to Montalcino, where he became the denomination's first certified organic estate in 1996.

Located just below Gianni Brunelli's Podernovone estate, Salicutti's vines average 450 meters (1,476 feet) above sea level in a mixed soil of clay, sand, and rock fragments, all with south and southwest exposures. Not wanting to intervene with chemicals in the vineyards, Leanza deep ploughs the vineyards in autumn, uses only organic fertilizer when necessary, and lets grass grow between the rows to create competition among the vines and to stop erosion. Self-taught in the art of winemaking, Leanza shuns selected yeasts for fermentation and is adamantly against any techniques he feel forces the wine, including clarification and filtering. He prefers to age in French wood, employing 500-liter tonneaux of various ages as well as 10- and 20-hectoliter botti of Allier oak. He also has one 40-hectoliter botte of Slavonian oak. "French wood gives a richer taste profile, and though I actually prefer large French oak casks, where the wine can age more slowly at its own pace, realistically, I can't wait years before I can sell the wine," explains Leanza. He ages his Brunellos for a total of thirty-three months, first in the smaller barrels, proceeding to the biggest. Rosso, on the other hand, is aged entirely in tonneaux, new and used, for eighteen months. These are some of the best Brunellos, and while they have the *tipicità* I love in Brunello, at the same time, they defy any other definition such as "traditional" or "modern," "classic," or "international," and are very much in a league of their own.

Production

Total surface area: 11 ha (27 acres)
Brunello: 3.5 ha (8.64 acres), 6,000 -9,000 bottles
Rosso: 6,000–9,000 bottles

Brunello "Piaggione." This is the Salicutti calling card. Made from the Piaggione vineyard, this Brunello is decidedly Burgundian in style with earthy yet delicate aromas and layers of strawberry, cherry, and mineral on the palate.

◉ *"Piaggione" Riserva 2004.* As of 2011 this was the only Riserva that Leanza has ever made. It is stunning, complex, and delicious, with intense earthy and varietal aromas and rich creamy fruit and seductive minerality. Should age beautifully, and was already delicious upon its release in 2010.

Rosso. Salicutti's Rossos are quintessential: floral, vibrant, and round with ripe fruit. They simply cry out for food.

Terralsole

Villa Collina d'Oro 168
53024 Montalcino (SI)
Tel. +39 0577 835764
www.terralsole.com
info@terralsole.com

Swiss-born Mario Bollag is an adventurer of sorts, and a definite risk taker. Bollag first came to Montalcino in 1975, fresh from studying art in France, and bought a small apartment in Sant'Angelo in Colle, his base, where he could relax and study the bucolic countryside. Although he fell in love with Montalcino, he wasn't ready to settle down just yet, and soon left to open an art gallery in San Francisco, followed by numerous jobs including a stint in the Caribbean as a pilot, then running his own bike-touring company in Nepal where he organized extreme mountain-biking expeditions.

While his pre-Brunello experiences were exciting and rewarding, and judging from the exotic art that fills his beautiful stone villa recently built in the area's traditional style, highly successful, Mario often thought of Montalcino. In 1982 he returned to the town and created his first winery, Il Palazzone, which he later sold to the then CEO of Time Warner and later Citigroup chairman, Richard Parsons. After the sale, Bollag turned around and created Terralsole, which he runs with his American wife, Athena. Terralsole is the last farm on a high ridge on Montalcino's southeastern crest overlooking Castelnuovo dell'Abate, with a spectacular view of Mount Amiata and the Valley of Sant'Antimo.

In 1997 Mario planted vines in two very different areas, half around his new property, and half in the Sesta area between Castelnuovo dell'Abate and Sant'Angelo. "The vines planted around the winery in the Pian Bossolino vineyard are 420 meters above sea level, ensuring a strong variation between day and night temperatures that create intense and ample bouquets and elegance, while the vines grown in the Sesta area are situated lower, averaging 300 meters high and the area is much warmer. The Sesta grapes always mature perfectly and naturally reach high sugar levels," explains Mario. The heavier clay soil in Sesta also lends the wines rounder structure, while the more infertile, stony soil around the winery generates greater elegance and complexity. Blending grapes from the two areas produces powerful but refined Brunellos with mouthwatering, ripe fruit.

Mario and I don't always see eye to eye on wine styles, but I respect and enjoy his efforts to bridge the gap between classic Brunellos that often need years to mature, even once they hit the market, and rounder, more approachable Brunellos. The balance is very difficult, and Mario still remembers the first time I tasted his 2000 vintage at the 2005 Benvenuto Brunello, when I told him he had the best "Super Tuscan" at the tasting. Needless to say, Mario was not pleased, but he handled the jibe with incredible grace, and got my point: his first vintages, very dark with exotic wood-driven sensations, pushed Brunello's natural profile to the brink. Rather than avoid me, however, Mario sought me out at ensuing editions of Benvenuto Brunello to have me try his wines, and I happily observed as he reined in excessive oak and extraction in subsequent vintages.

Mario, who studied winemaking in Bordeaux once he became a full-time winemaker, and also uses the services of Paolo Vagaggini, carries out a cold soak before fermentation to extract color and intensify aromas. Regarding aging, Bollag has exchanged his barriques for 600-liter tonneaux made of Troncais oak. Although I usually go for the more traditionally crafted Brunellos, Terralsole's polished Brunellos are stunning and approachable with mouthwatering fruit and a whisper of oak and spice as well as Sangiovese's earthiness and minerality, which had been masked in earlier vintages.

Production

Total surface area: 50 ha (123.5 acres)
Brunello: 5 ha (12 acres), 25,000 bottles
Rosso: 2 ha (5 acres), 14,000 bottles

Brunello. These Brunellos perfectly bridge the divide between classic Brunellos and more internationally styled bottlings. Ripe but restrained dark fruit sensations with layers of spice and hints of chocolate and oak. While Terralsole's Brunellos flex some muscle, they also possess flair and finesse. Enjoyable upon release, the firm's Brunellos also boast age-worthy structures. In exceptional years, such as 2001, Mario produces a Riserva from the best grapes selected in the vineyards.

Rosso. Bright, with ripe dark fruit and a whisper of oak. Fresh acidity and with impressive tannic strength, but still very friendly.

Cerbaiona—Diego Molinari

Località Cerbaiona 146
53024 Montalcino (SI)
Tel. +39 0577 848660

When Diego Molinari left his job as a pilot with Alitalia in 1977, after having spent his last few years with the airline as a captain flying weekly routes to North America and dealing with continuous jetlag, he decided he wanted a drastic lifestyle change. Already a big fan of the great wines of Burgundy, Molinari decided to try his hand at winemaking, and set his sites on Brunello and Montalcino, where he found the tiny Cerbaiona estate southeast of town. His vineyards border Giulio Salvioni's La Cerbaiola estate; according to Molinari, the properties were one at the beginning of the last century. Molinari planted Cerbaiona's east-facing vineyards, situated on average at 350 meters (1,148 feet) above sea level, in 1977. Diego, in his characteristic and refreshingly nonchalant attitude to winemaking, no longer remembers which clone he chose, nor does he much care since whatever it is it has adapted wonderfully to Cerbaiona's terrain. The calcareous marly soil in Diego's vineyards is typical of the rest of the original zone just south of the town, with more stone and "thankfully not much clay," according to Diego, and is one of the reasons these Brunellos are more about depth and elegance and less about power.

Once he arrived in Montalcino, Diego befriended Giulio Gambelli, who "taught me how to make and age Brunello," says Molinari, whose first Brunello was from the 1981 vintage. Although Gambelli consulted for Cerbaiona until a few years ago, his advanced age has forced him to cut down his consulting activities and Diego has now hired the help of young enologist Valerio Coltellini. Unsurprisingly, given Gambelli's tutelage, Molinari shuns chemicals in the vineyards as well as selected yeasts for alcoholic fermentation. "In 2000, a really hot year, the sugar levels were very high and I was worried about problems with fermentation. So I decided to experiment with selected yeasts for my IGT wine, to see how it would come out. I'll never do it again, and I'm glad I didn't try that on my Brunello. Not to say that the wine was bad, it was just very different, with unrecognizable aromas and flavors. It didn't smell or taste like my wine," explains Molinari.

It should be noted that Molinari makes wine above all for his own pleasure and for the pleasure of his ferociously faithful customers, who fight over the small number of bottles available each year. These are very artisanal wines, and I mean that in a good sense. They are terroir-driven and vintage-driven: when the vintage is excellent, so are Molinari's wines, and when the vintage is less than extraordinary, so too are the wines, but they are always genuine. No matter what the vintage brings, Molinari selects only the best grapes and makes wine with as little intervention as possible, without compensating tough harvests by adding a little extra acidity here or powdered tannins there. In a time when so many wines are drawn up in a boardroom before grapes are even harvested, I find Molinari's approach to winemaking inspiring, if not downright courageous. When the vintage cooperates, Cerbaiona's Brunellos are delicious, complex, and truly memorable.

Production

Total surface area: 14.5 ha (36 acres)
Brunello: 1.6 ha (4 acres), 8,000 bottles
Rosso: 0.8 ha (2 acres), 5,000 bottles

Brunello. Cerbaiona's Brunellos are all about complexity and perfume rather than sheer muscle. Intensely floral and earthy bouquets take on tertiary aromas of leather and tobacco as they age, as would be expected in such a traditionally crafted Brunello. Succulent and bright cherry-berry flavors are replaced with dried fruit, fig, and tealeaf and tobacco nuances. Given the tiny production, Molinari never makes a Riserva but only uses the best grapes for his straight Brunello.

Rosso. Alluring perfumes of violet, with bright wild-cherry flavors with vibrant acidity and supple tannins. This is as easy-drinking, delicious, and approachable as Rosso was intended to be.

Salvioni—La Cerbaiola

Giulio Salvioni
Piazza Cavour 19
53024 Montalcino (SI)
Tel. +39 0577 848499
aziendasalvioni@libero.it

Although Giulio Salvioni's modest cellar is right in the center of town and this is the position indicated on the Consorzio's producer map, his vineyards are on the family's Cerbaiola farm to the southeast, bordering Diego Molinari's Cerbaiona estate. For years, Giulio's father made modest wine for family and friends from La Cerbaiola's southeast-facing vineyards, situated at 420 meters (1,377 feet) above sea level, where the soil is marl mixed with friable rock. Realizing that their land held great Sangiovese potential, in the early 1980s Giulio decided to funnel his almost limitless energy into serious winemaking. After revamping the vineyards and fitting out his cellars, he expanded production and released his first bottled Brunello in 1985. Ever since his debut vintage was released, Giulio's tiny but exclusive production has enjoyed a cult following across the globe.

Giulio can best be described as a modern-day traditionalist. He recoils from the very thought of aging Brunello in barriques, though he nevertheless criticizes those who age in very large and very old botti, preferring instead to age his Brunello in mid-sized 20-hectoliter botti, made exclusively of Slavonian oak. Giulio ages his wines anywhere from the mandatory two years up to three years or even more, depending on the structure of the vintage. Like most traditionalists, Salvioni is not only a staunch defender of Brunello's 100 percent Sangiovese-only pedigree, but also of Brunello's elite image. "Brunello is a *signore* who always shows up wearing a tuxedo, and who demands respect," argues Salvioni.

To maintain the tipicità of his wines, Salvioni refuses to use selected yeasts or filter his wines. The results are age-worthy Brunellos of impeccable class and breeding, with ample bouquets and layers of earthy, ripe fruit with great depth of flavor and purity.

FIGURE 7. Giulio Salvioni's tiny amount of handcrafted Brunellos have a cult following across the globe. Photograph by Paolo Tenti.

Production

Total surface area: 18.5 ha (46 acres)

Brunello: 4 ha (10 acres), 15,000 bottles (Rosso is also made in some vintages from Brunello vines)

Brunello. While recent vintages have marked a subtle shift to a darker and more concentrated expression of Sangiovese, quintessential Salvioni Brunellos have ample bouquets layered with violet, cherry, and tobacco, all of which carry over onto the palate, and older wines develop flint, leather, and goudron. These are extraordinary wines, with finesse and purity of fruit; based on the 1985, tasted in 2007, and the 1998, 1999, and 2001, all tasted upon their release, they are very cellar-worthy. Salvioni never makes a Riserva, preferring to use his best grapes for Brunello. The 2006 is beautifully perfumed, bold, and very structured and will be best after 2015.

Rosso. When the vintage is not worthy, Giulio, like only a handful of winemakers around the world, including Biondi Santi, declassifies his entire Brunello production to Rosso, as he did in 2002. In excellent years, he makes little or no Rosso, and varying amounts in other years based on the harvest results. When he does produce a Rosso from his Brunello vines, it is excellent, with more depth and structure than many but still very approachable and delicious.

Tenuta Le Potazzine

Tenuta Le Potazzine
53024 Montalcino (SI)
Tel. +39 0577 846168
www.lepotazzine.it
tenuta@lepotazzine.it

Giuseppe Gorelli and his wife, Gigliola, run this charming winery a few miles southwest of town just before the road turns toward Tavernelle, in an area known as Le Prata. The Gorellis, who also run La Vineria, a wonderful trattoria and enoteca serving up local dishes in the center of Montalcino, make focused Brunellos with heady aromas and succulent wild cherry-berry fruit. While they are enjoyable upon release, Le Potazzine's Brunellos have the structure to stand up to cellaring as well.

Giuseppe, a trained enologist and agronomist, comes with a wealth of Brunello experience. He worked for the Consorzio for years, and his father, Giancarlo, founded the family's first farm, Le Due Portine, in 1971, which made its first Brunello with the 1987 vintage. Giuseppe oversaw the winemaking at his father's firm until the family sold the estate in 1999. In 1993, Giuseppe and Gigliola bought their current property, where they planted 3 hectares (7.4 acres) of vines. The high altitude at Le Potazzine of 507 meters (1,663 feet) and the rocky, iron-rich, and well-draining soil produce elegant wines with exquisite aromas. In 1996, the couple bought another 1.5 hectares of vineyards much further south, near Sant'Angelo in Colle, where the warmer temperatures, lower vineyard altitude of 300 meters (984 feet) above sea level, and flaky, schistous soil produce round, muscular wines. When Sangiovese from the two vineyards are blended together, these Sant'Angelo in Colle grapes inject structure into the more delicate and perfumed wines coming from the Le Prata vineyards around the winery.

The Gorelli's two daughters, Viola and Sofia, were also born in 1993 and 1996, respectively, and the couple decided to celebrate this propitious coincidence by renaming the winery after their two daughters. They chose Le Potazzine, the local name for the brightly colored and vivacious birds that

FIGURE 8. Giuseppe Gorelli of Tenuta Le Potazzine, one of Montalcino's rising stars, makes elegant Brunellos with exquisite aromas. Photograph by Paolo Tenti.

live in the Tuscan countryside and that their maternal grandmother fondly called her granddaughters.

In the cellar, Giuseppe prefers a long vinification process of about thirty days for Brunello and Rosso (thirty-five for Riserva), consisting of spontaneous fermentation with only wild yeasts and without temperature control, and lengthy maceration, which according to Giuseppe allows him to better extract soft, refined tannins. To maintain these elegant tannins as well as Sangiovese's tipicità, Giuseppe ages his Brunellos in mid-sized and large Slavonian oak casks. Though in the past he experimented with barriques for his Rosso, he has now phased these out, preferring to age his Rosso too in small 10-hectoliter botti, because, he says, "Barriques are not suitable for

Sangiovese from Montalcino. Not only do they impart overwhelming wood sensations, they also make the wines age precociously."

Production

Total surface area: 10 ha (25 acres)
Brunello: 4.3 ha (10.6 acres), 16,000 bottles
Rosso: 0.3 ha (0.75 acres), 20,000 bottles
Riserva: 4,000 bottles

Brunello. Le Potazzine Brunellos are signature Montalcino bottlings, and like great producers all over the world, the small estate produces quality wines even in difficult vintages, such as 2002 and 2005, while in excellent vintages the Gorellis make some of the finest Brunellos in the denomination, with gorgeous aromas of leather, earth, and underbrush, and ripe cherry-berry flavors and fantastic depth. Their 2006 is exceptional, with heady aromas, mineral, and freshness. Best 2016 to 2026.

◉ *Riserva 2004.* At press time, this was the first Riserva the firm has ever produced. Exquisitely perfumed with violet, iris, earth, and spice. Vibrant structure with bright sour-cherry and mineral flavors impeccably balanced with fresh acidity and tightly packed but supple tannins. A gorgeous wine that will drink beautifully 2014–24 and maintain for decades.

Rosso. Bright, succulent, delicious, and so food-friendly, without the tannic backbone and high alcohol of so many of today's Rossos. Quintessential Rosso.

Villa I Cipressi

Località I Cipressi
53024 Montalcino (SI)
Tel. +39 0577 848640
www.villacipressi.it
hubert@villacipressi.it

About a mile south of Montalcino, heading toward Sant'Angelo, a steep unpaved road to the left brings you to Hubert Ciacci's Villa I Cipressi. Hubert's family started out as beekeepers more than thirty years ago, and today the firm makes a wide range of what I consider to be among the finest honeys in all of Tuscany, if not Italy, and its extra-virgin olive oil is also one of the very best in Montalcino and perhaps in the region.

To satisfy the many customers who buy his honeys, jams, and olive oil either directly at the estate or at his small shop in the center of Montalcino, in the 1990s Hubert added Sangiovese vines to his farming activities and began making Brunello with the 2000 vintage. His vineyards are divided between the south and southwest of the denomination, at Castelnuovo dell'Abate and between Tavernelle and Sant'Angelo, and both parcels have full southern exposures that help grapes attain ideal ripening. The average vineyard altitude, 350 meters (1,148 feet) above sea level, generates fine aromas while the soils, clay, silt, and sand confer both structure and naturally elevated alcohol levels, according to Hubert.

While in the past I have not always been overly impressed with Villa I Cipressi's Brunellos, finding them a little too simple and with very obvious alcohol, the 2005 Brunello demonstrated lovely balance and finesse, perhaps because the vines, now eighteen years old on average, had reached full maturity by 2005. Hopefully this will become the house style. Hubert carries out a conventional fermentation with a lengthy maceration on the skins in temperature-controlled stainless steel followed by two years wood aging in both barriques and botti for Brunello.

Production

Total surface area: 31 ha (76.6 acres)
Brunello: 3.5 ha (8.6 acres), 15,000 bottles
Rosso: 1.5 ha (3.7 acres), 5,000 bottles

Brunello. The 2005 and 2006 vintages seem to announce a new direction for Villa I Cipressi's Brunellos. If previous vintages struck me as being too simple and a bit mundane, the most recent vintages boast both finesse and sheer drinkability, with warm earthy and ripe berry aromas that carry over onto the palate with juicy and delicious black-fruit flavors accompanied by spicy overtones. Nicely focused, these Brunellos possess discreet aging potential, but should be at their peak at around the ten-year mark. In the best years, Ciacci also makes a special selection Brunello from the best grapes, called Zebras, named after a mural of zebras painted on the walls of the aging cellar.

Rosso. Aged for six to eight months in both barriques and casks, this is an even friendlier version of the Brunello, with vibrant, thirst-quenching flavors and just the right structure for all dishes. A whiff of oak adds another dimension without weighing it down.

L'Aietta

Francesco Mulinari
Via Mazzini 42
53024 Montalcino (SI)
Tel. +39 0577 849362
www.aietta.eu
fmulinari@aietta.eu

L'Aietta is the smallest Brunello bottling estate in Montalcino, but don't let this fool you: quality-wise, this young firm is one of the denomination's extraordinary albeit little-known gems. Founded in 2001 by Francesco Mulinari, a dynamic young winemaker who fell in love with viticulture and winemaking while still a student, the estate is named after a small, stony parcel of land situated among ancient stone terraces where imperial troops encamped during the siege of Montalcino in 1555.

The firm's two parcels of land are divided between L'Aietta, which lies beneath the fortified west wall of Montalcino, and Castelnuovo dell'Abate, totaling 1 hectare (2.47 acres). While the thirteen-year-old vines in Castelnuovo dell'Abate are trained with the ubiquitous spurred cordon, Francesco boldly decided in 2004 to plant his Aietta vineyard with the ancient *alberello* system: freestanding vines that resemble bushes, in a training system otherwise known as head training.

According to Mulinari, his unique choice of training system is due to the rugged terrain and rocky shelves beneath the soil. "The vineyard is really steep, with an altitude difference of 130 meters from top to bottom, while the high rock content just beneath the surface makes it impossible to drive support poles into the ground." While more modern training methods using poles and wires have proven impossible in the Aietta parcel, Mulinari also decided that bush vines would be the best for the vineyard's perennially dry, sandy topsoil because, as he says, they are the most resistant to drought conditions. The young winemaker also discovered that his *alberello* vines autoregulate their production, naturally producing just a few bunches of highly concentrated grapes. Their vicinity to the rocky ground and the heat captured in the stones also helps the grapes reach ideal maturation.

Francesco vinifies the two vineyards separately in stainless steel tanks, but forgoes temperature control and uses selected yeasts only in difficult vintages. He then ages his Brunellos for three years in Slavonian casks that range in size from 5 to 10 hectoliters, while the Rosso spends a year in the same type of cask. L'Aietta's Brunellos and Rossos are quintessential Sangiovese from Montalcino, with mouthfuls of wild cherry and mineral, and impressive structures and depth.

Production

Total surface area: 3 ha (7.5 acres)
Brunello: 0.3 ha (0.75 acres), 1,200 bottles
Rosso: 5 ha (1.2 acres), 1,300 bottles

Brunello. L'Aietta's Brunellos have hallmark Sangiovese perfumes of violet, rose, and leather with some truffle thrown in for good measure. Layers of wild cherry and spice greet the palate, with long, lingering finishes. The 2006 has an impressive structure and fantastic depth that will develop more complexity over the next ten years. Best 2016 to 2026.

Riserva. The firm's first Riserva, made from blending the best barrels from the 2007 vintage, is slotted for release in 2013.

Rosso. Intensely floral and bright with rich, ripe fruit, and fantastic, uplifting minerality and hefty structure. Fantastic and quintessential Rosso di Montalcino.

Tenuta Greppone Mazzi

Ruffino
Località Greppone
53024 Montalcino (SI)
Tel. +39 0577 6499703
www.rufino.it
info@ruffino.it

Tenuta Greppone Mazzi headquarters are situated—for now—just southeast of Montalcino in the heart of the historical Brunello production in an area known as "dei Greppi," after the rugged hills that characterize this part of Montalcino. Tuscan wine family Ruffino leased the estate in 1984, and at the same time acquired exclusive rights to the name Greppone Mazzi. However, with their long-term lease due to expire in 2013, the firm acquired property in Castelnuovo dell'Abate, where they plan on building a small underground wine cellar and eventually transferring production here where they will continue to make Brunellos under the Greppone Mazzi name.

Including the firm's leased holdings, current vineyards are situated between 210 and 420 meters (689 and 1,378 feet) above sea level in infertile soil made up predominantly of marl and schist. While the oldest vineyards date back to 1970, many of the estate vineyards have been replanted at five thousand plants per hectare. Ruffino's main focus for their Brunello production, however, is their 6-hectare (15-acre) Le Logge vineyard in Castelnuovo dell'Abate, just beneath Castello di Velona. "The vineyard altitude of 250 meters is ideal for perfect grape maturation, while the rocky, infertile soil naturally restrains grape production," explains Ruffino's managing director of estates Maurizio Bogoni. When Ruffino bought the parcel, the land was dedicated to olive oil and other crops, and the firm began planting a massal selection of Sangiovese from their other estates in 1998. Later, according to Bogoni, once newer clones became available, they planted VCR 23 and R 4 and R 5.

Like many Montalcino wineries, Greppone Mazzi experimented with barriques in the 1990s and the first years of the new century, then switched to larger tonneaux. Now they are aging 80 percent of their Brunello in large Slavonian casks and the rest in used tonneaux for three years. "We realize that barriques and Sangiovese are not a great match," says Bogoni. I must admit that in the past this estate did not always live up to its lauded reputation nor, given the position of its vineyards, its true potential. However, the recent turnaround in quality is evident: Greppone Mazzi turned out one of the best 2006 Brunellos, coinciding with the Le Logge vineyard going into full production and a return to classic winemaking.

Production

Total surface area: 120 ha (297 acres)
Brunello: 13.5 ha (33 acres), 50,000 bottles

Brunello. The estate only makes Brunello, no Riserva or Rosso. Many of my tasting notes of previous vintages point to a more commercial wine style, but the 2006 is gorgeous. Loaded with berry, licorice, and a hint of leather aromas and a creamy-cherry and spice palate, this is an extremely well-balanced Brunello with a lovely mineral finish. Best 2015 to 2026.

Casisano Colombaio

Località Casisano 52
53024 Montalcino (SI)
Tel. +39 0577 835540
www.brunello.org
info@brunello.org

Founded in 1990, this small winery is crafting delicious, ripe Brunellos with flair and finesse. Owned by Tatiana Schwarze and run by her son Riccardo Ciarpella, Casisano Colombaio is uniquely positioned on a natural terrace overlooking the Sant'Antimo valley with a clear view of the abbey just a few kilometers away, although you would never imagine this by looking at their position on the Consorzio's producer map. Surrounded by thick woods, this is another one of the denomination's isolated, untamed, and hauntingly beautiful settings accessible only by a rocky, steep dirt road. I was thankful I had a four-wheel drive for this visit.

The bulk of production comes from the firm's 19 hectares (47 acres) of registered Brunello and Rosso vines at the Casisano property, although they also own 1 hectare north of Montalcino. Average vineyard altitude is 400 meters (1,312 feet) above sea level, ensuring slow ripening and giving the wines both complexity and elegance, while southwest exposures and long hours of sunlight combined with frequent breezes ensure ideal ripening. Soil between the two properties is a mix of various clays interspersed with an abundance of rock fragments.

Since 1990, the firm has used the services of Paolo Vagaggini, who works with on-site winemaker Mario Generali. Temperature-controlled fermentation and maceration takes place in steel for twenty-five days, followed by three years aging in botti for Brunello. Rosso is aged in barrique for eight months.

Production

Total surface area: 53 ha (131 acres)
Brunello: 8.67 ha (21.4 acres), 58,000 bottles
Rosso: 7 ha (17.2 acres), 60,000 bottles

Brunello.   The estate's main focus, the Brunellos are finely crafted with rich, ripe fruit, hints of leather and tealeaf, and just enough vibrant acidity. While these tend to be ready upon release, that is not to say they won't age well.

Riserva.   In exceptional years, Casisano-Colombaio also makes a Riserva from a selection of grapes from La Colombaio vineyard north of Montalcino. While the firm's Riservas are powerfully structured, they also can have great depth and complexity, like the stunning 2001, but the 2004 is overripe and lacks vibrancy, apparently from extended hang time on the vine.

Rosso.   Bright and youthful with a tannic backbone and a whiff of oak.

MONTALCINO, NORTH

Surrounding Montalcino to the north as the slopes begin to descend, lies another area densely populated with small wineries. Here cooler weather dominates, and Brunellos with the most exquisite bouquets are produced. Vineyards in this area, almost all on steep slopes, are situated at mid- to high altitudes that average between 300 and 400 meters (984 and 1,312 feet) above sea level. The soil becomes predominantly calcareous limestone and clay from the upper Jurassic and lower Cretaceous periods, and as Professor Edoardo Costantini explains, soil composition in Montalcino's mid- to high altitudes are extremely intricate, resulting from the recurrent retraction and arrival of the ancient seas, which not only deposited marine fossils and marine sediment but also caused massive landslides that sent millions of metric tons of older, mineral-rich soil crashing down, thoroughly mixing layers of soil deposits originating from different geological periods. The differing altitudes and diverse exposures also create a variety of microzones, meaning that this fascinating area is difficult to define in terms of its growing conditions.

At altitudes above 300 meters (948 feet) a number of artisan estates make remarkably fragrant Brunellos that are naturally lighter colored and more complex rather than powerful, such as those made by Il Marroneto and

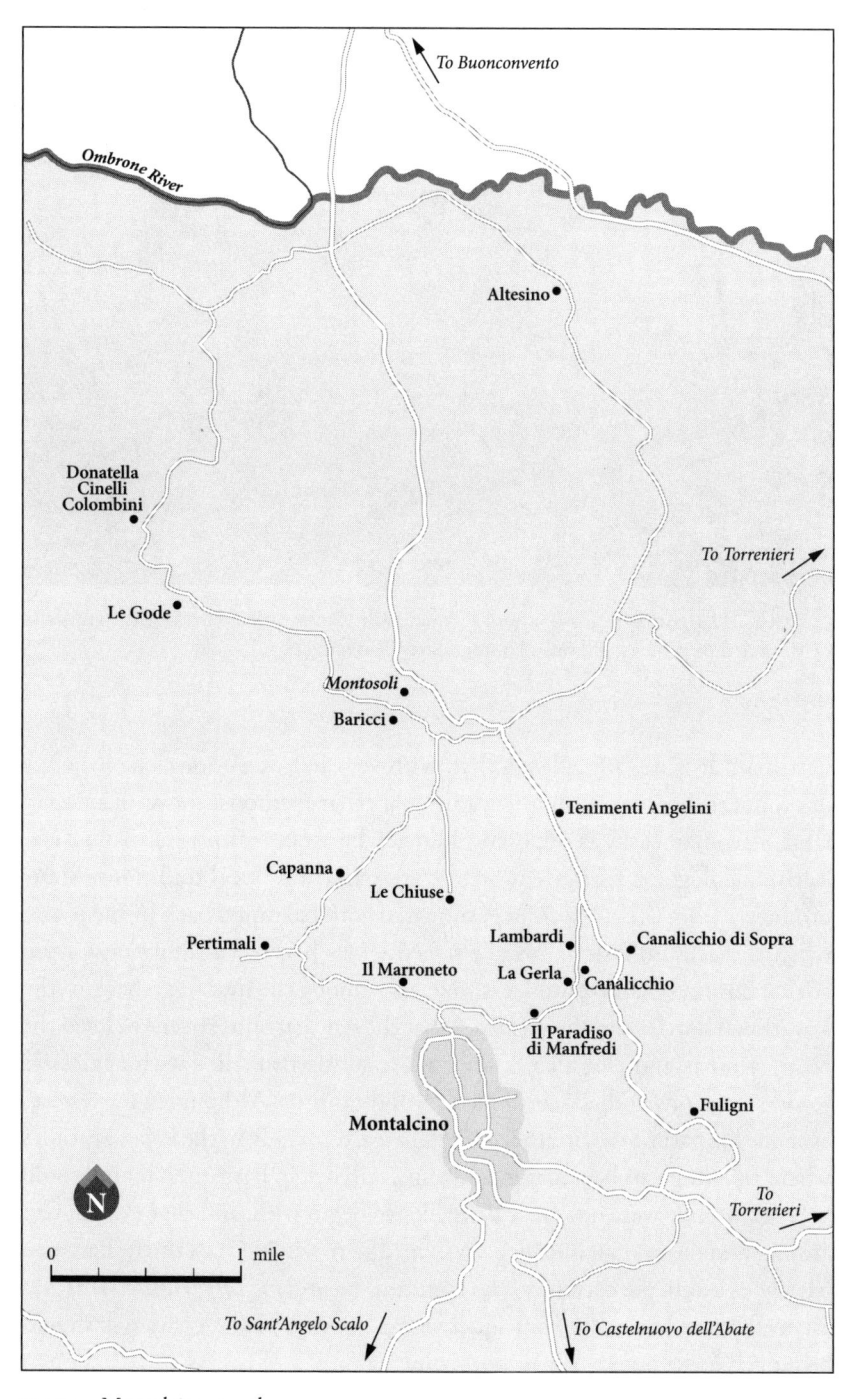

MAP 3. Montalcino, north

FIGURE 9. Large marine fossils found at Paradiso di Manfredi demonstrate the complexity of Montalcino's geology and soils. Photograph by Paolo Tenti.

Pertimali. It is no coincidence that, with very few exceptions, the majority of producers here employ more traditional cellar methods, above all aging in large Slavonian casks as opposed to French barriques. This is far from a collective ideology or a strictly romantic attachment to local traditions. Many producers from the subzone experimented with barriques back in the 1990s, when the denomination's heavily oaked wines began winning praise from critics, but these same producers were also among the first to go back to the traditional botti when they realized that the new barriques overwhelmed the heady aromas and elegance of their more subtle Brunellos with aggressive wood sensations and above all bitter wood tannins. Although a few estates even in this part of the original growing area, especially in the lower altitudes where ripening can be a major challenge, still age in barriques, many would agree that these were not great Brunellos to begin with, and that evident oak aromas and flavors can hide defects in mediocre wines. Or as the Italians say, barriques can make certain wines appear to be *un vino importante*. This was especially true back when barriques were a novelty, but excessive oak should be judged for what it really is: poor winemaking.

To the northeast is another prime zone for Brunello production around the area of Canalicchio, rising up to 300 to 330 meters (984 to 1,082 feet). Nearby estates are for the most part tiny family-owned operations, whose Brunello is not always easy to find. They produce earthy, sometimes austere Brunellos with extraordinary depth that need a few years to develop, depending on the vintage. Estates making particularly good terroir-driven Brunello include Il Paradiso di Manfredi, Canalicchio, Canalicchio di Sopra, and Lambardi.

Going further north, altitudes descend more and then rise again at the famous cru of Montosoli, a rounded hill with altitudes ranging from 280 to 350 meters (918 to 1,148 feet) that is spared the autumnal fog that often invades lower altitudes north of Montalcino. Single-vineyard Brunellos from Montosoli combine the power more often associated with Brunellos from the far southern reaches of the denomination, from the Sant'Angelo area, with the elegance of the original growing area. Montosoli Brunellos have very ripe fruit and earthy sensations, and while approachable at an earlier age, they also have the essential structure to age well. Perhaps the most famous producer with vineyards on Montosoli is Altesino, which bottles its single-vineyard Brunello only in the best years. With north-facing vineyards up to 340 meters (1,115 feet), the higher altitude gives a certain refinement to this hillside that is overall known for its muscle. Besides Altesino, Nello Baricci, the cru's modern-day pioneer, has Montosoli vineyards, as does Le Gode, while Capanna is just in front of this prime location.

Fuligni

Via Saloni 33
53024 Montalcino (SI)
Tel. +39 0577 848710
www.fuligni.it
brunellofuligni@virgilio.it

When Maria Flora Fuligni, a former schoolteacher with a doctorate degree in philosophy, took over the family's property in 1971 after her father passed away, she became one of the very first, if not *the* first woman in Montalcino to run an agricultural estate. "Even though I went to university to study, I always loved agriculture, which is why my five siblings asked me to take over the farm," explains Maria Flora today. She is, as the Italians say when they want to pay the utmost respect to one's wit and intelligence, *in gamba*. One can still imagine even today that this elegant and refined *signora* taught the boys a thing or two about running a business.

Maria Flora's father fell in love with Montalcino in the early 1920s while he was staying in the well-ventilated and salubrious hilltown to recover from malaria. In 1923, he bought a farm, known as Cottimelli after a sixteenth-century convent on the property, from Gontrano Biondi Santi, in what Maria Flora likes to call the "classic zone, where Brunello was born," and transferred his family from the Maremma to Montalcino. Fuligni also acquired an eighteenth-century palazzo in the town center; some family members still live there above the original aging cellars.

Fuligni's farm lies just two miles north of town. Although much of the land is still dedicated to olive trees, wheat, and other crops, over the years Maria Flora has focused much of her energy on Brunello. While her father had made wine for family consumption, his ambitious daughter began bottling the estate's Brunello in 1975, and since then has made major investments in both vineyards and winemaking, while slowly expanding production. The 12 hectares (30 acres) of vineyards are almost in a single block around the estate and the restructured convent, with east and southeast exposures that help promote ripening, at altitudes of between 350 and 400 meters (1,148 and 1,312 feet) above sea level. Average vine age is eighteen but the oldest vineyards are over thirty years old, planted at densities between 3,330 and 5,000 plants per hectare in Eocene soil composed of predominantly marl and rock with traces of clay. These are near-ideal growing conditions for Sangiovese to yield wines with ample aromas and structure.

Guided by consultant enologist Paolo Vagaggini, whose father consulted for the estate before him, Maria Flora's winemaking leans toward the traditional, with temperature-controlled fermentation in steel vats, lasting between eighteen and twenty-two days. For decades the firm aged its Brunellos solely in large botti but for the last few years Maria Flora, assisted by her nephew Roberto, a law professor at the University of Siena, has switched to 500-liter tonneaux and 7.5-hectoliter Allier barrels for the first four to five months, "to fix anthocyanins" that give wines their color, followed by two and a half years in Slavonian casks in the firm's suggestive aging cellars in the center of Montalcino. Fuligni's graceful Brunellos are consistently very good to excellent, but when they don't meet Maria Flora's rigid standards, she declasses the entire vintage to Rosso di Montalcino, as she did in 2002.

Production

Total surface area: 100 ha (247 acres)
Brunello: 10 ha (25 acres), 25,000 to 30,000 bottles
Riserva: 8,000–9,000 bottles
Rosso: 2 ha (5 acres), 12,000 bottles

Brunello.   Fuligni's vibrant Brunellos boast lovely floral aromas with racy acidity and supple tannins backed up by succulent berry fruit and mineral. These are very elegant Brunellos, more subtle than forward. Even though they drink well upon release, they do improve with age.

◊ *Riserva 2004.*   In great years, Fuligni produces a Riserva from the oldest vines. The firm's Riservas possess age-worthy structures that will maintain them for decades, and the 2004 is exceptional. Still somewhat closed when tasted in 2010, but offering delicate whiffs of violet and earth that need time to open up fully. Lush palate with raspberry and black-cherry-berry flavors and chock-full of spice. Still young and aggressive, but will develop into a beauty. Best after 2014 and should drink well through the next decade.

Rosso.   Named after the Ginestreto vineyard, Fuligni's Rosso is aged for six months in French tonneaux, which adds spice to the bright berry aromas and flavors. Very drinkable and food-friendly.

Il Marroneto

Località Madonna delle Grazie 307
53024 Montalcino (SI)
Tel. +39 0577 849382
www.ilmarroneto.it
info@ilmarroneto.it

Alessandro Mori makes some of the most elegant and age-worthy Brunellos in Montalcino. Austere in their youth, but already demonstrating extraordinary breeding and grace, Il Marroneto's wines are in for the long haul, as tastings with Mori back to the 1981 vintage have amply proven. Mori's father, Giuseppe, a Roman lawyer, bought the small estate just outside Montalcino's northern gate back in 1974, and Alessandro and his brother Andrea soon fell in love with Montalcino. At first, winemaking was solely a pastime for the family, until 1994, when Alessandro, who like his father and brother had become a lawyer, gave up his law career to make Brunello full-time.

Mori is a self-proclaimed traditionalist, who crafts classic Brunellos meant for lengthy cellaring in his modest cellar. "Brunello's fame derived from its reputation as a wine that improves with aging and that can last for decades, so I want to make classic Brunellos that will evolve and stand the test of time. Brunello should never be made as a ready-to-drink industrial beverage," argues the outspoken winemaker, whose Brunellos, tightly woven when young, blossom with age. He vehemently bemoans the trend toward fruit-forward and ready-to-drink Brunellos, contending, "The presence of notable acidity in many Brunellos is disappearing. What made Brunello famous all over the world is its elegance and capacity to evolve for years thanks to fresh acidity. But now there are Brunellos that are unnaturally flat and lifeless and will not age well. Elegance has been replaced by explosive fruit sensations and excessive alcohol, by a core of winemakers that are catering to critics' tastes to receive high scores."

All of the firm's vineyards are registered to Brunello, from which Alessandro makes his three wines. Il Marroneto's original vineyard, Madonna delle Grazie, planted in 1974 and named after the nearby eleventh-century church, is 400 meters (1,312 feet) above sea level and benefits from a combination soil of light sand, minerals, and marine fossils. In the best years, Mori bottles this small 1.6-hectare (3.9-acre) vineyard separately and as can be expected from classically crafted Brunellos made from vines at this altitude, this single vineyard bottling has enticingly floral bouquets in its youth that evolve into leather and tobacco with age. In 1998, Mori acquired another 4.4 hectares (10.8 acres) of vineyards in the same area, but at a lower altitude of 250 meters (820 feet), and from this vineyard he makes his straight Brunello and Rosso. Mori's Brunellos have naturally high acidity and tannins, and classic Sangiovese flavors of wild cherry, truffle, and mineral that over time take on tobacco, tealeaf, and fig flavors. Il Marroneto's wines are always superbly balanced with firm, tannic structures and bracing acidity that soften with time.

In the cellar, Mori, guided by Paolo Vagaggini, ferments his top Brunello, Madonna delle Grazie, in large Allier oak vats. The wine is then aged for forty-one months in botti, both French and Slavonian. Il Marroneto's straight Brunello and Rosso are both fermented in steel and aged in French and

Slavonian casks for thirty-nine and eight months, respectively. Alessandro is adamant about keeping his winemaking as simple as possible and uses no selected yeasts or any other added nutrients or powdered tannins. "In our wines everything is derived strictly from nature," according to the passionate winemaker, who is just as plainspoken about what he sees as the downside of making Brunello Riservas.

Though from 1980 to 1987 Il Marroneto turned out exclusively Riserva bottlings from the farm's original small vineyard, Alessandro now refuses to make a Riserva, concentrating instead on his Brunello and single vineyard bottling. "Over time, many firms started making Riservas with no real selection or criteria, and simply age their Brunello for a year longer. It has become almost a marketing gimmick, and to me Riserva no longer signifies a real selection or quality. To differentiate my top wine, I now make a straight Brunello and a single-vineyard selection," explains Mori.

Production

Total surface area: 9 ha (22.2 acres)
Brunello: 6 ha total (14.8 acres), 15,000 bottles
Brunello Selezione Madonna delle Grazie: 5,000 bottles
Rosso: 7,000 bottles

Brunello. These are classic, elegant Brunellos that need time to soften bracing tannins and almost pulsating acidity. All wild cherry, tobacco, and mineral sensations. Always a focused and vibrant wine.

❧ *Selezione Madonna delle Grazie.* Extremely elegant and more complex than the straight Brunello. The wine's youthful floral and earthy aromas evolve into leather and goudron over time, while the bright wild-cherry and tobacco flavors take on black tea, carob, and truffle nuances. Always impeccably balanced and can age for decades. The 2005 has a lovely bouquet and silky tannins, and will be best 2012 to 2020. The more structured 2006, with its hallmark floral and earthy perfume, needs time to come around but will evolve for decades. Best 2018 to 2030.

Rosso. A hallmark Rosso with a quintessential earthy and floral nose accompanied by sour-cherry flavors and energizing minerality. Bright and delicious, with just the right structure for enjoying upon release.

Canalicchio—Franco Pacenti

Località Canalicchio di Sopra
53024 Montalcino (SI)
Tel. +39 0577 849277
www.canalicchiofrancopacenti.it
info@canalicchiofrancopacenti.it

At first glance it would almost seem that Montalcino's producers purposely use and interchange various names that are common in the denomination, such as Canalicchio, or Sesta and Sesti, just to name a few, with the sole purpose of trying to confuse consumers. The Canalicchio winery for example, owned by Franco Pacenti, is situated in a historic microzone north of Montalcino known as Canalicchio, so named according to locals because of the canal that runs through the area. While Franco Pacenti named his winery Canalicchio, it is actually located in the area Canalicchio di Sopra, or Upper Canalicchio, but is not to be confused with the estate called Canalicchio di Sopra, which is across the street and below, at Casaccia. As you may have guessed, the two wineries were formerly a single estate, and family divisions have led to this rather puzzling state of affairs.

In 1988, Franco Pacenti took control of his share of the original family winery, Fratelli Pacenti, which was founded back in the end of the 1960s. Franco's inherited property included the traditional cellars, a stone chapel, and 36 hectares (89 acres) of land. Pacenti's vineyards have northeast exposures and are situated on average at 280 meters (919 feet) above sea level and are just a short ride away from his cellars. Plants are between seven and thirty years old, and most are the classic R24 clone planted between 3,333 and 4,166 plants per hectare, just right for Sangiovese according to most of Montalcino's producers. The soil is mixed between sand, schist, and light clay, which retains moisture and keeps the vines fresher than do hotter, drier areas with dense clay, further south.

Pacenti, who like so many of Montalcino's producers is guided by consulting enologist Paolo Vagaggini, is a traditionalist. After a classic fermentation of twenty-eight to thirty days, temperature-controlled, the Brunello is aged for three years in Slavonian botti, while Rosso is aged from eight to twelve months, again in botti. Pacenti makes perfumed, well-structured Brunellos that boast juicy fruit and sweet tannins. These Brunellos retain their complexity, but thanks to softer tannins can be enjoyed before many other Brunellos from the higher reaches of the original area. In very good years Pacenti also produces a Riserva version, from the oldest vines, with grape selection decided in the vineyard. Canalicchio's full-bodied Rossos are actually young Brunellos—they are made almost exclusively from the same vineyards as Brunello but are assigned Rosso status after fermentation. "Declassifying part of my Brunello production to Rosso ensures not only the best quality for Brunello, but also guarantees very good Rosso," according to Pacenti.

Production
Total surface area: 36 ha (89 acres)
Brunello: 9.3 ha (22.3 acres), 16,000 bottles
Rosso: 0.18 ha (0.45 acres), 15,000 bottles

Brunello. Classic floral aromas, with vibrant acidity, these are also big and round Brunellos with hallmark wild-cherry, leather, and truffle flavors. While they age well, they are also approachable upon release thanks to soft, ripe tannins.

Riserva. Made only in exceptional years, Canalicchio's Riserva is made from the estate's oldest vines that yield fantastic, concentrated flavors and great depth. With cellar-worthy structures, these need time to tame tight tannins and will age beautifully.

Rosso. These are serious Rossos, and are in reality declassified Brunellos that are released after only eight months to one year of wood aging. While they are lighter and fruitier than the firm's Brunellos, they often weigh in at 14 percent alcohol and have more of a Brunello rather than an easier-drinking structure one would expect in a Rosso.

Lambardi

Località Canalicchio di Sotto
53204 Montalcino (SI)
Tel. +39 0577 848476
www.lambardimontalcino.it
info@lambardimontalcino.it

At his Canalicchio di Sotto estate directly beneath Franco Pacenti's Canalicchio cellars, Maurizio Lambardi makes highly perfumed, refined, and expressive Brunellos with good concentration. Maurizio's father, Silvano Lambardi, another founding member of the Consorzio, bought the farm in 1965; after planting the vineyards with Sangiovese, he released the firm's first Brunello with the 1973 vintage.

Maurizio, a reserved man who is quietly passionate about making serious, classic Brunellos, is proud to point out that old land registries indicate that the Canalicchio di Sotto farm was already devoted to grape growing as far back as 1835. Today Canalicchio di Sotto's vineyards are in one of the most coveted spots in Montalcino, bordering directly on Le Chiuse's vineyards, once among Biondi Santi's most prized properties, which for years contributed to the exquisite aromas in the family's legendary Riservas.

The rich bouquets of Lambardi Brunellos are attributed to both vine altitude of 300 meters (984 feet) and to their northeast exposures, which create a long growing season and complex aromas. Vineyards, replanted between 1980 and 1995, are planted at surprising low densities, ranging from 2,564 to 4,166 plants per hectare, in a mix of tufaceous clay and stone soil, which lends these Brunellos ample body. In the cellars, Maurizio, under the guidance of Paolo Vagaggini, ferments in temperature-controlled steel tanks with selected yeasts, and ages Brunello between two and three years in medium and large Slavonian botti, one year for Rosso. Maurizio strongly believes in bottle aging for his Brunello as well. "Brunellos from this area benefit with more bottle age than other areas do because more time in the bottle helps develop and exalt their intense aromas," explains Maurizio. Selection is fundamental for Lambardi, and every year Maurizio bottles only about 25 percent of his Brunello production. While he declassifies some Brunello down to Rosso, wine that doesn't live up to his strict standards is sold off in bulk to other producers. Maurizio doesn't make Riservas, preferring to put his very best grapes into his Brunello every year.

Production
Total surface area: 22 ha (54 acres)
Brunello: 6 ha (15 acres), 10,000 bottles
Rosso: 8,000 bottles

Brunello. This is the focus of Maurizio's attention, and obsessive selection of only the best grapes in the vineyards and the best wine in the cellars guarantees that these Brunellos are always outstanding. Lambardi Brunellos are all about perfume and finesse, with lovely violet, iris, and earthy aromas, and bright succulent sour-cherry, berry, and mineral flavors. These are very enjoyable even upon release, although they improve with another few years and will age well up to ten to fifteen years.

Rosso. This is a hallmark Rosso, and although made from declassifying part of the Brunello production, it is always bright, easy-drinking, and crying out for food. Floral breeze and delicious creamy-cherry fruit restrained by fresh acidity and firm tannins.

Canalicchio di Sopra

Località Casaccia 73
53024 Montalcino (SI)
Tel. +39 577 848316
www.canalicchiodisopra.com
info@canalicchiodisopra.com

Across the street and directly below Canalicchio and Lambardi, the Canalicchio di Sopra estate was originally founded back in 1962 by Primo Pacenti, who was joined by his son-in-law Pier Luigi Ripaccioli in 1987. Primo Pacenti's grandchildren, Francesco, Marco, and Simonetta, have run the estate since 2001, bringing new ideas that have improved quality without interfering with the tipicità of their wines or breaking from the customs passed down from their father and grandfather. The younger set also continues to trust the advice of Paolo Vagaggini, who has consulted for the estate since the 1990s.

Canalicchio di Sopra has vineyards in two of the most enviable positions in Montalcino's original growing area, in the highest reaches of Canalicchio and also on the Montosoli hillside. The two different areas boast contrasting growing conditions that, when blended together, balance beautiful aromas and finesse combined with structure and ripe fruit. The firm's vineyards in Canalicchio, which average 320 meters (1,050 feet) above sea level, have northeast exposures that are ideal in this area for generating complex aromas, and soil composed of clay, marl, and sand. Their vineyards near Le Gode at

Montosoli, on the other hand, enjoy southeast exposures that offer more consistent ripening, and clay soil interspersed with limestone and a strong presence of rock. Plant age varies from those just replanted in 2009 to the oldest vines, now thirty-two years old, and density ranges from 3,000 to 4,500 plants per hectare.

While vineyard location and management may be the key to Canalicchio di Sopra's polished, well-structured Brunellos, the Ripacciolis combine a healthy mix of tradition and innovation that lets the vineyards best express themselves. Temperature-controlled fermentation with skin maceration takes place in stainless steel and lasts twenty days, while the Brunello is aged between thirty-two and thirty-six months in 30-hectoliter Slavonian botti. Rosso, on the other hand, is aged for about a year in both botti and 7.5-hectoliter French barrels. In exceptional years, like 2004, the firm also makes a Riserva.

Production

Total surface area: 60 ha (148 acres)
Brunello: 13.8 ha (34 acres), 18,000–35,000 bottles
Rosso: 1.2 ha (2.96 acres), 25,000 bottles
Riserva: 5,000–6,000 bottles

Brunello. This is the mainstay of Canalicchio di Sopra, and has it all: wonderful aromas, elegance, and power with vibrant fruit and ripe, brooding tannins lifted by energizing minerality. While these Brunellos can often be enjoyed upon release, they also have good aging potential.

Riserva. Made only in exceptional years, Canalicchio di Sopra's Riserva hails from a selection of the most structured wines destined for Brunello after three years of aging. But as Francesco Ripaccioli points out, the Ripacciolis vinify and age all the vineyards separately, and wine that ends up as Riserva almost always comes from their oldest vineyard. Their 2004 Riserva is a superb wine, with earth, leather, and black-fruit aromas accompanied by succulent dark-fruit flavors, sour cherry, and mineral. Very focused, with great structure and a firm tannic backbone. Best 2014 to 2024.

Rosso. Most of the estate's Rosso is a declassification of part of their Brunello production, and tends to have a very Brunello-like structure. While it is still a very vibrant Rosso, I preferred it before they started using 30 percent tonneaux, since it had more typical Sangiovese character and less oak sensations.

Le Chiuse

Località Pullera 228
53024 Montalcino (SI)
Tel. +39 055 597052
www.lechiuse.com
info@lechiuse.com

Although they may not know it, anyone who has enjoyed older bottles of Biondi Santi Riservas have already had contact with this small estate. For years the *podere,* north of Montalcino, was in the Biondi Santi family and its oldest grapes were used in the Riservas for their fine aromatic qualities. When Tancredi passed away in 1970, the farm went to Franco Biondi Santi's younger sister Fiorella, who leased it to Franco Biondi Santi until her death in 1986. Franco continued to cultivate, harvest, and vinify Le Chiuse's grapes for his Greppo Brunellos until 1990.

After this, Fiorella's daughter Simonetta Valiani, who had renovated the farm and built a winery, took over the estate, which she runs with her husband, Nicolò Magnelli, and their son Lorenzo. According to Simonetta, her grandfather Tancredi begged his daughter never to sell the farm, because "this is where the famous Brunello for the Riservas was born." Simonetta guards her heritage and continues with the family's traditions. Many of the vines registered for Brunello and for Rosso are planted with BBS 11, the clone chosen at Greppo, but also from mother vines chosen in Le Chiuse's vineyards in the 1970s, along with a sprinkling of VCR 23, VCR 6, and VCR 24, biotypes identified by Vivai cooperativi Rauscedo.

Simonetta follows organic farming principles and keeps yields well below the established minimum. Vineyards are situated at 300 meters (984 feet) above sea level and benefit from northeast exposures, with vine age averaging twenty years. Soil at Le Chiuse is an intricate combination of marl, sand, and clay mixed with marine sediment, all of which conspire to produce rich but graceful wines with heady floral and earthy aromas. They also have the structure for lengthy cellaring, thanks to lithe but firmly packed tannins and abundant acidity.

Le Chiuse is guided by outside enologist Attilio Pagli, who works with other Tuscan firms including Moris Farms and Michele Satta, and cellar practices balance innovation with tradition at Le Chiuse, including long soaks both before and after fermentation in stainless steel, without the use of selected yeasts. Aging for all the wines takes place in 25-hectoliter botti, half of which are Slavonian oak, half Allier. While Brunello ages for three years, the Riserva, made only in top years, ages for four, and Rosso sees six to eight months in botti.

Production

Total surface area: 18 ha (44.5 acres)
Brunello: 5.8 ha (14 acres), 20,000 bottles
Rosso: 0.7 ha (1.7 acres), 10,000 bottles
Riserva: 3,000–4,000 bottles

Brunello. All the enticing floral aromas one would expect from Brunellos hailing from this area, as well as mouthwatering cherry and plum flavors. This usually benefits from more aging to tame teeth-coating tannins. Alcohol is often very conspicuous. Best fifteen years after the vintage but can age longer.

Riserva. Made only in top vintages. The estate's best Riservas so far, 1995, 1997, 1999, and 2001, demonstrate great breeding and class with complex aromas and cellar-worthy structures that should keep them fresh for decades. Wonderful depth of flavor dominated by irresistible fruit, but need years to tame aggressive massive tannins.

Rosso. Ethereal aromas of rose and violet, and bright acidity, but this has more of a Brunello-like structure with packed tannins and noticeable alcohol that make this less food-friendly than many Rossos.

Padelletti

Via Padelletti 9
53024 Montalcino (SI)
Tel. +39 0577 848314
www.padelletti.it
padelletti_claudia@yahoo.it

In Montalcino, there are traditionalists and there is Padelletti. This is one of Montalcino's oldest families; documents demonstrate they already had vineyards in Montalcino in 1571. The family has produced generations of doctors, lawyers, judges, and university professors who often went to live abroad but who always eventually came back to Montalcino to tend to the family's once-vast holdings. In the nineteenth century they had thirteen *poderi*, including the several farms in the Canalicchio area that have since changed hands. Carlo Augusto Padelletti, one of Brunello's pioneers, also helped improve living conditions in Montalcino decades before the Brunello economy would transform the town from one of the poorest to one of the richest in the province. In 1899, Carlo Augusto reportedly brought electricity to the center of Montalcino by constructing an internal combustion engine fueled by gases generated by the burning of waste from the timber industry. He later created other industries to modernize Montalcino's agricultural production, including an electrically powered flour mill.

During the first half of the twentieth century, the small amounts of Brunello that Padelletti produced were for family consumption, until Carlo Augusto joined ranks with Tancredi Biondi Santi and many of Montalcino's other landholders in the 1920s and became part of the Cantina Sociale Biondi Santi e C. The two world wars and phylloxera thwarted production and this cooperative cellar broke up in 1944. Carlo Augustos's son Guido replanted the vineyards in the 1950s, specifically with making Brunello in mind.

Claudia Susanna Padelletti runs the firm today, after working for years in the banking industry. Her vines, on average twenty-five years old, are located at the family's Rigaccini podere to the northeast of the town, at the foot of Montalcino's hill and directly east of the fortress. Vineyard altitude is 400 meters above sea level, guaranteeing sharp day and night temperature changes that generate fine and focused aromas, while calcium-rich clay soil lends full but elegant structure.

The Padellettis' cramped but functional cellars are still located beneath the family's sixteenth-century home in the town center, where fermentation is carried out in glass-lined cement tanks and aging takes place in—you guessed it—30-hectoliter Slavonian botti for two years, and one in 30-hectoliter botti of French wood, the firm's only break with rigid tradition. The house philosophy is decidedly hands off, with only wild yeasts allowed for fermentation.

Production

Total surface area: 8 ha (20 acres)
Brunello: 4 ha (10 acres), 7,000 bottles
Rosso: 2 ha (5 acres), 12,000 bottles

Brunello. Padelletti rarely makes a Riserva, meaning that most years only the best grapes go into Brunello, the firm's most important wine. These Brunellos have a range from earthy to exquisite aromas depending on the vintage, and their charming 2004 demonstrates a floral bouquet with hints of talc and incense. Palate is very Sangiovese: ripe wild-cherry fruit with ripe sweet tannins and a long licorice finish. Delicious now but will age well too.

Riserva. Padelletti's vibrant 2004 Riserva has richer aromas and more depth and weight than Brunello, as well as a very cellar-worthy structure. Before this, the last Riserva was 1997, underscoring the firm's commitment to selection. The 2004 boasts all the earthy Sangiovese nuances one would expect from a traditionally crafted Brunello: black-cherry, floral, and leather aromas accompanied by round cherry-berry flavors, leather, and truffle. Refreshing acidity and very firm tannins will keep this drinking well through the 2020s.

Rosso. Rosso is declassified from Brunello and is everything this junior partner should be: vibrant, floral, and friendly with mouthwatering fruit. This will accompany everything from *pasta pomodoro* to white meat dishes, even *baccalà*.

Il Paradiso di Manfredi

Via Canalicchio 305
53024 Montalcino (SI)
Tel. +39 0577 848478
www.ilparadisodimanfredi.com
ilparadisodimanfredi@interfree.it

The tiny Il Paradiso di Manfredi farm, run by three generations of a close-knit and delightful family, makes the most soulful Brunellos in the entire denomination. Florio Guerrini, a retired math professor, along with his wife, Rosella, a former elementary school teacher, and their two grown daughters, Silvia and Gioia, lovingly tend the vineyards that encircle their home and cellars, and among them share all the winemaking and business responsibilities. Rosella's father, the late Manfredi Martini, who worked for years in Biondi Santi's Greppo cellars, and her mother, Fortunata, purchased the Il Paradiso farm in the 1950s and together founded the firm back in 1959. Manfredi, one of the twenty-five founding fathers of the Brunello Consorzio in 1967, believed in the strictly traditional, noninvasive winemaking approach that

FIGURE 10. The Guerrini family makes traditionally crafted and soulful Brunellos of great depth at their Paradiso di Manfredi farm. Photograph by Paolo Tenti.

he learned firsthand while working at Biondi Santi, and passed this philosophy down to Rosella and her husband Florio. For many years after Manfredi passed away in 1983, the couple ran the farm and made wine together with Fortunata while they also held down their day jobs and raised a family.

Fortunata, as of 2011 ninety years old and still thriving, is immensely pleased that her daughter, son-in-law, and granddaughters are carrying on her late husband's wishes of handcrafting classic Brunellos that are meant for lengthy cellaring. The small winery, country home, and vineyards, rising up to 335 meters (1,099 feet) above sea level, are located just northeast of Montalcino's gates in one of the oldest growing areas in the denomination. Like his father-in-law, Florio refuses to use herbicides, pesticides, or chemical fertilizers in the vineyards. The pristine vines are over thirty years old, with roots reaching down as far as twenty-five feet beneath the surface, as can be seen by an exposed rock wall inside the small cellar, where roots from a former vineyard are clearly visible snaking their way down through the nooks and crevices in the rock bed. Here, far underground the vines seek out abundant minerals, nutrients, and water, and it is no coincidence that even in scorching drought years like 2003, Il Paradiso di Manfredi's Brunellos boast remarkable freshness. While this subzone can suffer in wet or cold harvests, like the catastrophic 2002 when torrential rain severely damaged grapes just before the harvest, since Il Paradiso is such a small operation, Florio was able to pick his entire crop just before the rains arrived.

Though Florio increased production since the estate first bottled three hundred bottles of Brunello in 1981, winemaking has changed little since Manfredi's time, even if Florio does consult with Brunello *maestro* Giulio Gambelli and employs the consulting services of enologist Paolo Vagaggini. Alcoholic fermentation takes place spontaneously, exclusively with wild yeasts, in resin-lined cement tanks using no temperature control. The wines are then transferred by gravity to large Slavonian oak barrels for aging that goes far beyond the required limits: fourteen months for the Rosso, a minimum thirty-six months for Brunello, and at least four years for Riservas.

Il Paradiso's Rossos, Brunellos, and Riservas are exceptionally earthy and vital, almost exhilaratingly alive, and need ample time to aerate, at least two to three hours in the uncorked bottle. After being poured, it is not uncommon to find what can be initially funky odors that soon transform into the most extraordinary mélange of new leather, marinated cherries, and truffle. Aromas and flavors continue to evolve and open up in the glass, a constant reminder to palates jaded by more industrialized bottlings that truly great wines have a life of their own. While the Rosso has fantastic structure and vibrant fruit, the Brunello is earthier, with leather, tobacco, and bracing but supple tannins. The Riservas, produced only when Florio, and not the Consorzio or critics, deems the harvest is exceptional, is richer, with more depth, boasting intense leather and meat-juice aromas, and a creamy fruit and mineral palate with big but sweet tannins. Il Paradiso's Brunellos are extremely complex, and benefit from lengthy cellaring, during which time they evolve dramatically with bottle age. As Florio succinctly puts it, "My Brunellos are not commercial wines, and I don't want them to be. Instead I want to make Brunellos that will allow the younger generations to relive the unique traditions and vocation of Sangiovese in Montalcino."

In a day when there is so much doubt over the authenticity of Brunello, and question marks over whose dark and inky Brunellos are the result of blending or of the newest generation of Sangiovese superclones, and when so many small and large producers overextract and overoak their wines in an attempt to be noticed by critics, it is refreshing to discover a winery like Il Paradiso di Manfredi. These distinct earthy and mineral Brunellos are the real thing; they are without a doubt Brunellos for connoisseurs.

Production

Total surface area: 3.5 ha (8.5 acres)
Brunello: 2 ha (5 acres), 7,000 bottles
Rosso: 2,500 bottles

Brunello. Il Paradiso di Manfredi's Brunellos have intensely earthy, floral, and truffle aromas, all of which carry over to the palate, along with ripe-berry flavors and mineral. Intense mineral purity, vibrant acidity, and firm tannins give these a cellar-worthy structure. These Brunellos are wonderful at the ten- to fifteen-year mark but age for far longer. The 2005 was already so enjoyable in 2010, but will maintain beautifully through 2020.

🅁 *Riserva.* In the best years, like 2000 and 2004, Florio makes a Riserva with more power and depth than the Brunello Annata. A tasting in 2010 of older Riservas back to 1985 show that these gain in complexity, thanks to concentrated violet and leather aromas with a hint of meat juices, and layers of ripe dark-cherry, mineral, tobacco, and truffle flavors balanced with hallmark fresh acidity and bracing tannins. The estate's Riservas need time to fully develop; they are best after fifteen to twenty years but can age and evolve slowly for far longer. The rich, velvety, and vibrant 2004 will be best after 2014, but will drink well for decades.

Rosso. Aged for one year in botti, Paradiso di Manfredi's Rosso is a lighter, brighter version of Brunello, with fresh acidity and supple tannins, that is best coupled with steaming plates of pasta or grilled chicken. Very food-friendly and delicious, this Rosso has some complexity but just the right structure for easy drinking.

La Gerla

Località Canalicchio
Podere Colombaio
53024 Montalcino (SI)
Tel. + 39 0577 848599
www.lagerlamontalcino.com
lagerla@tin.it

Right next to Paradiso di Manfredi is the charming La Gerla estate. Although it takes its name from the large, old-fashioned baskets that grape harvesters once strapped to their backs, the farm was formerly known as Podere Colombaio Santi, and was originally owned by the Biondi Santi family. After the death of Tancredi Biondi Santi in 1970, this small property was left to his eldest daughter, Tedina, who was not interested in winemaking and apparently sold it off to the first interested buyer, Sergio Rossi.

Rossi, who passed away in August 2011, was part of the wave of Milanese entrepreneurs that first descended on Montalcino in the early 1970s and included Gianfranco Soldera and later the Angelini family, among others. When Rossi left Milan for Montalcino to manage the Altesino-Caparzo estates, it was a new direction for him. He had previously been a successful business executive running the European branches of a major international advertising firm. After a few years in Montalcino, Rossi wanted his own property, and more importantly, his own Brunello label, so in 1976 he bought the Colombaio Santi podere. Ever the advertising executive, Rossi soon changed the name of the estate and created the La Gerla "trademark" in 1978. According to estate manager Alberto Passeri, by the time Rossi bought the property, both the vineyards and the buildings needed extensive restructuring, and Rossi set to work immediately by replanting the vineyards, then expanding the original cellar, restoring the stone villa, and eventually built a whole new cellar.

Besides the vineyards directly on the La Gerla property and just nearby, including their top Gli Angeli vineyard, which in great years is bottled separately, Rossi later acquired vineyards in Castelnuovo dell'Abate. "The areas are completely different. La Gerla's vineyards have northeast and east exposures, and the terrain is mostly marl and chalk. This is good for developing aromas, while the Castelnuovo dell'Abate vineyards have more sand and clay, and is very protected from the cold northern winds, so ripening is excellent. These grapes yield more intensity and structure," explains Passeri who is also the firm's agronomist. The average altitude of the vineyards together is between 270 and 320 meters (886 and 1,050 feet), and plants are between twenty-five and thirty years old—a combination that generates concentrated flavors.

Since the beginning, Rossi enlisted the services of consultant enologist Vittorio Fiore to make polished, focused Brunellos with wide appeal. Fermentation lasts fifteen days, and the estate's Brunellos are then aged in

Slavonian botti for three years, six months for Rosso, though the firm often experiments with new techniques in its quest to improve quality, including malolactic fermentation in barriques for its Riservas.

Production

Total surface area: 16 ha (39.5 acres)

Brunello: 11.5 ha (28 acres), divided between La Gerla and Castelnuovo dell'Abate, 40,000 bottles

Brunello Vigna gli Angeli: 6,000 bottles

Riserva: 6,000 bottles

Rosso: 25,000–30,000 bottles

Brunello. The Brunello Annata, generally a blend of La Gerla's vineyards and those at Castelnuovo dell'Abate, tends to have intense violet and iris aromas and ripe-fruit flavors. Good structure and firm but sweet tannins. In less than perfect vintages, such as 2005, most of the fruit comes from Castelnuovo dell'Abate, hence that year's unusually ripe fruit and heft. Best 2012 to 2015.

Brunello Vigna gli Angeli. This single vineyard selection is made only in select years, such as 2003 and 2004, with grapes from the one-hectare (2.47-acre) single vineyard Vigna gli Angeli that takes its name from the small Degli Angeli church. Plant age averages thirty years old, and the vines are severely pruned to further ensure low yields. This is a complex Brunello with an intense bouquet boasting spice, tobacco, and violet, and a warm, ripe palate balanced by bracing tannins. Best after modest cellaring.

Riserva. In exceptional years La Gerla also produces a Brunello Riserva gli Angeli made with 30 percent of top grapes from Vigna gli Angeli and about 70 percent of a selection of best grapes from Castelnuovo dell'Abate. However, an experiment with the 2004 Riserva, in which malolactic fermentation took place in barrique before aging in botti, left the wine overwhelmed with oak when tasted in 2010

Rosso. Made by declassifying wine destined to become Brunello, this is usually one of the top Rossos in the denomination. Very polished and approachable, yet has structure too.

Pertimali—Livio Sassetti

Azienda Agricola Pertimali 329
53024 Montalcino (SI)
Tel. +39 0577 848721
lsasset@tin.it

For generations, the Sassetti family grew grapes and made wine on their property in Sant'Angelo in Colle, but they were never completely satisfied with the results. In the early 1970s, Livio Sassetti sold the Sant'Angelo property and bought the Pertimali estate on top of a hill just northwest of town, an area Sassetti firmly believed was best suited for the complex, full-bodied, but elegant wines he wanted to craft. Livio's intuition was correct, and today he and his son Lorenzo, a trained enologist, make outstanding Brunellos that seamlessly unite power with elegance.

The small farmhouse and cellars sit below a high ridge and are encircled by vineyards averaging 270 meters (886 feet) high and that have northwest exposures. The ridge and nearby hills block humid marine breezes from the south, and according to Livio's son Lorenzo, who now runs the winery, an opening to the north generates a vortex of constant airflow that keeps vines dry and relatively free from powdery mildew. This northern airflow also brings cool air, crucial in the summer when it keeps grapes cooled down and fresh even in scorching years.

This constant airflow further allows the Sassettis to greatly reduce disease control treatments in the vineyards, where they strictly forbid both herbicides and insecticides. Besides an ideal location, which incorporates a complex soil composition of light clay, marlstone, sand, and marine fossils that impart notable minerality, Pertimali's Brunellos are also the product of a unique clone of Sangiovese that was already in the vineyards when Livio bought the estate. The vines, now replanted exclusively with Pertimali's own Sangiovese that has had decades to adapt to the environment, are between eighteen and thirty-six years old.

Lorenzo keeps things traditional in the firm's very modest cellars. He carries out temperature-controlled alcoholic fermentation in steel using only wild yeasts, followed by thirty-six months aging in large Slavonian casks for Brunello and Riserva. Pertimali's delicious and vibrant Rosso, which originates from the same Brunello vines, sees no oak, but spends a year in steel. "Rosso should be an easy-drinking wine, so I age it only in steel to exalt the fresh fruit sensations. Wood should be reserved for wines destined for lengthy aging only," argues Lorenzo.

Production

Total surface area: 14 ha (35 acres)
Brunello: 12 ha (30 acres), 40,000 bottles
Rosso: 15,000 bottles

Brunello. These are beautiful expressions of Sangiovese from Montalcino, with elegant, floral, and earthy aromas that morph into leather and tobacco with age. Vibrant black-cherry and berry palate with a great depth of flavors, balanced by athletic tannins and fresh acidity. Best after ten years, but drinks well for twenty, longer in great vintages.

Riserva. In great years, Pertimali produces a Riserva from a selection of the best grapes that are then vinified and aged separately. This has more concentrated fruit, earth, leather sensations, and wonderful age-worthy structure thanks to bracing tannins and acidity.

Rosso. Made with vines registered to Brunello. A delightful, delicious, and flexible Rosso, with bright candied-cherry aromas and flavors and surprising depth. Thoroughly enjoyable upon release, as Rosso is meant to be.

Capanna

Località Capanna 333
53024 Montalcino (SI)
Tel. +39 0577 848298
www.capannamontalcino.com
info@capannamontalcino.com

The Capanna farm has been owned by the Cencioni family since 1957 and has been bottling Brunello since the 1960 vintage. Patrizio Cencioni runs the estate and is a former president of the Brunello Consorzio, and his father, Giuseppe, who is still active at the winery, was one of the Consorzio's founding members.

Located to the north of Montalcino, sandwiched between Biondi Santi's celebrated Pievecchia and the illustrious Montosoli, La Capanna makes archetypical Brunellos and Rossos of consistent quality vintage after vintage. Though they are not among the denomination's flashiest or most sought-after bottlings, these Brunellos and Rossos are honestly made and reasonably priced, and demonstrate the floral aromas and cherry-berry earthiness of Montalcino's northern vineyards, combined with surprising power that comes from the Montosoli zone.

Capanna's Sangiovese has been selected from within the estate and is planted at 4,000 to 5,000 plants per hectare in the best sites, with marly soil rich in rock fragments, at altitudes of 270 meters above sea level. Under the guidance of famed Brunello consultant Paolo Vagaggini, the Cencionis keep it simple and conventional in the cellar, with a long fermentation lasting between twenty-five and thirty-five days in Slavonian oak vats for Brunello, followed by three years aging in 10- to 30-hectoliter Slavonian casks. Capanna also makes a Riserva in top vintages that is aged for at least four years in botti followed by one in bottle. Rosso, which mostly comes from declassified Brunello, is fermented partly in wood and partly in steel and is aged for one year in Slavonian oak barrels. They also make two fine Moscadellos from a clone native to Montalcino; a fresh version and a more structured late-harvest interpretation.

Production

Total area: 69 ha (170 acres)
Brunello: 12 ha (30 acres), 30,000 bottles
Riserva: 10,000 bottles
Rosso: 2.5 ha (6.2 acres), 28,000 bottles

Brunello. This is a classically crafted Brunello, with hallmark cherry, earth, and mineral sensations leaning toward leather and tobacco. With its more austere structure, which includes firm but ripe tannins and racy acidity, this always benefits from some cellaring and is usually prime between the ten- and fifteen-year mark, depending on the vintage, but has serious staying power.

Riserva 2004. In exceptional vintages, the winery also chooses the best grapes from their oldest vines and ages for more than four years in botti. The 2004 boasts big and beautiful Sangiovese aromas of fresh-tilled earth, leather, and mineral. Fantastic ripe dark-fruit flavors, with piercing minerality, mint, and licorice. Best after 2016 and will cellar for years.

Rosso. Lovely, floral, fresh, and bright with a tannic backbone. Very refined and delicious.

Moscadello. Using a Moscato clone native to Montalcino that was already in their vineyards when they acquired the property, Capanna produces a fresh and floral Moscadello that is a fresh dessert wine with a dry finish. They also make a late-harvested version that is fermented and aged in botti, with a big, round structure dominated by honey and apricot flavors. Pairs wonderfully with seasoned cheeses.

Baricci

Località Colombaio di Montosoli 13
53024 Montalcino (SI)
Tel. +39 0577 848109
Baricci1955@libero.it

On warm, sunny days, ninety-year-old Nello Baricci can inevitably be found sitting on the low stone wall in front of his small cellar, taking in the breathtaking scenery of his vineyards on one of Montalcino's greatest crus: Montosoli. This now legendary hill north of Montalcino is celebrated for producing powerful yet graceful wines of extraordinary depth. Montosoli rises up to over 350 meters (1,148 feet), where vineyards are safely out of reach of autumn fog that can afflict lower vineyards north of Montalcino, and it suffers less from spring frosts, allowing grapes to reach ideal ripening, which in turn generates firm but refined tannins. Montosoli's soil, a complex mix of marl, loam rock, and limestone, lends the wine its muscle and complexity. Although Baricci didn't know all this back when he bought the property, he did know that the wines hailing from Montosoli were of consistently superior quality.

Baricci has a wealth of local experience that only one who has worked Montalcino's land since he could walk could ever gain. He was born in 1921 on the Poggio Martelli farm, where his family were *mezzadri,* or sharecroppers. The whole family transferred to another podere, Scopone, in 1938, again to work as farmworkers for the proprietors, where Nello remembers, "We worked very hard all the time, but no matter how hard we worked, we were always in debt to the owners." Then, in 1955, as Italy's *mezzadria* system, no longer feasible or economically viable in postwar Italy, was beginning its

FIGURE 11. Nello Baricci, one of Montalcino's veteran Brunello producers, makes ripe delicious Brunellos from his Montosoli vineyards. Photograph by Paolo Tenti.

inevitable dissolution, Baricci bought his own farm on Montosoli. Fifty-five years on, he still recalls the sheer terror of taking out a mortgage to buy the property, thanks to revamped banking rules on lending aimed to encourage Italy's peasant farmers to become independent.

Following local customs, Nello initially cultivated a bit of everything on his newly acquired 12 hectares, from olive oil and grain to Sangiovese. But he always remembered that at Siena's early agricultural fairs, red wines labeled as Montosoli made by the Fattoria Montosoli, then owned by Guido Angelini, "always won first prize," so Baricci was well aware of his property's winemaking potential. One of the twenty-five founding members of the Consorzio, Baricci began replanting his vineyards in 1967. His first Rosso was from the 1968 harvest, and he began commercially bottling Brunello with the 1971 vintage released in 1976. After Baricci's Rossos and Brunellos hit the market, other producers, namely Altesino and Caparzo, noticed the great potential of Montosoli, where they quickly snapped up vineyards.

Baricci's 5 hectares (12 acres) of vines, replanted between 1985 and 2001, cut across the center of the famed hill and enjoy perfect south and southeast exposures. The average altitude of 280 meters (919 feet) above sea level is low enough for ideal ripening, but high enough to ensure a long growing season that generates complex bouquets, and as Nello points out, the stony soil in his vineyards gives the wine structure. Baricci, helped by his son Graziano, son-in-law Pietro, and grandson Federico, ferments in temperature-controlled steel tanks and ages his Brunellos for thirty-six months in large Slavonian casks, eight months for Rosso. Baricci doesn't make a Riserva, preferring to use the best grapes only for his Brunello.

These are traditionally crafted Brunellos, marked by earthy, gamey, and spicy aromas with creamy-cherry fruit and chewy tannins that mellow with time. They have the heft and depth found in Sangiovese cultivated in prime areas of Montalcino. Baricci is also an outspoken critic of Brunello's exploding production. "The denomination expanded too much, thanks to the pressure from some of the larger firms, who wield a lot of power in Brunello politics," argues the veteran, adding that in 1967 many areas now under vine were deemed unsuitable by agricultural inspectors who analyzed the area before growers could plant new vineyards once the wine became regulated under the DOC laws.

Production

Total surface area: 12 ha (30 acres)
Brunello: 5 ha (12 acres), 14,000 bottles
Rosso: 18,000 bottles

❧ *Brunello.* These traditionally crafted Brunellos boast earthy and heady aromas of wild cherry, underbrush, leather, and tobacco. The palate is always loaded with juicy dark fruit, leather, and truffle balanced by impressive depth, power, and freshness. The 2006 is fantastic, with layers of flavor and great length. Best 2014 to 2026.

❧ *Rosso.* These are among my favorite Rossos in the denomination. Declassed from Brunello, they are rich but bright. The 2007 and 2009 are exceptional, with succulent cherry-berry aromas and flavors punctuated with hints of tobacco, leather, and tea. These are delicious and enjoyable without the excessive alcohol sensations and overblown structure of so many Rossos made from declassifying Brunello.

Altesino

Località Altesino 54
Montalcino (SI)
Tel. +39 0577 806208
www.altesino.it
info@altesino.it

Altesino has been a stalwart and forward-thinking Brunello producer ever since Giulio Consonno bottled his first Brunello with the 1972 vintage. Consonno, who completely restructured the early fifteenth-century manor house and cellars in 1970, also brought the single-vineyard concept to Montalcino when he first vinified and bottled his 4.5 hectares (11 acres) of Montosoli vineyards separately in 1975.

Built in 1414, the grand Palazzo Altesino and its surrounding vineyards, woods, and olive groves were owned for centuries by the noble Tricerchi family before being bought by Consonno in 1970. In 2002, the Consonnos sold Altesino to Elisabetta Gnudi Angelini, owner of the adjacent Caparzo Brunello firm, effectively reuniting the two properties that before 1970 had been one contiguous estate. Angelini has made much-needed investments in the cellars and vineyards without altering Altesino's classic style.

Altesino's original vineyards northeast of Montalcino reach up to a maximum of 250 meters (820 feet) above sea level, and are at risk of autumn fog and spring frosts that can compromise production in adverse vintages. Realizing this, and wanting to add more structure to the wines, the former proprietor also acquired vineyards elsewhere in the denomination. Besides the aforementioned Montosoli, acquired in 1972 and 1973, where the thirty-year-old vines are situated between 350 and 450 meters (1,148 and 1,476 feet) and effectively out of harm's way, the firm also purchased vineyards in Castelnuovo dell'Abate and Sant'Angelo in Colle in the southern extremes of the denomination, where the warmer climate yields more muscular wines.

Altesino's basic Brunello is a blend of their vineyards in the various parts of the growing areas; in superb years they also produce a fine Riserva, aged for five years before release. But Altesino's greatness lies in its single-vineyard Brunello, Montosoli, made only in exceptional years, meaning that from 1975 to 2004, only thirteen vintages were deemed worthy of being bottled as single-vineyard Montosoli. This golden hill is not only Montalcino's answer to the Cote d'Or's Grands Crus, but is arguably the most famous single vineyard in Tuscany, and one of the most famous in Italy.

Montosoli pairs the heady floral perfumes and mineral complexity of Montalcino's oldest growing zone with the big chewy tannins and muscular backbone usually found in Montalcino's more southern wines. Montosoli is a classic example of the concept of terroir, because its success is its combination of high altitude, northwest exposure, and marly limestone soil that together yield remarkably powerful but graceful and aromatic Brunellos. Montosoli is also a perfect example of why Montalcino desperately needs to delimit its subzones and important microzones, because more and more producers in the general vicinity try to cash in on Montosoli's fame by claiming that their vineyards are actually on Montosoli. Or as one producer puts it, his hilltop vineyards are "a continuation of Montosoli," despite the fact that he is on a hill that is clearly detached and separated by a valley floor from the famed cru.

Production

Total surface area: 70 ha (173 acres)
Brunello: 25 ha (62 acres), 120,000 bottles, 15,000 bottles Montosoli
Rosso: 7 ha (17 acres), 50,000 bottles

Brunello.   Assembled from the firm's vineyards located in prime subzones throughout the denomination, this is a solid Brunello, with quintessential Sangiovese aromas and flavors. Bright fruit and brooding tannins, this is best drunk at around ten years, though it also has staying power. In outstanding vintages, Altesino also produces a Riserva, aged for one year longer in barrels and released a year later than Brunello *normale*. The Riservas also have more power and depth, and can age for decades.

▌*Brunello Montosoli.*   This is Altesino's flagship wine and perhaps Montosoli's finest expression. Well-structured, but also remarkably elegant thanks to the highest vineyard altitude on the famed hill, this is a Brunello lover's Brunello, of remarkable finesse and complexity. Best after ten years, but has the structure to age well for decades. The 2006 is superb, with earthy, floral, and leather aromas and rich, vibrant palate with spice and mineral energy. Big, ripe tannins. Best 2015 to 2025.

Rosso.   Made primarily from the youngest vines on the estate, those between seven and fifteen years old, this is a superb Rosso, with a classic floral nose and an elegantly extracted palate that is both fresh and vibrant. Ready and enjoyable.

Le Gode

Claudio Ripaccioli
Località Le Gode 343
53024 Montalcino (SI)
Tel. +39 0577 84857
www.legode.it
azienda.legode@libero.it

Located directly on the celebrated Montosoli hillside, Le Gode is another unsung jewel of Montalcino. Run by one of the nicest, most down-to-earth families in Montalcino, this small estate consistently turns out quintessential Brunellos that boast gorgeous aromas, great structure, and succulent, concentrated fruit flavors.

Founded in 1960 by Ilano Ripaccioli, the farm was bought during "the height of economic misery here in Montalcino," according to Ilano's son Claudio, who took over the estate in 1996. In the beginning, despite their fantastic location for winemaking, the family concentrated instead on what at the time was the more stable business of raising sheep and cultivating various crops—activities that allowed them to scrape out a living. Ilano planted his first vineyard in 1976, but like many of the vineyards at that time it was planted with *coltura promiscua* and the wine was for family consumption. Not long after this, Ilano realized the family's property sat on prime Brunello land, and throughout the late 1970s and 1980s, Ilano planted more Sangiovese vines in specialized vineyards, and began bottling Rosso di Montalcino with the fabulous 1990 vintage. The firm's first bottled Brunello was from the excellent 1995 harvest, still outstanding when tasted in 2010 with Claudio, his wife, Donatella, and their teenage daughter Carlotta, the latter already showing an active interest in wine and winemaking.

The secret to Le Gode's fantastic Brunello is the combination of having the good fortune to own vineyards on Montosoli, along with the wisdom and restraint to not botch up what nature has so generously provided, by employing invasive cellar techniques that can drastically transform if not downright smother the vibrant beauty and intense aromas of Sangiovese.

Le Gode's vineyards average 280 meters (919 feet) above sea level, high enough to avoid frosts and fog but low enough to ensure ideal maturation. The soil is a complex mix of various layers of marl, marine deposits, and clay, a confirmation of the continuously invading and receding ocean in past epochs. Claudio has replanted to reach the ideal density of 5,000 plants per hectare and average vine age in 2011 was around fifteen years. In the cellar, Claudio does nothing fancy, employing temperature-controlled fermentation for twenty-five days in steel tanks. He ages both his Brunello and Riservas, the latter made only in exceptional years, for three years in 25-hectoliter botti, seven months for Rosso.

Production

Total surface area: 16 ha (39.5 acres)
Brunello: 6.5 ha (16 acres), 10,000 bottles
Riserva: 3,000–4,500 bottles
Rosso: 6,000 bottles

Brunello. Hallmark Montosoli, with structure and elegance, and wonderful aging potential, as proven by tastings back to the fabulous 1995 vintage tasted in 2010, with some tasting highlights below.

✷ *2004.* Well-structured with ripe fruit and tobacco aromas accompanied by mouthwatering black-cherry and spice flavors. Brooding tannins will soften with time and are balanced with fresh acidity. Gorgeous. Best 2014 to 2024.

1997. While this has for the most part proven to be a grossly overrated vintage, this is an outstanding effort. Very focused, incredibly bright and youthful, with earthy aromas of leather and underbrush and succulent cherry and spice flavors. Fresh acidity and lively mineral sensations balanced with great depth and complexity. Should drink well until 2017.

Riserva. Made only in outstanding years, the Riservas have more power and structure, yet retain their grace and vibrancy.

2004. Enticing floral and eucalyptus aromas. Very ripe black-fruit flavors and spice with supple, velvety tannins. Wonderful balance and depth, great length. Should drink well from 2015 to 2030.

1999. Floral, earthy nose with lots of tobacco nuances. Earthy, ripe-plum and mineral flavors with silky tannins, and a long, smooth finish ending on a licorice note. Stunning. Best through 2019.

Rosso. Made from the Brunello vineyards, this is a brighter, more approachable, and mouthwatering version. Boasts both muscle and vitality.

Donatella Cinelli Colombini

Casato Prime Donne
53024 Montalcino (SI)
Tel. +39 0577 849421
www.cinellicolombini.it
casato@cinellicolombini.it

Donatella Cinelli Colombini, whose family has been making wine for hundreds of years and helped launch Brunello back in the early 1960s, not only has winemaking in her DNA, but she is a creative promoter as well. Ambitious and scintillatingly energetic, Donatella was one of the first in Italy to take charge of the dire, almost nonexistent state of wine tourism in the 1990s. At her own initiative, she founded the Movimento del turismo del vino association in 1993, and that same year invented the highly successful *cantine aperte,* an event that takes place across Italy, when hundreds of wineries open their doors to the general public on the last Sunday of May.

Keeping up with the unwritten but solid tradition of most of Italy's great wine families—that of not being able to work alongside parents or siblings—in 1998 Donatella left her family's Fattoria dei Barbi estate in the hands of her mother, Francesca, and brother Stefano, and struck out on her own after fourteen years of working with them. She created her own eponymous company, composed of the Il Colle estate in nearby Trequanda, and the Casato farm in Montalcino, a property already in her family for centuries. One of the most unique aspects of the winery is that it is one of the first in Italy to employ only women, and Donatella duly changed the original name of simply Casato to Casato Prime Donne (First Ladies). Here, a few kilometers directly north of Montalcino, Donatella's south- and southwest-facing vineyards are situated at 225 meters (738 feet) above sea level, where the Pliocene lay soil is mixed with gravel.

For many years, Donatella enlisted the outside consultancy of Carlo

Ferrini, and the wines were crafted in the famed consultant's highly recognizable style; very dark, dense, and extracted, with opulent fruit and very evident oak sensations accompanied by massive tannins you could chew on. These Ferrini-styled Brunellos seemed to have more to do with the enologist, and less to do with Montalcino, but since this was the prototype that garnered top scores from certain wine critics, you can't blame winemakers for trying this route. However, Ferrini left in early 2010 and Donatella replaced him with a young woman, Valerie Lavigne, who advises in-house enologist Barbara Magnani. As one of her first major changes in winemaking at the estate, Lavigne, who studied under the greats of Bordeaux, has openly declared that Brunello should be aged in large barrels and casks, not barriques.

To this end, Donatella had already begun replacing her barriques with tonneaux and large casks, and in fact hasn't purchased any barriques since 2004, about the time the tide began turning against excessive oak. Cinelli Colombini is also experimenting with isolating Brunello yeasts, and has even inaugurated an outside vinification area located in the Casato Prime Donne vineyards for part of her production. Dubbed "Vats in the Wind," open-topped steel vinification tanks, inoculated with two isolated strains of Brunello yeasts created in the laboratories of Oliver Ogar, are open to the winds on four sides. As I mentioned before, Donatella is indeed a marketing genius.

For now, in 2011, Donatella is fermenting with a mix of commercial yeasts, and is experimenting with the manufactured Brunello strains in both a conventional vinification cellar and her new outdoor project. Until Lavigne came in 2010, Donatella, still highly influenced by Bordeaux, was mixing up both Bordelaise and Tuscan traditions. She has since pulled back from barriques, instead aging her wine in French tonneaux the first year, small botti of 5 to 15 hectoliters the second, and twenty-year-old 40-hectoliter botti the third. Only occasionally "does a wine spend all three years in the small barrels." Given that Lavigne feels that large casks "are much better than barriques at preserving Sangiovese's aromas," I have high expectations that we can expect more terroir-driven wines coming out of the estate.

Production

Total surface area: 15.9 ha (39.2 acres)
Brunello: 9.2 ha (22.7 acres), 38,000 bottles
Riserva: 5,000 bottles
Rosso: 4.19 ha (10.3 acres), 25,000 bottles

Brunello. The 2005 straight Brunello was restrained, with less of the overextracted qualities of past vintages, and with pleasing aromas boasting plum, earth, and spice with ripe black fruit, spice, and vanillin oak flavors. Round with supple tannins. Should drink well until 2015. In excellent years, Donatella also produces a Riserva version, chosen from the best wine in the cellars, that has more structure and concentration. This usually needs more time to tame bracing tannins.

Brunello Prime Donne. This is a selection made by several prestigious women tasters, including sommeliers and masters of wine who get together a couple of times of year to taste the Brunello from the barrels, and decide the blend of top Brunello that will be labeled as Progetto Prime Donne. It is usually very fruit-forward; the latest vintages, while still vaunting evident oak, are showing signs of earth and mineral as well.

Rosso. This tends to have less oak influence, but still boasts lush fruit while retaining vibrancy and mineral sensations.

Tenimenti Angelini—Val di Suga

Località Val di Cava
53024 Montalcino (SI)
Tel. +39 0577 80411
www.tenimentiangelini.it
info@tenimentiangelini.it

In 1994 the Angelini family, manufacturers of pharmaceuticals and an international health-care products business, swooped into Tuscany on a winery shopping spree. That same year they purchased three separate properties in Tuscany's top denominations of Chianti Classico, Vino Nobile, and of course Brunello, acquiring the Val di Suga estate north of Montalcino. Although the original winery was founded in the early 1970s, owner Francesco Angelini took Val di Suga to a whole new level after he invested in updating both the vineyards and winemaking.

The Montalcino estate is divided into three distinct vineyard sites. Vineyards around the Val di Suga winery north of the town, positioned at 300 meters (984 feet) above sea level in predominantly clay and sand soil, yield more delicate wines with enticing bouquets. The Lago vineyard, right in front of the winery, was bottled as a single vineyard until 1999. It was then grubbed up thanks to the advanced age of the vines compounded by severe hail damage in 1997 that drastically reduced the number of vines, but Angelini plans on releasing it again as a single-vineyard selection starting with the 2009 vintage. The original acquisition of Val di Suga also came with the Vigna Spuntali vineyard in the other end of the denomination, halfway between Sant'Angelo in Colle and Sant'Angelo Scalo, where the warmer climate and the lower altitude of 250 meters (820 feet) produce full-bodied wines with succulent fruit. Besides having reached an ideal balance with the two vineyard areas, the 1997 hailstorm that wiped out the entire crop around the winery that year but left the Spuntali vines unscathed made the firm realize how important it is to have vineyards in different subzones. "Having vineyards only in one area brings the risk that hail or other damaging storms can destroy the entire production. Because we have vines in other areas, we minimize that risk," says Angelini. To further diversify its vineyard areas, in 1999 the firm purchased the San Polo vineyard in the Podernovone area, overlooking the valley of Sant'Antimo.

To increase concentration by lowering yields, Val di Suga's newer vineyards have been replanted at 7,200 hundred plants per hectare, very high density for Montalcino, but Angelini feels this will further improve quality, especially in their northern vineyards. In the cellar, enologist Fabrizio Ciufoli ferments in steel tanks for the straight Brunello, which he then ages for three years in botti and (a small amount) in seasoned barriques when there is not enough wine to fill an entire large cask. The fuller-bodied Vigna Spuntali, on the other hand, is fermented in resin-lined cement vats, and aged for two years in new barriques, as is the Vigna del Lago. Although the producer doesn't make a Riserva, its single-vineyard selection, Vigna Spuntali, and eventually the Vigna del Lago, are aged to all effects as a Riserva since they hit the market one year later than the Brunello Annata.

Production

Total surface area: 100 ha (247 acres)
Brunello: 40.7 ha (100.5 acres), 163,000 bottles
Rosso: 5 ha (12 acres), 60,000 bottles (the firm also buys grapes for Rosso from other Brunello growers)

Brunello. This is a very round, approachable, and reliable Brunello offering pretty floral aromas and ripe cherry-berry sensations. Aged for three years almost entirely in botti, a small percentage in recycled 300-liter barriques, Val di Suga's Brunello is a blend of the firm's three vineyard areas, creating a natural balance between aromas and structure.

Vigna Spuntali. This is Val di Suga's flagship wine and is only made in exceptional vintages from a selection of this vineyard's select grapes. Although they don't call it Riserva, Vigna Spuntali is aged to fit Riserva stipulations but the owners prefer to focus on the vineyard rather than aging requirements. This wine is all about ripe fruit, power, and complexity. The 2004 is superb, with its succulent black berry and spice and Sangiovese's hallmark earthiness and vibrancy. Great depth and length. Best after 2016.

Rosso. Very bright and drinkable with a refreshing structure that pairs beautifully with everything. Loaded with sour cherry and mineral. Delicious.

NINE

Bosco and Torrenieri

Although both these areas are in the far north of the growing zone, they have markedly different growing conditions between them and accordingly I have broken the far northern territory into two sections.

BOSCO

I would like to note that the name I have given this subzone is unofficial. *Bosco*, which means woods, seemed appropriate not only because of the area's dense woodland but also because *bosco* is part of the name of the area's two wineries.

According to Dr. Alessandro Benvenuti, the Siena-based geologist who prepared the Consorzio's lithological map of Montalcino, in strictly geological terms soil deposits in most of the northwestern corner of Montalcino, and stretching all the way down to the CastelGiocondo estate southwest of Montalcino, are more uniform than, other parts of Montalcino. "This is not to say that individual estates don't also have some geological deposits not shared with their neighbors, but these variations are more isolated when compared to other parts of the denomination. For the most part, this area contains what is commonly referred to as *galestro,* friable rock made from what is in essence petrified layers of calcareous clay," Benvenuti told me in 2010.

Based on Costanti's CRA-CNR soil map, Bosco, in the extreme northwestern part of the denomination, shows mixed results for Sangiovese, with soil in many parts of the area ranging from "scarcely suitable or not suitable" to "low frequency of suitable and very suitable soils."

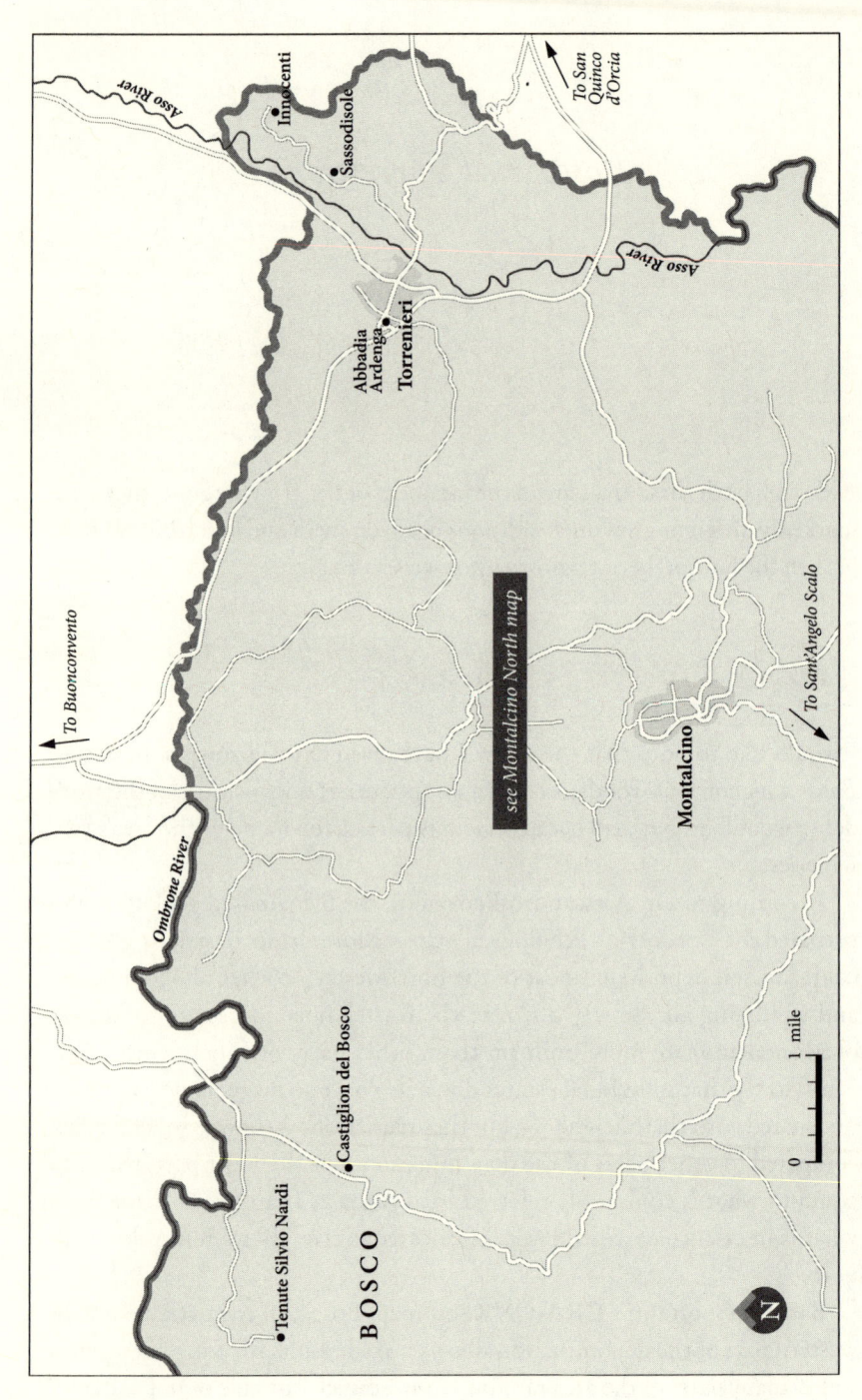

MAP 4. Bosco and Torrenieri

The Bosco subzone has cooler temperatures, with more precipitation than the rest of the denomination, and its lower-lying vines often suffer from damaging spring frosts and autumn fog. There are only two estates in this entire sprawling, wild subzone that is dominated by ancient woods.

Tenute Silvio Nardi

Casale del Bosco
53024 Montalcino (SI)
Tel. +39 0577 808269
www.tenutenardi.com
info@tenutenardi.com

Even though Silvio Nardi was one of the founding fathers of the Consorzio back in 1967, for years locals considered him as "the foreigner" who made Brunello, even though he hailed from the neighboring region of Umbria. As the first producer in Montalcino without roots there, Nardi effectively preceded the trend of massive outside investment by nearly a couple of decades. His family owned a thriving agricultural machinery business founded in 1895 by his father, who is credited with developing the Voltorecchio plow, which helped revolutionize Italy's agricultural sector. Nardi bought the 818-hectare (2,022-acre) Casale del Bosco estate in the extreme northwestern edge of the growing zone in 1950. In 1958, the agricultural industrialist bottled his first Brunello.

Vineyards this far north of Montalcino can suffer from fog and frost, so that grapes often have problems reaching ideal ripening. Even when the climatic conditions allow full ripening, Brunellos from this area yield less structure compared to vineyards further south of the estate. Perhaps it was for these reasons that in 1962 Silvio Nardi bought the Manachiara property, 25 kilometers (15.5 miles) away from Casale del Bosco and close to Castelnuovo dell'Abate, once again beating the trend of mixing grapes from different parts of the production zone by decades. Nardi realized that grapes from these more southern vines on his new property, particularly the exceptional Manachiara vineyard, would inject ripe fruit and muscle into his more delicate Brunellos from Casale del Bosco. In 1995 the firm first bottled the best fruit from Manachiara for its eponymous single-vineyard Brunello, which has become the winery's flag bearer.

Silvio's children inherited the large property in 1990, since when his

FIGURE 12. Tenute Silvio Nardi's Emilia Nardi, at her Casale del Bosco estate, where her father bottled his first Brunello in 1958. Photograph by Paolo Tenti.

youngest daughter Emilia has overseen day-to-day operations. The firm is divided into thirty-six vineyards between the two estates. Vineyard altitude is between 240 and 420 meters (787 and 1,377 feet) at Casale del Bosco, and the soil is of fluvial origin, predominantly jasper and a shale and clay mix. At Manachiara, where the climate is warmer and drier than Casale del Bosco, vineyards average 350 meters (1,148 feet) above sea level, with eastern exposures, and the soil is composed of sand rich in quartz over Pliocene clay. The Manachiara vineyard also boasts notable calcium content and especially good drainage, which sets it apart from the other vineyards. It also has the oldest plants, averaging over forty years old, which generate concentrated flavors. Much of Casale del Bosco was replanted in the late 1990s and in 2000 with new clones better suited for the estate's growing conditions and at higher densities of 5,200 plants per hectare, while older vineyards have densities of 2,200 plants per hectare.

Nardi, who is followed by a team including consultant enologist Mauro Monicchi and resident winemaker Pasquale Presutto, vinifies all the Brunello vineyards separately with fermentation carried out in steel for about twenty days. The firm ages both their Brunellos for one year in barriques and one year in botti and their Rosso in wood of various sizes and ages.

Production

Total surface area: 2,200 acres
Brunello: 50 ha (123.5 acres), 160,000 bottles
Rosso: 7 ha (17 acres), 50,000 bottles

Brunello. This is the mainstay of Tenute Silvio Nardi. It is usually a well-balanced Brunello, with power and ripe fruit from Manachiara restrained by the elegance derived from Casale del Bosco.

Manachiara. This has become the firm's calling card. Powerful and complex with fantastic depth and a lovely mineral purity. Rigid selection of Manachiara's best grapes consistently turns out a polished Brunello of impressive structure. Though Manachiara can be enjoyed early, it also has an age-worthy structure.

Rosso. This undergoes a short cold maceration before fermentation to extract aromas and fruit, and is a lovely, bright Rosso made for enjoying young.

Moscadello. A late-harvest Moscadello from the northern vineyards, this nectar spends six months in new barriques. Classic sensations of apricot and peach with spicy, toast, and nut sensations.

Castiglion del Bosco

Località Castiglion del Bosco
53024 Montalcino (SI)
Tel. +39 0577 807078
www.castigliondelbosco.com
info@castigliondelbosco.com

When fashion mogul Massimo Ferragamo and a select group of his friends bought the rambling and ramshackle Castiglion del Bosco estate in 2003, complete with its suggestive remains of a twelfth-century tower and the castle for which the property is named, the Italian wine press was rife with rumors and expectations over how the buyers would develop it. Extensive restoration was carried out on the older structures while new buildings, built in the same traditional Tuscan style, were seamlessly added. The result is an

FIGURE 13. The 4,500-acre Castiglion del Bosco estate, owned by Massimo Ferragamo and friends since 2003, is now a winemaking and golf resort after lengthy renovation. Photograph by Paolo Tenti.

impressive, exclusive, and incredibly expensive winemaking resort open to private members only.

According to Castiglion del Bosco's website, the estate will even allow its members the "unique opportunity" of picking and sorting grapes during the harvest, as well as to help out on the bottling line, which seems a rather innovative way to have wealthy people pay for the privilege of working for the estate for free, but perhaps that's just a rather practical view of this "members-only privilege." More appealing amenities, however, include staying in luxurious suites, using the on-site spa, and playing golf on the eighteen-hole course against the backdrop of what looks like a magnificent Renaissance painting.

On the winemaking side, Ferragamo and friends also spared no expense, hiring consulting enologist Nicolò D'Afflitto, who has longed work for the Frescobaldi family, and locally trained Cecilia Leoneschi as their in-house enologist. Their new, 39,000-square-foot winery is completely gravity-fed, and currently holds more than seven hundred barriques. The firm also invested in two sorting tables for rigid grape selection during the harvest. Fermentation for their two Brunellos and Rosso is carried out in stainless steel, and despite the rather large volume by Brunello standards, Cecilia claims that they don't use selected yeasts to start fermentation but let it occur naturally with wild yeasts. Aging for all the wines occurs in both new and seasoned French barriques; two years for the straight Brunello as well as for their single-vineyard selection Campo del Drago, and six months for Rosso. While they have stepped back from using the minimum 50 percent new oak they employed for their first 2003 vintage, the wines can still be dominated by new wood, in a style more reminiscent of the overoaked Brunellos that invaded the denomination for a decade, starting in the mid-1990s, rather than the terroir-driven style most Brunello consumers are looking for today.

Yet after driving around the large estate with Cecilia, I would be extremely curious, even excited, to try these wines without the heavy wood influence. The beautifully manicured vineyards face southeast, and at altitudes of between 250 and 350 meters (820 and 1,148 feet) above sea level, vines are subject to consistent breezes that keep fungal diseases at bay. Plants are still relatively young at fifteen, but Cecilia feels that vines peak between their eighth and twentieth years, and should be replanted when at around twenty to twenty-five years old. As is typical for this northern quadrant, the soil is dominated by sandstone and clay with a strong presence of flaky schist. The estate makes its Brunellos from their higher vineyards, those with more *galestro*. All the vineyards are registered to Brunello, but the firm uses grapes from the lower vineyards that have more clay for their Rossos because "clay yields less complex, more perfumed and more immediate wines," says Cecilia.

Production

Total surface area: 4,500 acres
Brunello: 48 ha (118.65 acres), 60,000 bottles
Vigneto Campo del Drago selection: 4,000 bottles
Rosso: 70,000 bottles

Brunello.   In terms of volume, this is the most important wine for the estate. While the oak is better integrated in great vintages such as the 2004, which is extremely polished, wood overwhelms the 2005.

Vigneto Campo del Drago.   A single vineyard selection, this is bigger and more complex than the Brunello *normale,* with good depth. But once again, oak dominates the senses.

Rosso.   This is actually a lovely wine, with floral aromas, bright fruit, and spice with a mere whisper of oak.

TORRENIERI

Torrenieri, in the extreme northeastern edge of Montalcino's growing zone, is without a doubt the most controversial subzone in the entire denomination. The controversy can be summed up in two words: compact clay. To be precise, the area around the Torrenieri village is composed of Pliocene marine clay deposits, sediments left from the sea that covered the area about 5 million years ago and that created a vast expanse of gray badlands and knolls.

For centuries nothing was cultivated, at least not on a large scale, in this dense clay, known locally as the Crete Senesi or simply as the *crete*. Its lunarlike landscape has been criticized and despised by locals for centuries; in 1864, Clemente Santi described the area in no uncertain terms as the "squalid and desolate Crete."[1] Santi and other agricultural luminaries of his day believed the total clearing of the area's once dense woods, combined with unchecked waterways flowing through the area that cause repeated erosion, conspired to create this clay wasteland, and researchers still hold to these theories today.

Seeing that Montalcino's nineteenth-century agricultural activities were confined to a central area within the Montalcino municipality that was delimited by woods (which greatly contributed to the local economy) and the crete, Santi suggested replanting woods on the latter's razed terrain, after first preparing the ground by mixing massive amounts of fertilizer with elements already present in the crete. He also suggested converting parts of the prairie to pasture land for cattle to try and regenerate the area, or at least give the barren space some function. In 1865, some function was in fact given to the hamlet when the railway lines inaugurated a station in Torrenieri that would become an important way stop on the line to and from Grosseto.

Although Santi's suggestions were not taken up, the clay itself soon spawned a thriving industry. A brickworks factory was created in Torrenieri at the start of the last century that eventually employed over a hundred people, and other smaller companies specialized in ceramic fixtures and building materials were established in Torrenieri over the years. But during the first decade of the twenty-first century, all succumbed to the global economic crisis and closed their doors. Today the area is littered with the abandoned hulks of these once-bustling factories.

For years Torrenieri's landholders watched from the sidelines as the Brunello boom largely passed this area by, until the late 1990s, when the Brunello vineyard registers briefly reopened, followed by European Community Regulation 950/97, which granted land planting rights to those under

FIGURE 14. Torrenieri is one of the most controversial subzones in the denomination, thanks to compacted clay, known locally as the Crete Senesi. Photograph by Paolo Tenti.

forty, and which was heavily exploited in Montalcino. Yet by this time, massive investment in the Brunello industry meant there was little available land left in the denomination, with the glaring exception of the crete.

Seeing that the Brunello production code simply states that Brunello grapes must come from "within the administrative territory of the municipality of Montalcino," and because Torrenieri has been incorporated into Montalcino since 1777, Torrenieri's property owners enforced their right under the regulations to plant registered Brunello vines and set up production on the crete. Up until the mid- to late 1990s, there was only one producer with Brunello vineyards in the Torrenieri area; most of the farms were instead specialized in other crops, mainly wheat. However, as in other areas of the denomination, after the above-mentioned regulation gave planting rights to those under forty, many Torrenieri families divided their holdings into several smaller farms, each given or "sold" to one of the younger family members who promptly turned their attention to Brunello production despite the challenging conditions.

Even though this same dense clay is also found in various parts of Chianti Classico's denomination, it is significant that Classico's winemakers are not allowed to plant registered vineyards in those areas. Classico's foresight underscores how a once-struggling denomination plagued by its poor image has made impressive strides toward greatly improving quality, while Brunello, wallowing in its success, let its guard down. Perhaps alarmed by what was happening in Montalcino, and specifically around Torrenieri, when Classico broke free from the larger Chianti denomination in 1996, its own regulations specifically excluded vineyards located in unfit terrain, including land on the crete. According to article 4 of their production code: "Vineyards situated in damp soils and on valley floors are considered unsuitable and cannot be entered on the said register. Terrains consisting predominantly of Pliocene clay, or in any case, markedly clayey [sic] are not suitable even if they are situated within the delimited zone." That a denomination would clearly exclude such terrain, most certainly at the expense of commercial interests for some wineries, emphasizes the validity of the many fierce criticisms aimed at attempting quality winemaking in Tuscany's compact clay.

So why wasn't the Crete Senesi excluded from Brunello production back when the early pioneers were hammering out the rules and regulations governing the denomination, or later in subsequent modifications? According to Abbadia Ardenga's veteran managing director Mario Ciacci, at the time, specifically excluding Torrenieri and its crete would have been like excluding Brunello production from being carried out on the moon—it seemed that unlikely. "In the early 1960s, when the founding fathers of the Brunello production code created the denomination's regulations, and later when the Consorzio was created, no one ever even imagined making Brunello in the Crete Senesi. It simply never entered our minds that anyone would ever attempt making Brunello in thick clay and mud," says Ciacci. "Abbadia Ardenga has always had property in Torrenieri but never thought of converting it to Brunello vineyards," continues Ciacci.

Recent wide-scale planting in the Torrenieri subzone is amply illustrated by the Consorzio's annual wine-producer map. Up until 1999, there were only two Brunello producers located in Torrenieri—Casanova di Neri and Abbadia Ardenga; the latter, however, only has cellars in Torrenieri but no vineyards. The 2005 edition of the same producer map lists fifteen producers in Torrenieri, including Abbadia Ardenga. Just as Montalcino's farmers denounced the area for centuries, today the majority of Montalcino winemakers condemn Brunellos hailing from vineyards situated in the crete for their general lack of both elegance and complexity, but mostly for their massive, bitter tannins that dominate the palate.

Unsurprisingly, according to the Sangiovese soil map compiled by CRA and CNR geologists led by Prof. Edoardo Costantini, most land in and around Torrenieri is classified as an "area with soil scarcely suitable and/or not suitable." There is a small amount of land "with low frequency of suitable and very suitable soil" and a sliver of land "with moderate frequency of suitable soil." The area's many critics also point out that in addition to the issue of compact clay, Torrenieri's damp lower altitudes are also unsuitable for Sangiovese, and it is undeniable that the best Brunellos from this area come from vineyards reaching up to and over 300 meters (984 feet) above the humid valley floor and fog that frequently plagues the lower elevations of this corner of the growing zone.

In defense of Torrenieri, local producer and agronomist Roberto Terzuoli of SassodiSole says singling out all of Torrenieri isn't fair since there are some parcels that are suitable in terms of both soil and altitude, and because it is not the only subzone plagued with areas offering poor conditions for Sangiovese. "Throughout Montalcino, there are Brunello vineyards planted where they shouldn't be, like along the riverbanks, and at very low altitudes. Torrenieri is really no different, with sites where it wouldn't be advisable to plant vineyards, but there also select areas here that are definitely suitable for Sangiovese," contends Terzuoli.

SassodiSole

Podere Santa Giulia 1°, 48/A
53024 Torrenieri-Montalcino (SI)
Tel. +39 320 2155091
www.sassodisole.it
info@sassodisole.it

This is one of the denomination's young Brunello estates to watch, and thanks to meticulous care in both the vineyards and the cellar, has a lot of potential. SassodiSole's vineyards rise up like a hillside oasis out of a sea of clay below, which, on the day I visited the estate, had been turned by long heavy rain into mud with the consistency of wet cement. Run by Roberto Terzuoli and his wife, Erika, the property was once part of the nearby Santa Giulia estate that was purchased in the 1960s by Roberto's grandfather and was then divided into two separate holdings when Roberto's father, Bruno, and his uncle inherited the original farm.

Roberto is a trained agronomist who gained valuable experience working for several years for Franco Biondi Santi before he began running his family's winery full time. "Soil is important, but so is sun exposure and altitude," says Roberto. The soil in SassodiSole's three Brunello vineyards, planted in 1997, is predominantly clay mixed with some rock fragments, and ripening is helped by full southern and western exposures assisted by scrupulous canopy management that does not include complete defoliation. Altitude averages 320 to 330 meters above sea level, where the vines benefit from constant breezes that keep humidity at bay. Breaking up the soil here is crucial, and Roberto emphasizes that rather than merely breaking the crust, he goes down 30 to 40 centimeters (12 to 16 inches). Reaching this depth not only helps against erosion, a constant challenge in Torrenieri, but also sends plant roots down further. Choosing the right combination of clones and more suitable rootstocks, which were not widely available until a decade ago, has also improved grape growing in Torrenieri. Terzuoli uses clones R24 and CH20 with Paulsen 775 rootstock. For this terrain, the agronomist also keeps density at 4,000 plants per hectare to avoid excessive shade among plants within the rows.

SassodiSole keeps things pretty much on the traditional side in the cellar, and Terzuoli uses only wild yeast for fermentation that takes place in steel under temperature control for twenty-five days, though he also believes in *délestage*, or the rack-and-return method of aerating fermenting wine to extract color and enhance fruit, but above all to soften tannins. Brunello aging is carried out for three years in 35-hectoliter Slavonian botti.

Production

Total surface area: 45 ha (111 acres)
Brunello: 3.6 ha (9 acres), 10,000–13,000 bottles
Rosso: 1 ha (2.47 acres), 7,000 bottles

Brunello.   SassodiSole's first Brunello was the 2001 vintage, and quality has improved each year as the vines age. These are powerful Brunellos, with tannic structures, balanced with good acidity, delicious ripe fruit, and spice. A tasting of the 2001, back in 2006 and then again in 2010, proved that these wines improve remarkably with cellaring. The 2004 is focused with concentrated flavors and powerful structure.

Riserva.   With the fantastic 2004 vintage, the winery also released its first Riserva. It is an outstanding effort, with intense floral and fruit aromas, ripe fruit, spice, and brooding, tongue-coating tannins that need time to soften. Best 2014 to 2024 and longer.

Rosso. The firm also makes a vibrant, delicious yet firmly structured Rosso from ten-year-old vines. Aged for one year in botti.

Innocenti

Località Citille di Sotto 45
Torrenieri 53024 Montalcino (SI)
Tel. +39 0577 834227
www.innocentivini.com
info@innocentivini.com

Founded in 1961 by Livio and his father, Sabatino, the farm originally produced cereal for animal feed, as well as a small amount of wine and olive oil for family consumption. A few decades later, Livio began producing more table wine, which he sold in demijohns. In the 1990s, his sons Massimo and Gianni joined the firm and replanted the vineyards and updated the cellar, producing their first bottled Brunello from the 1998 vintage.

The family's 5 hectares (12 acres) of vineyards are located in the higher reaches of Torrenieri, well above the damp valley floor, at 330 meters (1,083 feet) above sea level. Not only are they are out of reach of the dangerous spring frosts that often attack the lower vineyards of this subzone, Innocenti's vineyards also benefit from constant breezes that help keep the grapes dry and healthy while south-southwest exposures help ensure full maturation.

Massimo, who studied agronomy, and Gianni, who is in charge of the cellar, keep winemaking traditional. After temperature-controlled fermentation in stainless steel, the brothers age their Brunello and Rosso in 30-hectoliter Slavonian casks.

Brunello. Aged for thirty months in large Slavonian botti, these are big, muscular Brunellos, with very tannic structures and hallmark Sangiovese nuances. Should age well for ten years after vintage.

Riserva. Made with the best grapes already chosen while on the vines, it is no coincidence that that 1999, 2001, 2004, and 2006 Riservas all hail from the highest part of the firm's most mature vineyard. Aged for three years in large Slavonian oak. Lovely Sangiovese aromas, with massively tannic structures that require time to soften.

Rosso. Aged for ten months in botti, these Rossos are big and bright with hefty body.

Abbadia Ardenga

Via Romana 139
53024 Torrenieri (SI)
Tel. +39 0577 834150
www.abbadiardengapoggio.it
info@ abbadiardengapoggio.it

Abbadia Ardenga is one of Montalcino's historic firms; its roots go way back to antiquity. The illustrious and wealthy Piccolomini family, direct descendants of Pope Pius II, who redesigned his hometown of Pienza into a wonder of the Renaissance during his papacy in the fifteenth century, originally owned the property. The last surviving Piccolomini heir, a World War II pilot, was killed during the war in the early 1940s, and the estate was bequeathed to the Società esecutori di pie disposizioni, which runs the property along with other select properties and museums throughout Tuscany. It should be pointed out that only the firm's headquarters are in Torrenieri; their Brunello vines are north of Montalcino near Donatella Cinelli Colombini's Casato Prime Donne property.

Since the early 1960s, Mario Ciacci has managed the firm on a day-to-day basis. While he now claims to be semiretired, he is almost always present at the winery's ancient, meandering cellars in the center of Torrenieri, alongside his two grown sons, who are in charge of winemaking and vineyard management. Ciacci's wife, Santina Trilli, was the first and for years the only employee of the Brunello Consorzio and for more than a decade Mario assisted the newly formed association by conducting tastings and accompanying Giulio Gambelli on his many visits to the cellars of aspiring Brunello producers back in the early 1970s. Abbadia Ardenga consistently produced Brunello in the 1960s and 1970s, but then the firm took a production hiatus for almost two decades while it updated the cellars and replanted most of its vineyards, resuming Brunello production with the 1994 vintage.

Abbadia Ardenga has vast holdings throughout Montalcino, incorporating immense stretches of woods and hundreds of acres devoted to other crops including olive trees and grain. Their winemaking activity is tiny, however, with less than 10 hectares under vine and only half of this devoted to Brunello. Of all the land belonging to the estate, Mario explains, "We only registered the very best vineyards to Brunello production, in the rocky soil around the Ardenga Abbey." The land around the medieval abbey north of Montalcino, from which the firm takes its name, was another important stop for pilgrims traveling the Via Francigena and was also part of the extensive Piccolomini holdings. The firm's Brunello vines, of various ages but with the oldest over forty years old, average 200 meters (656 feet) above sea level. Even if this area frequently suffers in colder, wetter vintages, in good and outstanding years Abbadia Ardenga's Brunellos boast fresh aromas and elegance, which they maintain during hot harvests like 2000 and 2003 when grapes cooked in many other areas of Montalcino. These are classically crafted wines that are aged for thirty months in botti. Abbadia Ardenga has also created a museum of winemaking artifacts as well as an impressive collection of old vintages of Brunello from various producers, all housed in the firm's fourteenth-century building next to the cellars.

Production

Total surface area: 700 ha (1,730 acres)
Brunello: 5 ha (12 acres), 25,000 bottles
Rosso: 1.5 ha (3.7 acres), 12,000 bottles

Brunello.   This is the bulk of Abbadia Ardenga's tiny production, and in great vintages, these Brunellos are almost ethereal, with floral and leather bouquets. The palate boasts candied-cherry fruit and mineral, balanced by tightly wound tannins and invigorating acidity. Best after ten years.

Riserva.   In 2004, the firm produced its very first Riserva from a selection of the best grapes, with impressive structure and depth as well as creamy-cherry sensations. This still needs time to sort itself out thanks to aggressive tannins and bracing acidity. Should drink beautifully after 2015 and should drink well until 2020 to 2025.

Brunello Vigna Piaggia.   Starting with the outstanding 2001 harvest, the firm also vinifies and separately bottles grapes from the Piaggia vineyard, where vines are over forty years old, generating complex aromas, concentrated flavors, and velvety tannins.

Rosso.   This is a very pretty Rosso with a remarkably floral nose, ripe-berry, and mineral flavors. Pairs beautifully with virtually any dish.

TEN

Tavernelle

According to several of Montalcino's old-timers, including Abbadia Ardenga's Mario Ciacci, who in the 1970s often accompanied Bruno Ciatti and Giulio Gambelli as they traveled the denomination to inspect Montalcino's burgeoning wineries on behalf of the Consorzio, select areas near Tavernelle, particularly the area known as Santa Restituta, have long been known for their great potential for Sangiovese. Once again vineyard altitudes play a crucial role. Averaging between 300 and 350 meters (984 and 1,148 feet) above sea level, fresh nocturnal breezes cool down hot daytime temperatures during the growing season, generating aromas and complexity. The vineyards are also elevated far enough above damaging spring and autumn frost and fog, but when compared to higher areas, are just low enough to enjoy warmer temperatures that guarantee more consistent ripening. In fact, most producers in this area feel they have the best of everything: perfect altitude combined with complex and predominately rocky, well-draining soils as well as warmer, drier temperatures. According to the CRA-CNR map, select areas around Tavernelle have "a high frequency of very suitable soil" for Sangiovese cultivation.

Case Basse—Gianfranco Soldera

Località Case Basse
53025 Montalcino (SI)
Tel. +39 0577 848567
www.soldera.it
gianfranco.soldera@casebasse.it

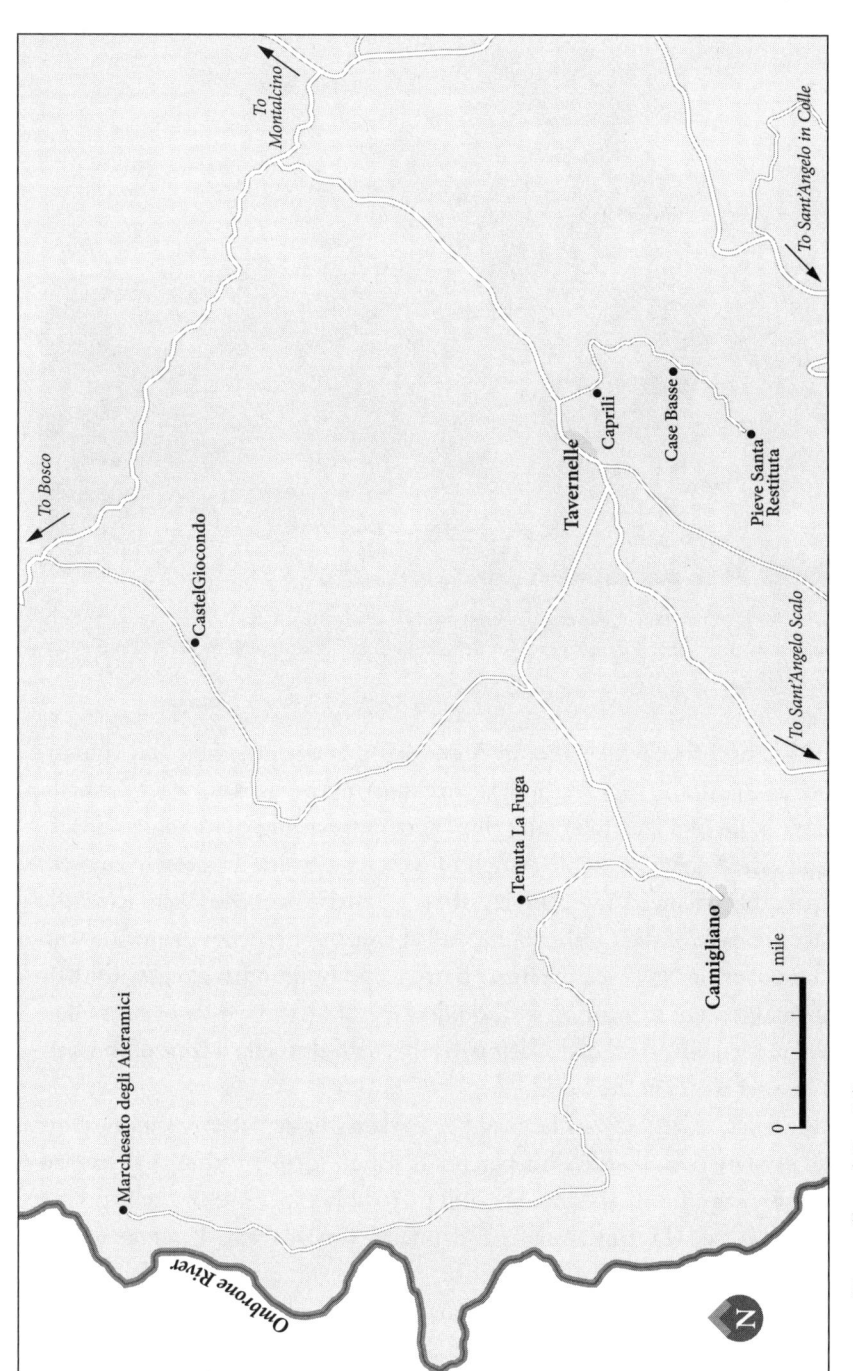

MAP 5. Tavernelle and Camigliano

FIGURE 15. Gianfranco Soldera, pictured at his Case Basse estate, is an outspoken traditionalist who says that barriques are "for deficient wines." Photograph by Paolo Tenti.

Perhaps no other winemaker in Montalcino is as outspoken and contentious as Gianfranco Soldera, and at the same time perhaps no other Brunello enjoys more of a cult following than bottlings hailing from Soldera's Case Basse estate near the small church of Santa Restituta. Delicately colored, impeccably balanced and complex, these exquisite Brunellos seem to be the exact opposite of their rather blunt and at times imperious winemaker, who is fond of criticizing even the finest Barolos and Burgundies along with their winemakers, not to mention what Soldera sees as all those inferior Brunellos. Soldera is equally fond of declaring that his own Brunello is "one of the only truly great wines in the world."

And yet, as abrasive as he may be, Soldera's undeniable passion—some may say fanaticism—fuels his perennial search for perfection that has led to these magnificent, memorable, and incredibly expensive Brunellos. True to form, he sells his tiny amount of Brunello, almost always Riserva, only to select private customers and a handful of shops and restaurants that he has personally chosen on the basis that they share his philosophy. Or, to repeat yet another Solderaism, "My wine, like all the finest wine in the world, is simply not for everyone."

Soldera came to Montalcino from Milan in 1972 as a successful insurance broker with the ambitious intention of finding the perfect location to make great wines, and discovered Case Basse. Although the land was totally abandoned and with no vineyards, Soldera was still somehow convinced that it would be perfect, and his intuition proved right. The hilly terrain, located at 320 meters (1,050 feet) above sea level, combined with a dry climate, long hours of sunlight, and full southwestern exposure, all ensure optimum ripening. According to Soldera, similar conditions in higher vineyards are simply destined to fail because "Sangiovese grown above 320 meters simply never reaches perfect ripening," while he dismisses Sangiovese grown at lower altitudes with a curt shake of his head and a wave of his hand. The estate's infertile soil of Eocene origin is not only well-draining and rich in minerals, but encourages roots from Soldera's 6 hectares (14.4 acres) of thirty-six-year-old vines and 2.5 hectares (6.1 acres) of ten-year-old vines to reach way down to the fresh water and nutrients located far beneath the surface.

Soldera and his wife, Graziella, have created a unique ecosystem on their estate to generate a natural balance and a healthy environment. To this end, Graziella has planted a magnificent 2-hectare (5-acre) botanical park, complete with more than fifteen hundred rose varieties and numerous other flowers and trees. An artificial lake and man-made birds' nests provide the perfect home for a multitude of bees, predator birds, insects, frogs, and snakes, which have developed a natural system of checks and balances. In winemaking terms, this means that Case Basse's grapes grow in an unspoiled environment teeming with life, allowing Soldera to ban pesticides and herbicides on the estate.

Soldera keeps yields remarkably low, roughly half of what the regulations allow, and he is obsessive about grape selection. Even though the estate's two vineyards, Intistieti and Case Basse, can produce more than 60,000 bottles, Soldera only bottles on average 15,000 bottles annually, and in difficult years such as 2002 this number drops to 6,000 bottles. Maniacal selection of only the best fruit is the rule at Case Basse; the firm's 2002 was exceedingly good, the best for the vintage in my opinion. Soldera is equally obsessive in the cellars, where the spitting out of even barrel samples is simply not allowed. Yet even at this stage, the still-evolving wines are so good, spitting is the last thing you would want to do, no matter how many wines you may have already tasted that day.

Soldera has enlisted the advice of Giulio Gambelli since 1976, and works closely with several universities, including the University of Florence, which conducts frequent analysis during all phases of vinification, from grape maturity to bottling. Soldera is quick to point out, however, that all decisions are his alone, and he keeps a natural approach to all aspects of winemaking. He was even behind the design of his recently constructed cellar, made entirely of rock and gravel without any cement plaster, a choice that he claims allows the walls and floor to "breathe" as well as naturally maintain a consistent temperature. Soldera's radically noninterventionist approach in the cellar includes only spontaneous fermentation with native yeasts, carried out in large Slavonian oak vats and without temperature control but frequent pumping over. Nearly all of Soldera's production is designated as Brunello Riserva, and ages between five and six years in large botti. Barriques, according to Soldera, are "for deficient wines," and are akin to blasphemy against Brunello.

Soldera is one of Montalcino's leading advocates for 100 percent Sangiovese only, and is widely credited by other local producers as having helped guide the Consorzio into the crucial 2008 vote that threw out any proposed changes to Brunello's production code. Although some of the larger estates have pointed their finger at him as being the whistle-blower that led to the investigation known as Brunellogate, Soldera adamantly denies the accusation.

Production

Total surface area: 23 ha (57 acres)
Brunello: 8.5 ha (21 acres), 15,000 bottles (Riserva)

Riserva. These are indeed among the finest Brunellos made. True Sangiovese, these luminous, ruby-red offerings, tending toward garnet, are lightly colored by today's black and inky standards, but this is the wine's natural color and is a sign of quality in Sangiovese, not a defect. Thanks to their long stay in large Slavonian oak, Soldera's Brunellos, almost always Riservas, boast heady aromas of leather, truffle, dried rose petals, earth, and tea. Fruit concentration varies from vintage to vintage. The palate is overall subtle, at times almost ethereal, but always delicious, with mineral purity and depth.

Pegasos and Intistieti. With the 2005 vintage, Soldera also made an IGT wine, from 100 percent Sangiovese that was declassified from Brunello because, according to Soldera, "a cask of Brunello matured precociously." Before Pegasos, Soldera occasionally produced a table wine called Intistieti from his youngest vines, or from wines that didn't meet his exacting standards for Brunello. Produced in the 1985, 1987, 1988, 1991, and 1992 vintages, these have become a cult collectors item. However, I found that Soldera's Pegasos IGT had extremely evident acidity and not enough fruit to back it up.

Pieve Santa Restituta

Località Chiesa di Santa Restituta
53024 Montalcino (SI)
Tel. +39 017 635158
info@gajawines.com

This stunning property, right next door to Soldera's Case Basse, is owned by none other than Angelo Gaja. Although Gaja is a tireless promoter of his Barbaresco and single-vineyard Langhe DOCs, he and his Brunellos have kept a surprisingly low profile in Montalcino, that is until Gaja wrote a letter (see chapter 6) to journalists and international wine publications during the height of the Brunello scandal. In the letter, Gaja supports allowing Montalcino's producers whose Brunello vineyards are not in ideal locations to be permitted to add other grapes besides Sangiovese to their Brunello. Although the letter stirred up bad feelings among the town's winemakers, it had little impact on changing minds, for despite his legendary status in Piedmont, Gaja plays a minor role in the politics of Brunellodom.

No one is quite sure why Gaja would suddenly be so concerned in the collective good of all the unfortunate Brunello producers who don't have suitable vineyards. This is, after all, a man who, despite being Piedmont's star producer, refused to contribute any considerations to subzoning even in his native Barbaresco, because, as he explains, his single-vineyard bottlings there are protected by registered trademarks, as are his single-vineyard bottlings in Montalcino, making subzones irrelevant for his wines. As Gaja further explained in 2008, in answer to my question on his thoughts on zoning Montalcino, "We've been invited to participate in subzoning projects in Montalcino but have refused because we don't want to interfere with projects that don't involve us."

Given his sudden and uncharacteristic interest in Montalcino's affairs, Gaja's letter had the effect—unintended I'm sure—of casting doubt over the suitability of his own vineyards for Sangiovese. But, having visited the manicured vineyards of Pieve Santa Restituta the week before Benvenuto Brunello in February 2010, supposedly the first journalist to visit after a massive five-year restoration, I can put to rest the assumption understand-

FIGURE 16. The fifth-century Santa Restituta church on Gaja's Pieve Santa Restituta estate. Locals say vineyards in this area have long been noted for great Sangiovese potential. Photograph by Paolo Tenti.

ably raised by some critics following Gaja's public appeal that perhaps his Santa Restituta vineyards are not ideally located for cultivating Sangiovese. I abstain, however, from making any judgment on vineyards he acquired in 2007 in Località Deserti, located between Montalcino and Torrenieri, which I haven't visited.

Named after the small parish church of Santa Restituta erected in the fifth century, Gaja's estate belonged to the diocese until 1972, when it sold the property, chapel and all, to Roberto Bellini, a businessman from Brescia who then sold it to Gaja in 1994. Gaja focused immediately on producing two Brunellos—Rennina, made from three separate parcels in the same area, and the single-vineyard bottling Sugarille. Sugarille is the more compelling and structured of the two, thanks to calcareous clay soil and southwestern exposure, while there is more sand in the Rennina vineyards, which produce a more delicate Brunello. Both vineyard areas average 300 meters above sea level. The newly acquired vineyards north of Montalcino will be used to make a straight Brunello. Gaja makes no Rosso and no Riserva.

In the cellar, Gaja's longtime enologist Guido Rivella consults while resident winemaker Francesca Arquint covers day-to-day operations. Fermentation is carried out in steel, and Brunellos age for one year in barriques and then one year in botti. However, the firm is also starting to use tonneaux, and will be slowly phasing out barriques, because "tonneaux are more respectful of Sangiovese," explains Arquint. It should be noted that the estate did not produce any Brunello in 2002 or in 2003 because Gaja did not think they met his rigid standards.

Production

Total surface area: 28.5 ha (70.4 acres)
Brunello: 25 ha (61.7 acres), 48,000 bottles

Brunello. The 2005 vintage, not one of the best vintages in Montalcino, is the first year the estate combined grapes from Sugarille and Rennina to make a straight Brunello. Up until this time they only made Brunello Sugarille and Brunello Rennina. This is also a calculated strategy to get consumers used to an undesignated Brunello because vineyards acquired in the northeast in 2007 will produce simply Brunello, while grapes from Pieve Santa Restituta will be for the cru selections.

Sugarille. This is the firm's flagship wine. Aromas range from eucalyptus, underbrush, and wood, with refined but concentrated fruit flavors and powerful, bracing tannins. Great length and striking depth of flavors are accompanied by evident but not overwhelming vanilla and oak sensations. This wine has incredible potential, and I look forward to trying future vintages once barriques have been phased out.

Rennina. Elegant aromas range from floral and incense to talcum powder. Lovely bright fruit flavors, but unlike the more structured Sugarille, Rennina's more delicate palate is overwhelmed by oak and wood tannins. Should greatly benefit with less obvious wood sensations once barriques are replaced by tonneaux.

Caprili

Podere Caprili 268
53024 Montalcino (SI)
Tel. +39 0577 848566
www.caprili.it
info@caprili.it

Caprili is an archetypical small Brunello estate, specialized in round, ripe, and earthy Brunellos with quintessential Sangiovese sensations. The Bartolommei family, originally from the nearby Grosseto Province, came to Montalcino at the beginning of the twentieth century and became sharecroppers on one of the several humble poderi that were then incorporated into the larger Villa Santa Restituta estate. Over the first half of the century, the family moved several times from one of the estate's tenant farms to another until they arrived at Caprili in 1952, along with all their livestock. This was toward the close of the sharecropping era, and in 1965, rather than give up farming and move to the city, Alfo Bartolommei instead bought the Caprili property from the Castelli-Martinozzi family, owners of Villa Santa Restituta. That same year, he planted his first vineyard, which he fittingly named "Madre," or Mother, and clones for Caprili's later plantings were selected from this original vineyard. Caprili's first Brunello di Montalcino was from the 1978 harvest, released in 1983.

The land is essentially the same as many other properties in the Santa Restituta microzone, hilly with mineral-rich Eocene soil composed mostly of limestone and silicate with a considerable amount of rocky fragments. Vineyards face southwest and average 330 meters (1,083 feet) above sea level, while vine age averages twenty years old and density is a modest 4,000 plants per hectare. Despite the small volume, the family works in collaboration with the University of Siena to select DNA from their best clones in their Madre vineyard to reproduce material for future vineyards that will maintain Caprili's Brunello characteristics.

Under the guidance of Brunello guru Paolo Vagaggini, the Bartolommei family adheres to the hands-off school of winemaking, gently guiding their grapes and wine through vinification and aging. They use no selected yeasts for temperature-controlled fermentation, which takes place in steel and lasts twenty-five to twenty-eight days. The firm ages its wines in 30-, 40-, and 60-hectoliter botti, three years for Brunello, four for Riserva, and eight months for Rosso.

Production

Total surface area: 59 ha (146 acres)
Brunello: 15 ha (37 acres), 27,000 bottles
Rosso: 30,000 bottles
Moscadello: 0.4 ha (0.99 acre), 2,500 bottles

Brunello. Most of the production is focused on Brunello, which boasts classic cherry-berry, leather, and underbrush aromas. These are round and rich, with succulent fruit flavors punctuated with spice and mineral. Already approachable upon release, they can also age well for another ten years and more in excellent vintages. Lovely and ripe. The 2006 is one of my favorites from the vintage. Rich and powerful with youthful tannins, this needs time to develop while vibrant acidity bodes well for aging. Best 2016 to 2026.

Riserva. In exceptional years, like 2004, Caprili also makes a Riserva, usually from grapes from the Madre vineyard. Riservas enjoy the same delicious, ripe fruit of the straight Brunello, but are more powerful and complex and will benefit with more cellaring. The 2004 will be best after 2014 and should drink well through the next decade.

Rosso. A declassification of Brunello, this is a serious Rosso. Bright Sangiovese aromas and flavors with more muscle than many Rossos, but with restrained alcohol that makes it just friendly enough, if a bit serious for Rosso.

Moscadello. The firm also produces a tiny amount of Moscadello, also fermented without selected yeasts. Intensely aromatic and floral Muscat nose, with a smooth, supple palate of tropical fruit and almond. An exquisite nectar that is not cloying but refreshing and lively.

ELEVEN

Camigliano

Heading west from Tavernelle, one descends toward the Camigliano subzone. At first the descent is gradual, then sharper the further southwest one travels toward the ancient hamlet of Camigliano itself and beyond, down to the railroad tracks and the rail station on Antinori's Pian delle Vigne property, where altitudes reach to only about 130 meters (426 feet). With the exception of Sant'Angelo Scalo, parts of the Camigliano zone have some of the lowest registered Brunello vines in the denomination. According to the Consorzio's consulting geologist, Alessandro Benvenuti, soil in and around Camigliano is made up of marine deposits from the Pliocene epoch, as is that of Torrenieri, but here the soil is composed of sand as well as clay, although at least one large Camigliano property claims to have Eocene soil of shaley marl. This mix of soils is reflected in the CRA-CNR Sangiovese soil map, where parts of the subzone, especially to the north and east of the eponymous village, have "moderate frequency of very suitable soil," while land to the west of the village is divided into "areas with low frequency of very suitable or suitable soils" as well as "areas with soils scarcely suitable or not suitable."

Average temperatures in Camigliano are warmer and drier than areas closer to Montalcino, resulting in faster and more consistent ripening. Because of the higher temperatures and lower altitudes, Brunellos from this subzone generally have lower acidity and higher evident alcohol than their neighbors further north, making them more approachable upon release but with less aging capacity than many would expect from Brunello. While some of the wines from this area can be powerfully structured with dense blackfruit flavors, generally speaking Brunellos from this area are not as complex as other subzones; while some of its Brunellos are very good indeed, others can be described as two- if not even one-dimensional. Although there are only eight estates in this subzone, a few are among Brunello's largest volume producers, namely the Frescobaldi's CastelGiocondo property, which is the second largest estate in Montalcino in terms of overall production. On its own, this subzone generates about 20 percent of the entire Brunello output. When combined with the Sant'Angelo subzone, these two areas alone generate nearly 50 percent of the entire Brunello production, though there are some who would say this is a conservative estimate.

CastelGiocondo—Marchesi de' Frescobaldi

Località CastelGiocondo
53024 Montalcino (SI)
Tel. +39 0577 84131
www.frescobaldi.it
info@frescobaldi.it

Although the Frescobaldis have been in the Tuscan wine business for over seven hundred years, their Brunello adventure began only in 1989 when they acquired CastelGiocondo, one of Montalcino's most historic and impressive properties. Constructed in 1100 to guard the road that led to Siena, CastelGiocondo was revamped into a leading Brunello estate in the 1970s, when it was acquired by a group of European investors who started bottling Brunello with the 1975 vintage. After purchasing the property the Frescobaldis ambitiously replanted at higher densities in an effort to upgrade quality, and engaged their trusted friend, the celebrated enologist Nicolò d'Afflitto, who consults at the family's other estates as well.

CastelGiocondo is the second largest Brunello producer both in terms of acreage, with a whopping 152 hectares (375 acres) devoted to Brunello, and in terms of Brunello bottle output according to the Consorzio's 2009 statistics. The substantial property stretches up to the far northwest and extends southwest, down toward the hamlet of Camigliano. Since CastelGiocondo spans parts of two subzones, this property has a unique combination of growing conditions that set it apart from both the rest of the Camigliano subzone as well as from points further north. Overall, CastelGiocondo has warmer, drier temperatures than Castiglion del Bosco, its closest neighbor to the northwest, but more complex soil and higher vineyard altitudes than much of Camigliano, making the extensive domain, set in the midst of thick woods, perhaps more of a microzone in its own right as opposed to part of

FIGURE 17. Owned by the Frescobaldis since 1989, CastelGiocondo dates back to 1100. It is now the second-largest Brunello producer in terms of acreage and volume. Photograph by Paolo Tenti.

a single subzone, but for geographical reasons and simplicity, I've listed the estate as part of Camigliano, the closest area.

Due to its unusual position, CastelGiocondo boasts a wide range of growing conditions, unusual within the confines of a single estate even in a territory as varied as Montalcino. Vineyard altitudes for Brunello range from 250 and 450 meters (656 and 1,476 feet) above sea level, and soil composition is mainly what locals refer to as *galestro,* the friable or flaky schist soil, and marl with sandy clay and limestone. According to Alessandro Benvenuti, in purely geological terms, CastelGiocondo shares the same *galestro*-rich soil as much of the northwest quadrant where Castiglion del Bosco is located. Yet much of CastelGiocondo also shares the warmer, drier temperatures of Camigliano.

While the estate's first-generation vineyards were planted at 3,000 vines per hectare back in the 1970s, vineyards replanted since 1993 have 5,500 vines per hectare. In the cellar, the Frescobaldis employ many of the latest, international winemaking methods while they also retain some tradition. After gentle crushing, Brunello ferments in temperature-controlled steel tanks for ten to twelve days followed by skin maceration for twenty-five to thirty days to extract more color and polyphenols. Aging takes place partly in barriques and partly in botti. For years CastelGiocondo's bottlings have tested the limits of Brunello's tipicità, thanks to their inky purple color, exotic aromas, and massive structures dominated by evident alcohol and oak, even though the 2005 Brunello and the superb 2004 Riserva seemed to hail a more classic expression of Sangiovese and an elegant style that still boasts impressive structure. As Lamberto Frescobaldi, who is in charge of winemaking and works closely with Nicolò d'Afflitto, told me, "For the 2004 vintage, we carried out less extraction and used far less new oak for aging. The result was a more elegant, delicate Brunello." However, the firm's 2006 Brunello, the most recent as of 2011, as well as the Frescobaldis' 2006 Luce della Vite Brunello from their neighboring eponymous estate, instead show a disappointing swing back to the hyperbolic, highly oaked, and extracted style that had for years been the firm's hallmark. The polar opposite when compared to CastelGiocondo's 2005 and 2004 Riserva, the inky dark, heavily oaked, densely concentrated, and high-alcohol 2006 CastelGiocondo has left many critics and consumers confused, since the estate's house style now seems to oscillate wildly from release to release.

Production

Total surface area: 815 ha (2,013 acres)
Brunello: 152 ha (375 acres), 280,000 bottles
Rosso: 13 ha (32 acres), 300,000 bottles

Brunello. This is the estate's most important wine in terms of volume. Rich and fruit-driven, with the exception of the 2004 and 2005, these often show evident alcohol and in my opinion too much oak that masks Sangiovese's vibrant, subtler charms. Both the 2004 and 2005, however, are well balanced, showing brighter, earthier sensations and less oak and alcohol, and should hold up with modest cellaring. The 2006 instead had very evident alcohol and wood sensations, and was unbalanced between low acidity and aggressive, drying tannins.

Riserva Ripe al Convento. This is made only in top years and from select grapes from CastelGiocondo's best and highest vineyards, located in the section of the property known as Ripe al Convento, where vineyard altitude generates extreme day and night temperature changes. Ripe al Convento 2004 boasts layers of intense, multifaceted aromas of fresh berry, violet, earth, and spice. Classic wild-cherry and mineral flavors, with a firm but ripe tannic backbone, great depth, and long, lingering finish. A stunning wine. While enjoyable upon release, this will benefit from another ten years aging.

Rosso.   Campo ai Sassi is made from the estate's youngest vineyards and from declassifying Brunello vines. With its more supple tannins and streamlined structure, this is a friendly and youthful Rosso to drink immediately or age one to two years.

Tenuta La Fuga

Località Camigliano
53024 Montalcino (SI)
Tel. +39 055 859811
www.tenutefolonari.com
folonari@tenutefolonari.com

Tenuta La Fuga's Brunello odyssey first began when Gabriella Cristofolini and her husband acquired the estate in 1985 and started making Brunellos that combined the sheer muscle usually reserved for Brunellos from Sant'Angelo with the finesse found in the more northern subzones. In past years, some of my top-scoring Brunellos have been from this small jewel of an estate, especially the Riservas from the 1997, 1999, and 2001 vintages.

Tenute Folonari, the firm owned by Ambrogio and his son Giovanni, purchased La Fuga in 2001 a year after the Tuscan Folonari scions, of Ruffino fame, split up the family's original firm and divided their collective assets. The various family members then went on to create their own separate holding companies, each comprised of a number of prestigious winemaking estates. La Fuga is the smallest property out of the eight separate wineries that make up Tenute Folonari, but even so, despite its boutique dimensions, is part of Tenute Folonari's global business plan. This is not to say that passion is by any means lacking, only that Giovanni's attitude toward the wine industry as a whole is decidedly more practical, almost corporate, when compared to the more philosophical demeanor displayed—at least in front of journalists—by many of Montalcino's more artisanal winemakers.

Tenute Folonari is apparently keen to anticipate market trends to help them craft top-quality wines from their various holdings that will have wide consumer appeal. While this is certainly an understandable approach, it is not without risk. Predicting consumer whims is always a challenge for winemakers, but becomes excruciatingly difficult for Brunello producers given that the wine hits the market five calendar years after the harvest, six for Riservas. So trends that perhaps dominated the international wine scene when Brunello grapes were picked can change drastically by the time the wine is finally released after its mandatory aging period.

Given the firm's market-driven approach, it is therefore no coincidence that La Fuga's Brunellos and Riservas made since the Folonaris acquired the estate have transformed from quintessential Sangiovese offerings that amply demonstrated their warmer climate origins without losing their varietal pedigree into more internationally styled bottlings with more exotic aromas and an almost sweet, high-alcohol palate. As Giovanni told me when I visited the estate a few years ago, "Dense and powerfully structured wines are what the market wants," adding that wines should also be ready to drink upon release.

The estate undoubtedly has the raw material for making fantastic Brunellos, and in my opinion La Fuga is one of the best-suited of all of the subzone's estates to make extraordinary Brunellos, as earlier vintages have amply demonstrated. La Fuga's vineyards average 260 meters above sea level, where frequent breezes keep grapes fresh and healthy while full southeast exposures lead to ideal ripening. According to Giovanni, the loamy clay soil, spiked with rocky fragments, lends elegance to the overall muscular structure. Vines, between twelve and eighteen years old, are planted at densities of 5,500 plants per hectare, what most Montalcino producers say is the perfect planting density for Brunello. The estate believes in low yields and rigidly selects harvested grapes on a sorting table.

After temperature-controlled fermentation in steel, skin maceration lasts twenty to twenty-five days for Brunello and one month for the Riserva. Aging for Brunello and Rosso takes place in both tonneaux and 20- and 25-hectoliter botti made with French wood, three and a half years for Brunello and a year for Rosso, while the Riservas age for at least three and a half years in 500-liter French tonneaux, although botti may used in some vintages.

Production

Total surface area: 10 ha (24.7 acres)
Brunello: 6.5 ha (16.1 acres), 30,000 bottles + 5,000 Brunello Riserva
Rosso: 1.5 ha (3.7 acres), 6,000 bottles

Brunello. This is the main focus of production. These are deeply colored with black-fruit and plum aromas along with herbs and spice that all carry over to the palate along with bracing tannins. Best to drink five to ten years after release. The 2004 was already very evolved in 2010, almost portlike, with plum, vanilla, coffee, chocolate sensations, and drying tannins. The 2005, a vintage that yielded more delicate wines across the denomination, offered more quintessential Sangiovese nuances of ripe black cherry, eucalyptus, spice, and still somewhat aggressive tannins. Should drink best 2012–16. The 2006 instead inky dark with massive tannins and very evident alcohol, lacking Sangiovese's hallmark vibrancy.

Riserva Le Due Sorelle. The firm's Riserva hails from the best grapes in the Due Sorelle vineyard, named in honor of Giovanni's mother and aunt who are the official owners of La Fuga. For several years this was one of my favorite Brunellos, thanks to rich, wild-cherry, and truffle aromas, hints of leather and forest floor, with layers of juicy, ripe-fruit flavors balanced with bracing tannins and quenching acidity. The 2004 Riserva, however, seems to be the firm's effort to "please the market" back when the wine was conceived, judging by its inky dark hue, plum, and vanilla aromas, and the overripe palate that was so in vogue in the first decade of the new century. Well-integrated but nonetheless evident oak and alcohol top this off. While this style may still have a certain appeal with some consumers, I don't think this is what most wine lovers are expecting when they pay the hefty price for a Brunello since, in my opinion, it's rather anonymous.

Rosso. Ripe but vibrant, with fresh berry-strawberry sensations, this Rosso comes from the estate's youngest and lowest-situated vines. Both enjoyable and refined with a tannic backbone and fresh acidity.

Marchesato degli Aleramici

Podere Il Galampio 376
53024 Montalcino (SI)
Tel. +39 0577 849078
www.marchesatodeglialeramici.it
info@marchesatodeglialeramici.it

The Marchesato degli Aleramici–Il Galampio estate is in the furthest reaches of Montalcino's southwestern corner, and not only marks the boundary of the denomination, but the property also straddles the border between the Siena and Grosseto Provinces. My visit here had a dubious start. After setting out after dark and in the pouring rain from another estate just north of Montalcino, and getting lost on the long road from the hamlet of Camigliano to the estate, I was convinced after a few miles of following the railroad tracks that run past Pian delle Vigne that I must have somehow taken a wrong turn, although that would probably have landed me in the river. After almost an hour's drive from Montalcino, the last twenty minutes on a bumpy unpaved road in the middle of the woods, I reached my destination. I was relieved to see that the vineyards were not right next to the tracks or along the riverbed, but on a gentle slope facing the Ombrone River below.

The estate, with its rustic Old West–styled entrance, is owned and run by a rather eccentric and jovial family. Filippo Fedriani, the *simpatico* son of the founder, seemed not to notice the torrential rain or the February cold as he led me around the property. The family descends from the noble Aleramici clan from Piedmont, which at one time counted the castle of Barolo among their holdings, at least according to Filippo. Filippo's father, Giacomo, an engineer born in Genova, founded the estate in 1986 and immediately planted Brunello vines. Lately, however, eighty-one-year-old Giacomo is not often at the farm, but instead, as an international ski champion, continues to compete and win gold medals around the world, these days in the masters class—a fact that yet again fuels my wholly unscientific observation that perhaps drinking Brunello may be behind the uncanny energy and advanced years of many of the denomination's octogenarian producers.

Surrounded by thick woods, the Fedrianis' Marchesato degli Aleramici property, locally known as Il Galampio, lies in the wildest part of Montalcino's production zone and is smack in the middle of the Il Bogatto Nature Reserve. According to Filippo, the sloping terrain, the nearby woods, and the vicinity of the Ombrone River conspire to create a unique microclimate for this normally torrid subzone. "The refreshing humidity from the woods and the breezes generated by the river give us cool nights that relieve hot daytime temperatures during the growing season, and especially over the last decade, as we feel the effects of global warming here in Montalcino, this has been crucial. In cooler years however, we can sometimes have a problem reaching ideal ripening because of the same humidity and cool nights," admits the forthright Filippo. He further notes that while land in much of Camigliano is closed in by the woods and is located on flat terrain, Il Galampio's vineyards are in an open space where the woods give way to the river, which in turn generates frequent ventilation that keeps grapes healthy.

Fedriani explains that even though many areas of Camigliano have a lot of clay mixed with sand, Il Galampio's soil also consists of marl with a strong presence of rock fragments. Vineyards, located at 140 meters (460 feet) above sea level, are planted at 3,800 plants per hectare and are on average twenty years old. The Fedrianis enlist the help of consulting enologist Lorenzo Landi, and together they prefer to keep things traditional in the cellars. Fermentation takes place under temperature control in both steel tanks and resin-lined cement vats. Aging occurs exclusively in botti, three years for Brunello, four years for Riserva, and one month for Rosso.

Production
Total surface area: 50 ha (123.5 acres)
Brunello: 9 ha (22 acres), 40,000 bottles
Rosso: 20,000 bottles

Brunello. As to be expected from traditionally crafted Brunellos, these boast Sangiovese's quintessential sensations of berry, earthiness, spice, and mineral. The estate's Brunellos are not powerfully structured or particularly complex, but their bright fruit and ripe tannins render them thoroughly enjoyable upon release.

Riserva. Made from a selection of the best grapes in top years, this is decidedly more structured and complex than the Brunello Annata, with creamy raspberry-berry aromas and flavors, leather and earth sensations, and loaded with spice. Should age well for ten years after release.

Rosso. Made from Brunello vines, this is lovely, delicious, and very drinkable thanks to vibrant, ripe-fruit, and refined structure.

TWELVE

Sant'Angelo

Differences between Sant'Angelo and the original growing areas around Montalcino, in terms of winery profiles, climatic conditions, soil, Brunello styles, and aging potential, can only be described as extreme. While almost exclusively small wineries populate the sometimes-vertiginous slopes in the rest of the denomination, Sant'Angelo, in the denomination's far south-southwest, is dominated instead by large-scale operations such as Il Poggione, Argiano, Col d'Orcia, and the industrial-sized Banfi. Although a sprinkling of small wineries and vineyards hug the hillsides climbing toward the hamlet of Sant'Angelo in Colle as well as the middle altitudes, the bulk of production originates from extensive tracts of vineyards spread out on the subzone's flat plains far beneath the hamlet. According to even the most conservative estimates of average bottle numbers, the subzone of Sant'Angelo alone makes between 35 and 40 percent of total Brunello output.

Climatic conditions are decidedly more Mediterranean in Sant'Angelo, the collective name for the large growing area that encompasses land from Sant'Angelo in Colle, a tiny village 444 meters (1,457 feet) above sea level, all the way down to and including the sprawling, low-lying terrain of Sant'Angelo Scalo, so named for the now defunct village train station situated beneath the hamlet. Sant'Angelo is the hottest and driest subzone in the denomination. Torrid sea breezes blowing inland from the Maremma push summertime temperatures higher by 3 to 4 degrees centigrade (5.4 to 7.2 degrees Fahrenheit) than the more elevated reaches closer to Montalcino, and rainfall in Sant'Angelo is also markedly lower, with an average of 500 millimeters a year as opposed to the 700 millimeters average for the entire denomination. These warmer, drier conditions allow more consistent and

FIGURE 18. Sant'Angelo in Colle's steep slopes nearest the village are home to mostly small-scale wineries, while large-scale operations dominate in low-lying areas further south. Photograph by Paolo Tenti.

faster ripening for Sangiovese in Sant'Angelo, where the crop is harvested on average ten days to two weeks earlier than areas further north.

However, climate change is now exaggerating the already hotter, drier conditions, so that summertime temperatures have become almost sizzling over the last decade. According to Col d'Orcia's agronomist Giuliano Dragoni, certain vineyard practices that were used to improve quality from the late 1980s until the first years of the new century have now been reduced or abandoned because of the extreme heat and lack of rain. "In 1988 we began planting grass between the rows to reduce plant vigor by creating competition for the water and nutrients in the soil. This method helped us reduce grape thinning and green harvests, and produced less bunches and higher quality grapes, but we don't use this system much anymore. Since 2000, the area has noticeably hotter and drier temperatures and planting grass risks causing severe heat and water stress to the vines," explained Dragoni while we walked through Col d'Orcia's Poggio al Vento vineyard. Other producers in Sant'Angelo have told me that planting at very high densities in Sant'Angelo can often cause stress to the vines, as well as generate excessive alcohol and lower acidity given the extreme temperatures.

Based on the geological map compiled for the Commune of Montalcino in 2009 by Dr. Stefania Mencacci, calcareous soils from the Upper Cretaceous epoch surrounds much of Sant'Angelo in Colle. Miocene clay, and to a much larger extent more recent Pliocene marine deposits of clay and silt, dominate most of the subzone, while the alluvial plains along the riverbanks in the far southwest—which, according to the locals, were for the most part cultivated with grain and other cereals until the 1970s—are composed of sand deposits. The CRA-CNR Sangiovese soil map rates the areas closer to the village of Sant'Angelo in Colle as having a "high frequency of very suitable soil," with land located mid-hill rated as having both "moderate frequency of very suitable soil" as well as a "high frequency of suitable soil." The same map rates the poor draining soil around Sant'Angelo Scalo in the lower and furthest reaches of the growing zone as an area having both "low frequency of very suitable and suitable soil" and "scarcely suitable or not suitable soil." A further challenge to Sangiovese production around much of Sant'Angelo Scalo is the severe erosion caused by drastic manipulation of the land that flattened the once gently rolling hills to create easy-to-maintain vineyards.

In years with exceptional climatic situations, such as 2002 and 2003, the differences between Brunellos from Sant'Angelo and Montalcino can be dramatic. While the higher reaches near Montalcino were devastated by torrential rain just before the harvest in 2002, the southern reaches suffered far less. Not only did they get less rain thanks to the barrier created by nearby Mount Amiata, but because ripening is faster here, most estates had already picked much of the crop by the time the worst of the rain hit, and since the area dried out faster thanks to the warm sea breezes, the remaining grapes escaped rot and were picked after the deluge. In contrast, the torrid 2003 vintage proved to be a difficult but decent harvest for the areas around Montalcino, while down in the lower reaches of Sant'Angelo vines suffered severe stress from the prolonged heat and drought. The extreme conditions caused many grapes to dry into raisins while still on the vines, producing wines that were more concentrated than usual with even higher evident alcohol, lower acidity, and very bitter tannins. "In 2003, grape selection was crucial, as tannins often did not mature perfectly because the plants were too stressed. Through rigorous hand selection before, during, and after the harvest, we achieved good quality but we discarded 50 percent of our grapes," Pablo Harri, Col d'Orcia's enologist until late 2009, told me in 2006. Col d'Orcia's proprietor, Francesco Marone Cinzano, like most winemakers from Sant'Angelo, prefers his Brunello 2002 to 2003, the exact opposite of what winemakers closer to

Montalcino will tell you. Almost without exception estates in Sant'Angelo would like to see irrigation made legal to combat broiling summertime temperatures. "While they might not need irrigation at the smaller wineries farther north toward Montalcino, here we risk vines dying during periods of excessive heat and drought," argues Marone Cinzano, who would like to see emergency irrigation, allowed in many of Italy's denominations, to be permitted in Montalcino, where it is prohibited under the strict production code. In recent years, global warming has further aggravated the problem of excessive heat and prolonged dry spells throughout central Italy, but the consequences could prove dire for this already scalding part of Montalcino.

Altitude is once again a crucial factor in quality, with most of the best wines in Sant'Angelo hailing from the higher vineyards. It is surely no coincidence that close to Sant'Angelo in Colle there exists a long tradition of winemaking and the area hosts several of the denomination's pioneering estates including Il Poggione and Lisini. Besides the presence of more calcareous soil in the most elevated vineyards, the mid- and high altitudes produce wines that combine depth and finesse with powerful structure along with richly concentrated fruit. Even though Brunellos from all of Sant'Angelo are generally more approachable than Brunellos from areas closer to Montalcino thanks to ripe tannins, the best Brunellos from select vineyard sites are also surprisingly age-worthy. Case in point: boutique producer Lisini has vineyards starting at about 300 meters (984 feet) reaching up to 400 meters (1,312 feet), just below the hilltop hamlet of Sant'Angelo in Colle, and the estate's deeply garnet-hued, round, and hefty Brunellos reflect their southern muscle but are balanced with bright acidity thanks to higher vineyards. Tasting back to Lisini's extraordinary and complex 1971 and 1975 Riservas, the predecessors to Ugolaia, prove that these southern Brunellos indeed stand the test of time, as do Col d'Orcia's Poggio al Vento Brunellos from a single vineyard at 350 meters (1,148 feet), which impeccably poise strength and grace.

In contrast, Brunellos from Sant'Angelo's low-lying vineyards in the Sant'Angelo Scalo part of the subzone are much darker, higher in alcohol, with noticeably lower acidity and greater immediacy than the comparatively austere style of other zones up north. Excessively low yields, picking grapes when they are overripe, and overextraction during vinification can further exaggerate this already fuller style. Approachable and forward upon release, they do not, however, have the essential structure for lengthy aging, and though muscular, Brunellos from Sant'Angelo's lowest areas are simple if not downright one-dimensional, lacking the depth and complexity expected in Brunello. Many producers in this part of the subregion prefer aging in barriques to shore up the wines with wood-driven sensations, presumably to create a more interesting wine, or at least the illusion of a *vino importante*. A number of Brunello producers throughout Montalcino's denomination question the validity of allowing Brunello to be made in this area, criticizing the apparent lack of foresight of the denomination's founding fathers. "The pioneering producers who created the production code excluded all land above 600 meters because of issues with ripening. But they should have excluded land in low altitudes down along the river beds and railroad tracks in Sant'Angelo and other parts of the denomination since these are also not good conditions for Sangiovese," argues Giulio Salvioni.

Given the remarkable differences within the single subzone on so many levels, knowing the producer, and therefore where the vineyards are located as well as the house style, is perhaps more crucial in Sant'Angelo than anywhere else in the denomination.

Col d'Orcia

Località Sant'Angelo in Colle
53024 Montalcino (SI)
Tel. +39 0577 80891
www.coldorcia.it
info@coldorcia.it

Col d'Orcia is another one of Montalcino's genuinely storied estates, with Brunello-making roots tracing back to the early decades of the twentieth century, and its commitment to research and improving quality over the last few decades has greatly contributed to the success of modern-day Brunello. In terms of acreage under vine, it is the third-largest Brunello producer, after Banfi and CastelGiocondo. Despite its large dimensions, owner Count Francesco Marone Cinzano and his longtime estate manager, Edoardo Virano, run the estate much like a small family-run winery, with scrupulous attention to detail in the vineyards and rigid grape selection—remarkable given the size of production. The firm's most famous wine, Riserva Poggio al Vento, made only in exceptional vintages from old vines from a breathtakingly beautiful single vineyard that is also home to a centuries-old oak tree, is

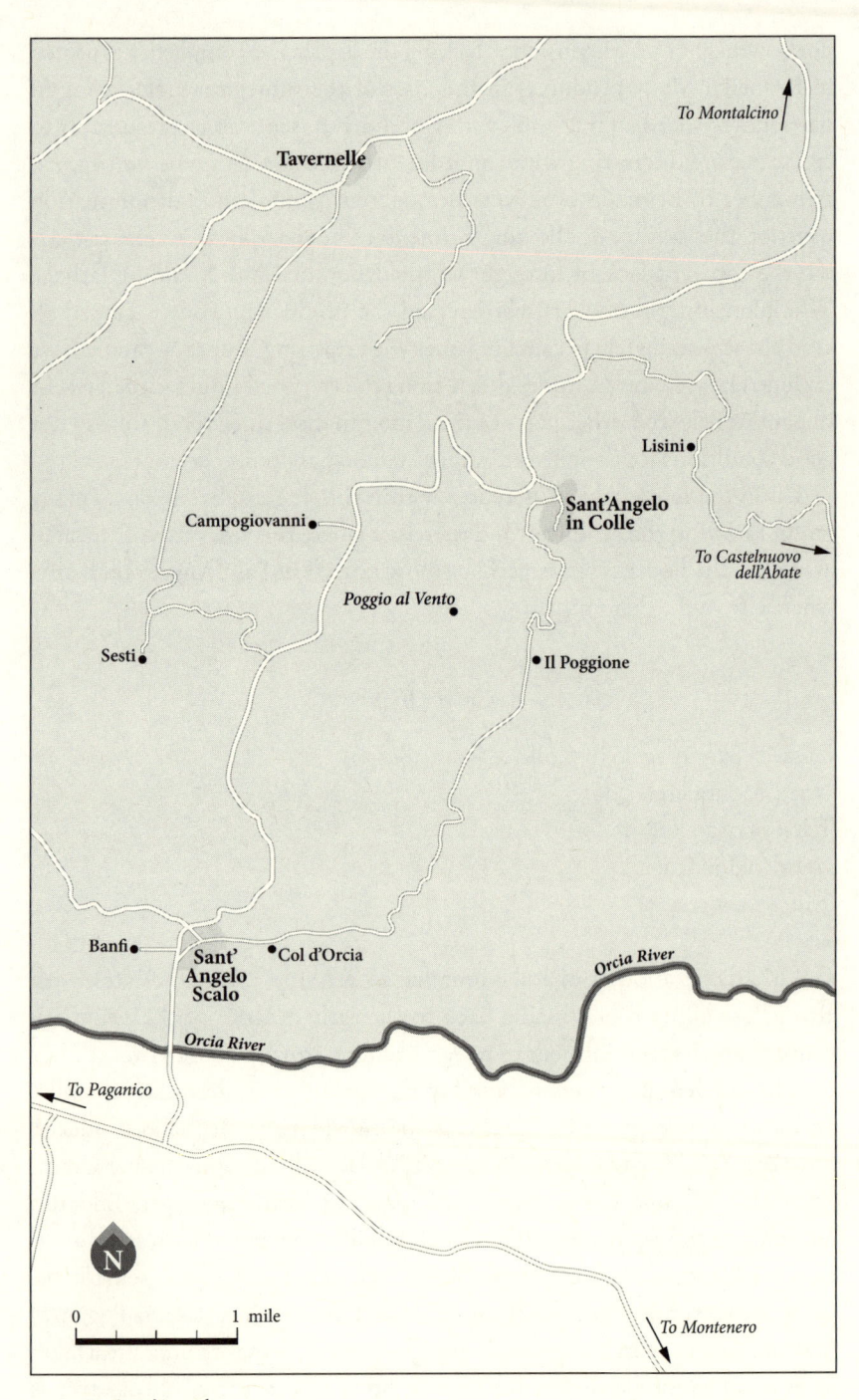

MAP 6. Sant'Angelo

FIGURE 19. Col d'Orcia's celebrated Poggio al Vento vineyard yields remarkable Riservas of restrained power and complexity. Photograph by Paolo Tenti.

hands down one of the finest offerings in Montalcino, thanks to its captivating equilibrium between power and grace, ripeness and restraint.

Before Francesco's father, Count Alberto Marone Cinzano, bought the property in 1973, Col d'Orcia was incorporated with what is now the Il Poggione estate. The single firm, called Fattoria di Sant'Angelo in Colle, presented several Brunello vintages at Siena's first wine exhibition in 1933. The large estate was owned by the Franceschi family who in 1958 divided the property among family members. Today the Franceschis still own half of the original holdings where they created their Il Poggione estate.

Although all winemakers claim that the real quality of their wine starts in the vineyard, Col d'Orcia practices what many others merely preach. For years they have been at the forefront of research and experiments with training systems, plant density, planting grass between rows, clonal research, and the suitability of certain rootstocks in particular soils. Working closely with University of Florence's Dr. Bandinelli, the estate selected two excellent clones from their own genetic material chosen from the Poggio al Vento vineyard, Sg Cdo-4 and Sg Cdo-6. In 1997 the estate replanted several vineyards with these selected clones at high density and saw a noticeable improvement in quality. The firm also has worked with Professor Attilio Scienza at the

University of Milan to select the best spots for new vineyards and the most compatible rootstocks for their terrain.

Col d'Orcia balances these high-tech studies with sound principles, such as a strictly manual harvest of all 106 hectares (262 acres) dedicated to Brunello and Rosso, followed by careful grape selection on a sorting table. Col d'Orcia's enological team is led by outside consultant and Sangiovese specialist Maurizio Castelli, and in-house winemaker Antonino Tranchida (replacing Pablo Harri, who left in late 2009 to dedicate his energy to his wife's Montalcino farm, Ferrero). Together they combine a wise use of modern technology with sound tradition. Col d'Orcia's custom-made steel fermenting tanks are large and squat rather than tall and narrow, and allow more contact between skins and must in order to optimize extraction of both color and polyphenols. Brunello aging takes place for three years in botti of various dimensions of both Slavonian and Allier oak.

Production

Total surface area: 540 ha (1,333 acres)
Brunello: 81 ha (200 acres), 300,000 bottles
Rosso: 25 ha (61.7 acres), 250,000 bottles
Moscadello: 3 ha (7 acres), 9,000 bottles

Poggio al Vento Riserva. First released as a single-vineyard bottling in 1982, this is the glory of Col d'Orcia, with only about twenty thousand to twenty-five thousand bottles produced exclusively in excellent vintages. Situated at 350 meters (1,150 feet) above sea level with south-southwest exposures, Poggio al Vento's 5.5 hectares (14 acres) were replanted in 1974 with a selection of the best plants that were already present in the vineyard. Although vine density of 3,000 plants per hectare is low by today's standards, the advanced age of the vines, over thirty-five years old, generates concentrated flavors and aromas while calcareous, well-draining soil lends structure.

Poggio al Vento is aged for four years in botti of both Slavonian and French wood followed by lengthy bottle aging that lasts anywhere from eighteen to thirty-six months. Only released in excellent vintages, this is one of the few Brunellos from Sant'Angelo that needs at least a decade or more before displaying its true magnificence and attaining perfect harmony. Seeing as this is one of the truly great Brunellos, below are tasting notes from tastings in 2005, 2009, and 2010 of some of the top vintages. Before the firm began putting the name of the vineyard on the label, the estate's excellent Brunello Riservas were made almost exclusively from Poggio al Vento grapes, and these notes are included as well.

🞯 *Poggio al Vento 2001 Riserva.*   Intense bouquet of rose, violet, earth, leather, and incense. Concentrated berry flavors balanced with firm but ripe tannins. Long licorice finish. Great depth, fantastic length. Powerful and complex, still incredibly young and vibrant, this will age beautifully. Best 2015–30 and beyond.

Poggio al Vento 1999 Riserva.   Rich perfume of berry, leather, and earth. Succulent and earthy black-cherry flavors with licorice and spice balanced by big, sweet tannins. A striking wine that while delicious now, will drink beautifully through the 2030s.

1985 Riserva.   In this absolutely outstanding vintage in Montalcino, Col d'Orcia made both Poggio al Vento and a Brunello Riserva from a selection of the only best grapes in the other vineyards. A dense garnet color and initially closed bouquet slowly reveals enticing layers of goudron, tobacco, and leather fragrances. Delicious palate of dried cherry, tobacco, and licorice with supple tannins. Fabulous depth and length. A wonderfully compelling wine.

1982 Poggio al Vento Riserva.   This was the debut Poggio al Vento bottling. After always coming in first in in-house tastings of the separate vineyards, starting with this vintage, Marone Cinzano decided to bottle the vineyard apart, and with good reason. Tasted in 2010, this youthful wine still boasted an intense fragrance of leather, graphite, truffle, and tobacco. Dried cherry marinated in spirits ruled the palate along with *zabaglione* cream and pastry. Impeccably balanced with a long mineral finish. Delicious now but has enough energy to maintain for years to come.

1980 Riserva.   Made with Poggio al Vento grapes, this is concentrated, almost portlike, with intense prune, tobacco, and truffle aromas that carry over to the palate. Long sweet black-tea and fig finish. Velvety smooth with still lingering fresh acidity will allow this to keep for another decade at least.

1979 Riserva.   Lovely perfume of earth, flint, and *vin santo*-like aromas. Stunning depth, with still succulent fruit flavors, mineral, and tobacco. Lovely, fresh acidity keeps this remarkably youthful. Will drink well for at least another decade, if not more.

1969 Riserva.   Gorgeous nose of incense, prune, plum, tobacco, and underbrush. Dried fruit, tobacco, and mineral palate. Still holding on, though at the end of its long span.

Brunello.   This is Col d'Orcia's most important wine in terms of production, and is produced every year. A reliable Brunello, this is decidedly more approachable than Poggio al Vento. However, in excellent years even the Brunello improves dramatically with some bottle age. The 1999 tasted in 2010 was vibrant and fresh, with rich berry flavors and supple tannins and the firm's hallmark licorice notes, and should drink well for at least another decade if not more. The delicate 1991, not an outstanding vintage despite its four-star rating, also tasted in 2010, was complex, loaded with underbrush and spice and surprisingly bright fruit.

Rosso.   Col d'Orcia makes two Rossos, the single-vineyard, barrique-aged Banditella, and a straight Rosso aged for one year on botti. While the Banditella may appeal to certain palates, the Rosso *normale* is a wonderful expression of youthful, unfettered Sangiovese.

Moscadello.   The firm also makes an outstanding late-harvested Moscadello called Pascena that is fermented and aged in barriques. Aromatic, smooth, and full-bodied, this would pair beautifully with seasoned cheese or fruit tarts.

Il Poggione

Sant'Angelo in Colle
53024 Montalcino (SI)
Tel. +39 0577 844029
www.tenutailpoggione.it
info@ilpoggione.it

Il Poggione is one of Montalcino's largest and most well-known estates, and one of the best in terms of value and quality. In particular the firm's straight Brunellos are not just reliable and quintessential Sangiovese bottlings from Sant'Angelo, they have a surprising, indeed almost a shocking staying power belied by their easygoing approachability. Apart from being one of the five largest Brunello houses, Il Poggione boasts a bona fide Brunello history. The estate is part of what used to be known as Fattoria di Sant'Angelo in Colle, which in 1933 presented various vintages of Brunello at the first Italian wine fair held in Siena. The Franceschi family acquired the estate in the late nineteenth century from the Servadio family, who had acquired the property some years earlier from the noble Della Ciaia family. The original property was much larger, incorporating what is now Col d'Orcia, and was divided between members of the Franceschi family in 1958 to create two separate estates. Today Leopoldo Franceschi, along with his wife, Lidia, comprise the fifth generation to run this family affair. Although the original firm was already making Brunello in the first half of the twentieth century, production was greatly reduced in the 1930s after phylloxera ravaged Montalcino's vines, followed by the outbreak of the Second World War and the passing of the Front, which completely halted production for years.

Il Poggione's modern-day rise to fame came after they hired the late Pierluigi Talenti in 1959. Talenti was a far-sighted man whose quality standards established a new era for the winery, for Sant'Angelo's growing zone, and for Montalcino when he came to work at the estate. After he passed away in 1999, his protégé Fabrizio Bindocci, who has looked after the vineyards since the mid-1970s, took over winemaking as well and is now joined by his son, Alessandro.

Getting ripe fruit is not a problem in this sun-drenched area of Montalcino, where Il Poggione's vineyards range from 150 meters (492 feet) above sea level up to 400 meters (1,312 feet). Summer temperatures are noticeably higher here than growing areas further north and precipitation is much lower. If winemakers in the original growing areas have to worry about achieving ideal ripeness in cool or wet vintages, the biggest challenge for Sant'Angelo's winemakers is balancing ripe fruit with freshness and not allowing fruit to become jammy or cooked, as well as controlling naturally high alcohol levels. Il Poggione usually finds the right equilibrium thanks to careful vineyard management that includes keeping vine density down to anywhere from 2,800 to 5,000 plants per hectare and training on a double-arc to further boost maturation through increased sun exposure. Many of Il Poggione's clones have been chosen from their own genetic material on the estate. In the early 1980s, Il Poggione began a long collaboration with Italy's famed Rauscedo vine nursery, and after experimenting with twenty estate Sangiovese clones, two, VCR 5 and VCR 6, both biotypes of Montalcino, were selected from the estate's Paganelli vineyard and remain among the most important clones for Brunello production. True Montalcino biotypes with many decades if not centuries to adapt to the growing area, these clones are known for their high anthocyanins, ripe fruit, and round tannins. The same care and almost paternal defense of the estate's clones, originating with Talenti and passed down to Bindocci, spread over to the firm's Moscadello. After hunting down the few remaining plants left on the estate back in the 1960s and slowly reproducing and replanting, Il Poggione now has 3 hectares (7 acres) of original Moscadello di Montalcino clones.

Bindocci has kept things fairly traditional in the cellar but he has made a few changes since Talenti's reign. Brunello and Riserva are aged in large botti, but instead of Slavonian oak they are now made with French wood. The Rossos, on the other hand, are aged partly in botti and partly in barriques, which Bindocci feels makes them more approachable sooner. Brunello, made from vines over twenty years old and aged thirty months in oak, is very approachable and enjoyable young, but tastings back to the mid-1960s have demonstrated a remarkable aging potential as well. The Riservas, made only in the best years and from grapes from their Paganelli vineyard 200 meters (656 feet) above sea level, can be outstanding in classic vintages, but they also can suffer from a lack of vibrancy in warmer years.

Production

Total surface area: 590 ha (1,457 acres)
Brunello: 63 ha (155.6 acres), 180,000–220,000 bottles
Riserva: 30,000–40,000 bottles
Rosso: 27 ha (66.7 acres), 200,000 bottles

Brunello.   Given the production average of 200,000 bottles a year, the quality achieved by the estate is quite impressive. Il Poggione Brunellos capture the bright, cherry-berry and earthiness of Sangiovese mixed with the ripeness and density achieved in Sant'Angelo, and while they are often quite enjoyable even upon release, the following tasting notes from 2009 and 2010 assess their surprising aging potential.

1997.   While many Brunellos have already completely faded from this highly overrated vintage, this still has sweet fruit to accompany the more advanced aromas of saddle leather and prune. Soft tannins and just a flash of acidity left, so drink now, as it won't improve beyond this point.

1991.   Fresher than the 1997, with better fruit and tannins and livelier acidity. Long licorice finish. Drink now through 2015.

1988. Still aggressively tannic, with chewy, marinated, cherry-fruit flavors and a lovely vein of acidity. Should drink well through about 2025.

1970. Loaded with leather and tobacco sensations and hints of *vin santo* and liqueur. Dried cherry and spice, but the palate still retains some fresh acidity to carry on for a few more years, though this is past its prime.

1967. While the first bottle was oxidized, the second was impressively bright for a forty-three-year-old at tasting time. Compact garnet color with some brick on the edge, with a gorgeous nose of incense, cherry liqueur. Prune and plum flavors, with lovely balance and sweet tea finish. Still has enough structure to march on for another few years at least.

Riserva. Today many Montalcino winemakers merely age a certain lot of Brunello for an extra year and call it Riserva. Il Poggione's Riserva, however, is a true Riserva, made only in the best vintages and selected in the vineyard. Grapes for the Riserva come exclusively from the I Paganelli vineyard, situated at 200 meters (656 feet) above sea level. Planted with estate clones in 1964, this vineyard has supplied most of the newer vineyards with Il Poggione's own genetic stock. Il Poggione Riservas are big and round with almost overripe tannins and concentrated fruit. While the 2001 and 1999 were excellent, the 2004 suffered from a disappointing lack of freshness and vibrancy that was fatiguing.

Rosso. Quite a structured Rosso, with ripe fruit, spice, and firm tannins.

Moscadello. Even though most of Montalcino's Mosacadellos are late-harvest bottlings, Il Poggione instead makes a delightful, floral, and refreshing sparkling Moscadello di Montalcino from original estate clones saved from extinction. According to Bindocci, the grape's naturally high sugar content makes it a perfect sparkler.

Banfi

Castello di Poggio alle Mura
53024 Montalcino (SI)
Tel. +39 0577 840111
www.castellobanfi.com
info@banfi.it

Founded in 1978 by American brothers John and Harry Mariani, Banfi is not only the biggest Brunello producer—by far—in terms of both extension and volume, it has also stirred up more controversy and debate than any other producer in Montalcino. Consumers, buyers, and journalists either shower the firm with praise or fiercely criticize it, with little middle ground. Even if the colossal firm, one of the biggest private wineries in Europe, turning out an annual total of over ten million bottles of wine of various designations and extending over a whopping 2,900 hectares (71,000 acres), a third of which are under vine, has undoubtedly helped bring the once obscure Brunello to tables around the world, the estate's critics blame Banfi for turning Tuscany's most elite wine into a mass-produced beverage. Then there are those detractors who blame Banfi for the Napa-ization of Montalcino thanks to its extensive plantings of more than 500 hectares of international grapes combined with a heavy reliance on custom-sized 350-liter French barriques that can often overwhelm the wines.

Montalcino winemakers themselves grumble that the Goliath of Montalcino wields too much power in local politics, not in the least because voting rights in the Brunello Consorzio, as in all Italian unions, are based on volume. In this case, that means hectares under vine, sales and bottle numbers. Based on the latter criteria, Banfi (which depending on exact bottle numbers and sales usually has the equivalent of approximately sixty votes, while the average small to mid-sized winery has the equivalent of a mere three votes) has far more voting power than any other firm in Montalcino. In other words, not only can Banfi's vote potentially sway elections and decide final outcomes on critical issues within the Consorzio; they are almost always able to lock in candidates of their choice for key positions on the board. And if Banfi's highly publicized involvement in the Brunellogate scandal, in which they, along with several other leading estates, were accused of violating Brunello's production code (for which they were eventually cleared), reinforced fierce tensions within the denomination, Banfi's founders created dissension and hostility from the very beginning.

Those residents old enough to remember still shudder when they recall how bulldozers were called in to flatten much of the rolling hillside on the Marianis' newly acquired property, allowing them to plant thousands of acres of easy-to-manage vineyards and create what resembled a great swath of California wine country. Although these days the winery proudly promotes its commitment to the environment, witnesses to the unprecedented, and today unthinkable, ecological damage that resulted from razing the hills have not forgotten the destruction. The late Luigi Veronelli, the legendary and outspoken Italian wine critic, often referred to this episode in the denomination's history as "the rape of Montalcino's hills and the destruction of terroir." Apart from purely romantic idealism, according to geologists, the firm's early disregard for the natural landscape has generated severe erosion and long-term harm in the vineyards. "Since the soil dates from the Pliocene epoch, it's extremely rich in marine deposits and therefore has a high salt content underneath the top layers. Where the soil around Sant'Angelo Scalo has been drastically manipulated, this high salt content has been brought up to the surface. From a strictly geological point of view, this is not an ideal condition for grape vines," explains Professor Edoardo Costantini of Florence's Istituto Sperimentale per lo Studio e la Difesa del Suolo (Institute for the Study and Defense of Soil). Granted, back when the hills were callously mowed down, Brunello production was not the object of Banfi's Master Plan.

Instead of concentrating on the denomination's flagship red, the Mariani brothers, famed U.S. importers of easy-drinking Lambrusco, the sales of which helped them amass a substantial fortune, and Ezio Rivella, their enologist and estate manager, who hails from Piedmont where he earned his reputation as the "wizard of white wine,"[1] were convinced that American tastes were veering toward sweet, sparkling whites like Asti Spumante. They duly decided to dedicate most of their land to mass-produced Moscadello, and only a small percentage of their extensive holdings to Brunello, to appease the locals. Their decision set off an uproar in Montalcino, where winemakers had been working tirelessly for over a decade to produce and promote their world-class red wine. According to the late Piero Talenti, shortly after he arrived in town, Rivella attended a town meeting where he implored Montalcino's residents, many of whom were Brunello makers while others had created spin-off businesses including restaurants, wine shops, and hotels from the burgeoning Brunello tourist trade, "to pull up their Brunello vines and plant Moscadello, because this wine was the real future for Montalcino. For their part Banfi would buy all the Moscadello grapes from the other farmers."[2]

The citizens reportedly wrote letters of outrage to the mayor at that time, Mario Bindi, and tried to block the arrival of Villa Banfi, as it was then known. The local citizens lost their plea, and Rivella planted 350 hectares (865 acres) of Moscato. The plants, sent down from his native Piedmont, were

FIGURE 20. Banfi's enormous vinification cellar. With annual production over 10 million bottles from different designations, including nearly 1 million bottles of Brunello, Banfi dwarfs Montalcino's other estates. Photograph by Paolo Tenti.

cultivated in vineyards planted in the firm's low-lying and flattened terrain around Sant'Angelo Scalo, in what is the hottest area in the entire denomination. Banfi also planted French grapes Cabernet, Merlot, and Chardonnay, but only dedicated a mere 35 hectares (86 acres) to Brunello. Over the next few years, as the transplanted Moscato grapes struggled in a drastically different climate from their indigenous growing area, American palates took a completely different direction: rather than wanting fizzy, light, white wines, the U.S. market instead demanded serious, full-bodied reds.

What the locals still refer to as Banfi's "colossal flop" was then turned into one of Italy's greatest success stories, as the massive Moscadello project was shelved and the Moscato vines were essentially beheaded and then regrafted with Sangiovese and French grapes. Since low-lying vineyards are not well-suited areas for Brunello vines, the firm now dedicates these areas not only to international grapes but also to Sangiovese that, they say, is destined for Banfi's range of blended Super Tuscans. As the firm's Brunello production took on its unexpected primary role, in the mid-1980s the estate teamed up with the University of Milan and poured massive amounts of resources into Sangiovese clonal research to help improve their production. Starting with the astonishing number of 650 individual clones, the firm's team of researchers narrowed the field down to 15, and then finally 6, which Banfi registered in 1996 so that other firms could have access to them. Today their clones, Janus 10, Janus 20, Tin 10, Tin 50, BF 30, and BF 10, are widely available and their Poggio alle Mura vineyards were planted with a selection of these clones in 1992.

The massive property has a wide range of vineyard altitudes, with vineyards starting just above the riverbanks. Vines for their basic Brunello are as low as 120 meters (394 feet), although average altitudes for their entire range of Brunellos are between 200 to 250 meters (656 to 820 feet). Besides the clay that dominates this part of the subzone, according to Banfi they have found twenty-nine distinct soil zones, ranging from pure clay to clay mixed with sand and rock. The firm also has several large irrigation pools, another source of local hostility since irrigation is strictly forbidden for Brunello vines even during severe droughts. For their part, Banfi says these irrigation pools are used only in the first few years, when Brunello vines are not yet in production, and for their IGT wines, whose more flexible laws allow irrigation. Cellar techniques include malolactic fermentation for all Brunellos in custom-made 350-liter barriques, and aging for the most part occurs in the same size barriques, though 50 percent of the straight Brunello is aged in Slavonian botti. These are Brunellos geared for what Banfi evidently feels Americans and other international palates want: overripe fruit with massive, chewy tannins and indiscernible acidity, accompanied by wood-driven sensations including oak, vanilla, and coffee suppported by evident alcohol.

Banfi has also created a large tourist complex, including a luxury hotel, tavern, and gift shop, centered around its eleventh-century castle, Poggio alle Mura, which the Marianis modestly renamed Castello Banfi after they acquired it in 1984.

Production

Total surface area: 2,900 ha (7,100 acres), 850 ha (2,001 acres under vine)
Brunello: 170 ha (420 acres), 700,000-plus bottles
Rosso: 28 ha (69 acres), 700,000 bottles
Moscadello: 45 ha (111 acres), 36,000 bottles

Brunello. In a good year, Banfi turns out more than 700,000 bottles of their straight Brunello, or about 10 percent of the denomination's entire bottled Brunello production. It is almost impossible for Sangiovese to excel

FIGURE 21. Banfi acquired the Poggio alle Mura property in 1984 and renamed it Castello Banfi, where they created a tourist complex centered around the eleventh-century castle. Photograph by Paolo Tenti.

in mass production, and despite being beefed up with evident wood sensations, in my opinion these are entry-level bottlings that will appeal more to wine drinkers than wine lovers.

Poggio alle Mura. About 60,000 bottles produced from the vineyards beneath the castle, this is the first wine made with three of Banfi's selected clones. Dark and inky wine and loaded with ripe black-fruit sensations, this is more robust than refined, thanks to massive tannins, evident alcohol, and obvious oak. While this wine surely has a loyal following among consumers and critics alike who love sheer power and the not so subtle nuances of new wood, I'm not sure why there is so much fuss over clonal selection if in the end wood is going to dominate both aromas and flavors.

Poggio all'Oro. Made exclusively from the eponymous vineyard, this is the estate's top Brunello and is released as a Riserva, usually in amounts of about 50,000 bottles. While I would not define this as a terroir-driven wine, it is definitely the best of the firm's Brunellos with Sangiovese's cherry earthiness and mineral peeking out of the dense concentration. Lots of power with a hint of finesse.

Lisini

Podere Casanova
53024 Sant'Angelo in Colle (SI)
Tel. +39 0577 844040
www.lisini.com
azienda@lisini.com

Boutique winery Lisini makes quintessential Brunellos that perfectly demonstrate their exclusively Sangiovese origins. Given the cult status and high demand of Lisini's Brunellos, these bottlings easily put to rest the idea that what the people really want is a little Merlot blended into their Brunellos. Rather than overoak, overextract, or overripen, the firm prefers to craft its classic offerings with the denomination's tried and true winemaking methods.

The Lisini and Clemente families have owned land in both the Chianti area and in the commune of Montalcino since the sixteenth century, and later combined their holdings when the two families were united by marriage. Though for many years the Montalcino property generated income through lumber and olive oil, Lodovico Lisini realized the area's great potential for red wine. In the 1930s he planted his first Brunello vines in the higher reaches of his estate located between the hamlets of Sant'Angelo and Castelnuovo dell'Abate, and some of these original vineyards are still in production today. Lodovico's enterprising daughter Elina took over the estate upon his death, and she became not only one of the founding "fathers" of the Consorzio but, in 1970, its first and so far only woman president. Elina was active until she passed away in 2009 at the impressive age of ninety-three, which helps fuel my ardent hope, since I enjoy drinking Brunello so much, that the wine is somehow related to longevity, and the relatively high number of octogenarians and even nonagenarians at several Montalcino estates seems to be more than a mere coincidence.

Elina's nephews and heirs Lorenzo and Carlo Lisini Baldi, who have been active at the winery for years, have ensured that the estate remains true to its roots by turning out finely crafted traditional Brunello. For more than twenty years they were guided by outside consultant Franco Bernabei, one of Tuscany's most celebrated enologists. "After we started with Bernabei in the early 1980s we had a noticeable increase in quality, thanks to higher planting densities, better training systems, and better winemaking," says Lorenzo. But according to Lorenzo, over the last few years Bernabei had less and less influence on the estate, and the firm recently parted ways with their friend on the best of terms. Today all winemaking responsibilities rest solely in the capable hands of Lisini's in-house enologist, Filippo Paoletti. The firm does, however, continue to seek out the advice of veteran Giulio Gambelli, *il maestro* to some of Montalcino's star producers.

Most of the estate is planted with its own genetic material, though they are also experimenting with other clones in their newer vineyards. Plant age averages between ten and sixty years old, generating a healthy but not excessive concentration, and the firm still has a tiny, isolated parcel of vines hailing from the mid-nineteenth century. Surrounded by olive groves, these ancient vines were miraculously never attacked by phylloxera, despite their original rootstocks. Though for years Lisini bottled this vineyard separately as "Prefilossero," an intriguingly complex but subtle wine with rich balsamic notes, production is now too low and the remaining grapes go into Brunello.

Vineyard altitude averages 350 meters (1,150 feet) and is key to achieving both ripe tannins and freshness. Lisini is refreshingly and unabashedly traditional—they make no excuses for abhorring the black, inky, and oaky Brunellos that many of their neighbors prefer. Fermentation is performed in glass-lined cement tanks that hail from the early 1970s, and some stainless steel, with maceration on the skins lasting twenty to twenty-eight days. Aging is carried out exclusively in large Slavonian botti for three to three and a half years. According to Lorenzo, botti are the only true way to age Brunellos, or as he matter-of-factly explains, "Using barriques for Brunello is like adding cream to tomato sauce—they both mask the defects of poor quality ingredients."

Production

Total surface area: 154 ha (380 acres)
Brunello: 15 ha (37 acres), 30,000 bottles
Rosso: 1.7 ha (4 acres), 20,000 bottles

Brunello Ugolaia. Made only in the best years, this is the firm's *fiore all'occhiello* or pride and joy. Made with grapes hailing from the Ugolaia vineyard, this bottling replaced the firm's Riserva, which was also made from the 1.5-hectare (3.7-acre) Ugolaia plot. I've tasted back to Lisini's magnificent 1971 Riserva, still youthful with great depth of flavors, and can confirm the wine's wonderful cellaring potential. The firm later decided to underscore the importance of the vineyard rather than the extra year of aging, and first released

Brunello Ugolaia starting with the 1990 vintage. Made with what are the oldest vines on the estate, Ugolaia ages from thirty-six to forty-two months in Slavonian botti, followed by at least eighteen months in bottle before being released. In its youth, Ugolaia has a deep, dense, garnet color that is typical from wines from this area, and a lovely concentration of ripe, wild, and sour cherry and plum accompanied by a strong tannic backbone and bright acidity. Production is usually between 3,000 and 6,000 bottles, depending on the vintage.

1971 Riserva (tasted in 2006). Leather, truffle, and mineral aromas with surprising cherry fruit for this advanced age. Silky-smooth tannins balanced with a dazzling vein of acidity will maintain this for a few years more. Long tea and fig on the close.

1973 Riserva. At first rather closed, but slowly reveals a classic bouquet of leather and tar. Fresher-than-expected acidity, with dried fruit flavors. Has completed its journey, but a great expression from a difficult vintage.

❧ *1975 Riserva* (tasted in 2010). Gorgeous bouquet of truffle, leather, maple syrup, carob, and tobacco. Shockingly youthful with creamy-cherry, fig, and black-tea flavors. Surprisingly vibrant with still fresh acidity and sleek, smooth tannins. Stunning depth of flavors and long, lingering finish. A fabulous wine still going strong. At its top but should maintain for years.

1998 Ugolaia. Intense aromas of violet and iris, with lively acidity balanced with ripe dark-fruit flavors and firm but developed tannins. Now through 2030.

1999 Ugolaia. A superb effort with rich, sour cherry, earth, leather, and mineral. Supple tannins and fresh acidity give this great aging potential. Best 2014–30.

Brunello. Even if Lisini Brunellos don't have the hefty structure of Ugolaia, these are no lightweights, boasting firm tannins and considerable alcohol that are restrained with fresh acidity and elegance. Lovely and quintessential sour cherry and whiffs earth and leather even when young. Best at the ten- to fifteen-year mark.

Rosso. Lisini Rossos are always approachable, with lovely floral aromas and delicious fresh-berry flavors and fresh acidity. They cry out for food and can be paired with almost anything. Though they have the structure for modest aging, they are best enjoyed young while they are bursting with fruit.

Sesti

Località Castello di Argiano
53024 Montalcino (SI)
Tel. +39 0577 843921
www.sestiwine.com
elisa@sesti.net

Giuseppe Sesti, whose rich and powerful Brunellos are among the few that appeal to both Sangiovese purists looking for earthy, sour cherry, and complexity and to international palates craving layers of rich, dense fruit, is Montalcino's "accidental" Brunello maker. In 1975, when Sesti bought the splendid Castello di Argiano property, complete with a disintegrating but authentic medieval castle and tower, a ninth-century church, and a villa with a tree growing through the roof and pecking chickens milling about the sitting room, Brunello was the last thing on his mind. Or almost.

Sesti, a historian of astronomy, was merely looking for just the right country retreat where he could settle down with his young family and write scholarly tomes on the heavenly bodies. When he arrived in Sant'Angelo and stumbled on the ruins of Castello di Argiano, part of a chain of castles that served as watchtowers when it was built in the thirteenth century, he felt the mystic connection he was looking for. Besides writing several successful books, he also found an unexpected "side job." For by the late 1970s and throughout the 1980s, the charismatic Sesti, who speaks fluent English, was in high demand among local producers who enlisted him to translate for them during visits by the many foreign importers, distributors, and journalists who had begun descending upon the wineries scattered around the hilltop town. "I really did it because after many hours of translating for the wineries and the visiting importers and journalists, I was awarded with: The Lunch. For me this was a highly anticipated event, especially when the producer's wife brought out steaming plates of *pinci* with tomato and garlic sauce, followed by wild boar and pecorino cheese, all accompanied by old and recent vintages of Brunello," recalls Sesti.

By the late 1980s, after more than a decade of interpreting for winemakers and agronomists and tasting their wines, Sesti realized he was sitting on prime Brunello land, and planted his first vineyard in 1990. Thanks to the vast knowledge he had accumulated on grape growing and cellar practices, he also knew just what kind of Brunello he wanted to make. Sesti preferred

FIGURE 22. Astronomer and winemaker Giuseppe Sesti of Castello di Argiano, crafts rich, powerful Brunellos using traditional methods. Photograph by Paolo Tenti.

traditionally crafted wines, and rejected barriques and other cellar practices he felt were just a trend, or as he succinctly phrases it, "I want to make wines that taste like they are from *here,* and not wines that taste as if they could have been made just anywhere." With the help and guidance of a local grape grower, Sesti planted several hectares of Brunello vineyards with a clone discovered through experiments with massal selection on the nearby Il Poggione estate.

The tepid microclimate of this part of Sant'Angelo, halfway between Sant'Angelo in Colle and Sant'Angelo Scalo, naturally generates fruit-forward wines while the vineyard altitude of 350 meters (1,150 feet) above sea level reins in excess. Soil composition of sand mixed with quartz and light clay gives the wines an energizing mineral purity. Unsurprisingly, given Sesti's passion for astronomy and astrology, his winemaking is dictated by the phases of the moon. However, he is quick to point out that he does not adhere to Rudolf Steiner's biodynamic principles. "Steiner's astrologic calendar is not precise because it doesn't take into account the gradual progression of the stars over the years. This throws off the entire astrological calendar, which Steiner used as his guide," argues Sesti, who is today assisted in the winery by his daughter Elisa.

Sesti's winemaking is best described as ultranatural; he uses no herbicides

FIGURE 23. The mystical Castello di Argiano property, complete with a disintegrating but authentic medieval castle, boasts prime growing conditions for superb Brunellos. Photograph by Paolo Tenti.

or chemical pesticides, and only natural fertilizer. He uses no selected yeasts for fermentation, and keeps sulfites to the bare minimum. He also racks and bottles only during the waning moon, which he claims generates less shock, and thereby reduces the amount of sulfites needed to preserve the wine. Sesti's earthy Castello di Argiano's Brunellos, which by the way are not to be confused with wines from the nearby Argiano estate owned by Noemi Cinzano, are often enjoyable even upon release but benefit from more bottle aging. They age well for ten to twenty years after the vintage, more for the Riservas.

Production

Total surface area: 102 ha (252 acres)
Brunello: 4.2 ha (10.3 acres), 15,500 bottles
Rosso: 2 ha (4.9 acres), 10,000 bottles

Brunello. These are wonderful wines of great character, with dense, delicious fruit and striking depth. After spending four years in traditional botti, these wines also demonstrate whiffs of leather, earth, and mineral, all seamlessly balanced with rippling, velvety tannins and bright acidity. While enjoyable upon release, these will maintain well for at least a decade and more, though great vintages, such as the stunning 2004, will age longer. Whether it be the unique location, careful vineyard management, conservative cellar practices, or more likely the fortuitous combination of all the above, Sesti even made an outstanding Brunello in 2002 that in 2010 was still very much alive with uncommon heft and complexity for the vintage. The 2006 was loaded with leather and balsamic aromas and ripe cherry-berry, spice, and mineral flavors. Fantastic depth. Well balanced with big, brooding tannins and fresh acidity. Best after 2016, and will age beautifully for a decade more at least.

Riserva Phenomena. In the best years, Sesti makes a fabulous Riserva, called Phenomena, whose label design is ever changing to reflect the most important astronomical event that occurred during the year of the vintage, such as the 2003 that colorfully demonstrates the planet Mars crossing the constellation of Aquarius. Even more important, however, is what is in the bottle. Sesti's Phenomena, made from grapes hailing from the vineyard that excelled in that given vintage, are aged for up to five years in botti, and even if some warmer vintages are approachable upon release, their full structure, firm tannins, and fresh acidity also make them unquestionably cellar-worthy. In 2010, I gave the 2004 one of my highest marks, 18.5 out 20, with the following note: "Gorgeous nose of earth, plum black cherry, and leather. Beautiful, sweet, and supple tannins; great balance. Fantastic depth and length." This should drink well through 2025–30 and longer.

Rosso. Aged for eighteen months in botti, this is an outstanding Rosso that combines structure and drinkability thanks to delicious fruit, fresh acidity, and mineral.

Campogiovanni

Società Agricola San Felice
Località Campogiovanni
Sant'Angelo in Colle
53024 Montalcino (SI)
Tel. +39 0577 3991
www.agricolasanfelice.com
info@agricolasanfelice.it

FIGURE 24. Vineyard at Campogiovanni estate with Sant'Angelo in the background. Although owned by insurance giant Allianz, Campogiovanni is run like a family winery. Photograph by Paolo Tenti.

The San Felice company, perhaps best known for its Super Tuscan Vigorello and its Chianti Classico, acquired the already established Campogiovanni estate in the mid-1980s. Despite being owned by the insurance giant Allianz, San Felice's estates are managed with the care usually reserved for family-run wineries.

Campogiovanni lies halfway between Sant'Angelo in Colle and Sant'Angelo Scalo, where vineyard altitudes range between 250 and 300 meters above sea level, perfect for attaining both ideal ripening and for maintaining enough fresh acidity. Their soil is a complex blend of mineral rich clay dominated by silt and sand, laying over beds of sandstone and marl, all of which conspire to allow grapes to mature slowly and develop ideal ripening and complexity. While the older vineyards planted in 1976 have lower densities of 3,300 vines per hectare, those planted after 1998 are 8,500 vines per hectare, exceedingly high for Montalcino, but it seems to work for them.

My first impression of Campogiovanni's Brunello over ten years ago was one of intense concentration and rather low acidity. However, recent vintages show more restraint and fresher acidity. The firm's Brunellos lately combine striking depth of succulent fruit and spice with enveloping, ripe tannins, all lifted by pleasant acidity and energizing minerality. Their single-vineyard Riserva Il Quercione is a great wine with both structure and finesse.

Production

Total surface area: 65 ha (160 acres)
Brunello: 14 ha (35 acres), 70,000 bottles
Rosso: 6 ha (15 acres), 40,000 bottles

Brunello. Aged for three years in botti, this wine transcends the borders of labels such as traditional or innovative. It is what it should be—an excellent example of Mediterranean Sangiovese, with all the black-cherry, earthy-mineral notes and spice one would expect from a Brunello hailing from Sant'Angelo. While these are already enjoyable upon release, the best years hold up to modest aging as well. The firm's 2005, a lean year in most of the denomination, showed impressive structure for the vintage, while the 2004 showed dense cherry-berry with round, sweet tannins and cherry liqueur–like flavors and will drink well through 2015.

Riserva Il Quercione. A true Riserva made in the vineyard, and in this case, from the Il Quercione vineyard, a 2.5-hectare (6.1-acre) plot situated at 250 meters (820 feet) above sea level. Released only in exceptional years, and in tiny amounts of around 3,000 bottles, this wine has more structure than the Brunello Annata, and gripping complexity. Fermented and aged in 500-liter French tonneaux, the wine's Sangiovese aromas and flavors, and soft velvety tannins beautifully support the well-integrated oak nuances. Should drink well for fifteen to twenty years after release.

Rosso. Friendly and round with succulent berry flavors balanced by just enough fresh acidity.

THIRTEEN

Castelnuovo dell'Abate

About 10 kilometers (6 miles) southeast of town along the crest of the hill coming down from Montalcino one arrives at the hamlet of Castelnuovo dell'Abate, one of the most picturesque and, in terms of Brunello production, one of the most exciting of Montalcino's subzones. Centered around the twelfth-century Abbey of Sant'Antimo, this subzone is defined by multifaceted growing conditions that create Brunellos with rich fruit, penetrating mineral, and gripping complexity. The best vineyards face south, southeast, and west, and those near the delightful Castello di Velona that face Mount Amiata have average altitudes of 200 to 450 meters (650 to 1,475 feet) above sea level that virtually guarantee ideal ripening. Although the zone benefits from warm temperatures, it doesn't suffer the scorching heat of Sant'Angelo to the west because the ridge descending from Montalcino and rising above the Sant'Antimo valley blocks hot sea breezes while the flowing Orcia River below generates cooling winds at night. These vivid contrasts in day and night temperatures prolong the growing season, aiding the development of complex bouquets while creating impeccable balance. Castelnuovo dell'Abate also enjoys a complex mix of soil or as Roberto Colacicchi, a professor of geology at the University of Perugia, explains, the microzone "has an unusual combination of ancient and recent soil deposits." Most of the best vineyards have calcareous marl with shale formations known in technical terms as "Castelnuovo marl formation," according to Dr. Mencacci's geology map. This enviable combination has led to the most varied and complex soil situation in the entire denomination, and according to the CRA-CNR Sangiovese map, the entire subzone is considered an "area with moderate diffusion of highly suitable soil."

With its supreme growing conditions, Castelnuovo dell'Abate Brunellos

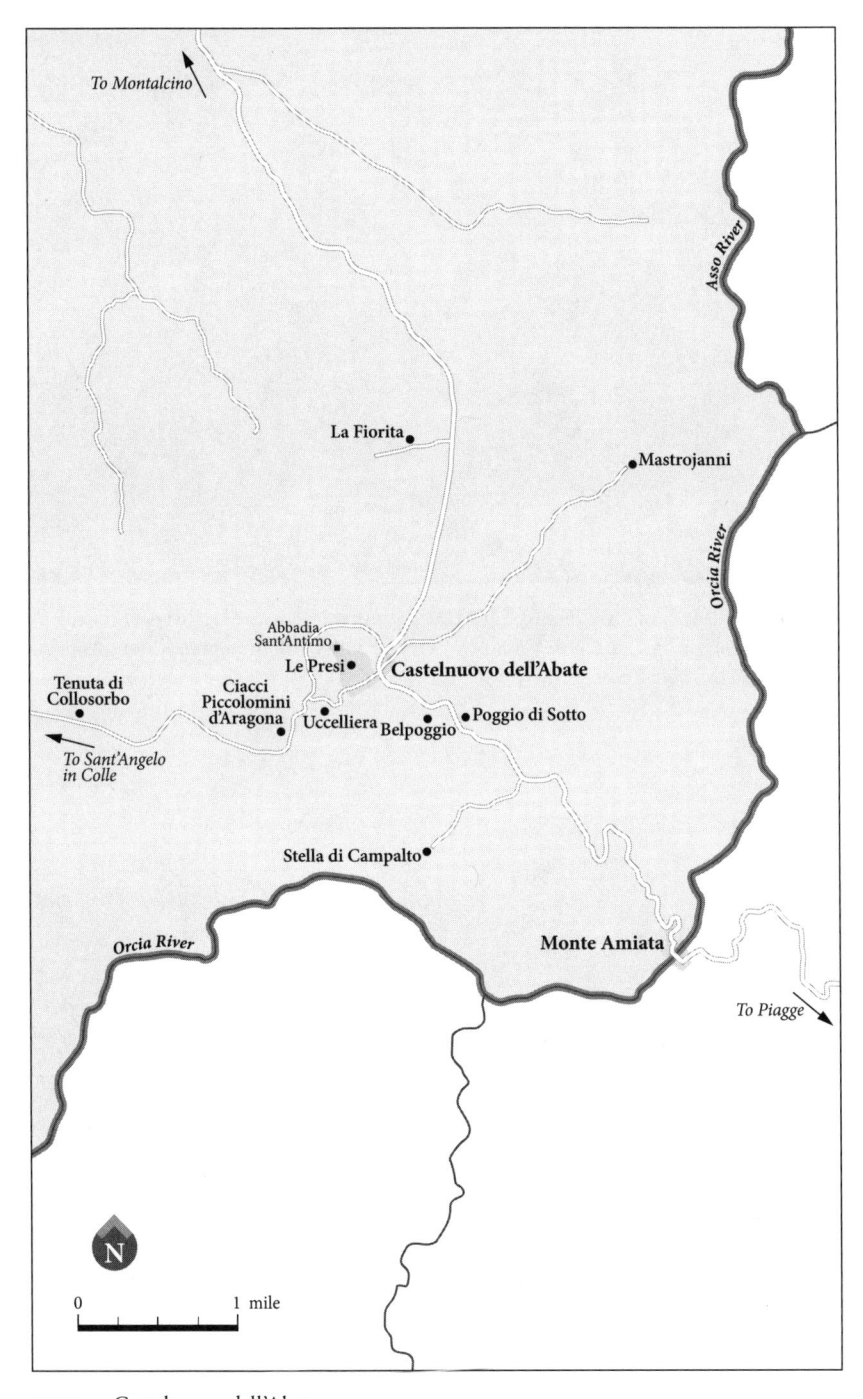

MAP 7. Castelnuovo dell'Abate

FIGURE 25. Many of Castelnuovo dell'Abate's prime vineyards are located near the splendid eleventh-century Castello di Velona that crowns a high hill in front of Mount Amiata. Photograph by Paolo Tenti.

FIGURE 26. The beautiful hamlet of Castelnuovo dell'Abate is making some of the most remarkable Brunellos in the denomination. Photograph by Paolo Tenti.

have an earthy elegance that beautifully combines power and grace. It is therefore somewhat surprising to learn that the area's full potential remained untapped for years, until pioneering firm Mastrojanni released its first Brunello in the mid-1980s, stunning critics and other winemakers alike with its depth, elegance, and balance. Local farmers from the hamlet suddenly took a serious interest in winemaking, which up until then had been a rather primitive affair carried out on a tiny scale to produce wines strictly for family consumption. Producers from other parts of Montalcino also took note and began snapping up land to plant Brunello vineyards, whose grapes would eventually be blended with their other Brunello vineyards to add body to more delicate wines from further north, just as Silvio Nardi had been quietly doing for years, though it would be decades before the firm would bottle Manachiara separately. Outside investors also came to Castelnuovo dell'Abate, starting with Piero Palmucci, who acquired the Poggio di Sotto estate where he crafts gorgeous Brunellos that have become one of the benchmarks for the entire denomination.

Mastrojanni

Poderi Loreto e S. Pio
Castelnuovo dell'Abate
53024 Montalcino (SI)
Tel. +39 0577 835681
www.mastrojanni.com
info@mastrojanni.com

Back in 1975, when Roman lawyer Gabriele Mastrojanni bought 90 hectares of land on a high ridge in Castelnuovo dell'Abate and founded his winery overlooking the valley where the Asso and Orcia Rivers merge, he may not have realized that he was opening up what would become one of the most provocative areas in Montalcino's growing zone. He did realize, however, that he wanted to make top-quality Brunello. Not only did he succeed, but soon after he released his 1979 vintage in 1984, other established producers flocked to the area to plant or acquire vineyards while newcomers bought estates and created wineries directly in the hamlet.

After Mastrojanni passed away, his heirs couldn't agree on how to run the estate and sold it in 2008 to Gruppo Illy, Italy's most exclusive coffee dynasty. Although Illy is based in Trieste, Montalcino was not a new frontier for the firm; former vice-president of the company Francesco Illy already owned a small property in Montalcino, Podere Le Ripi, and other family members have always had a strong interest in fine wine. This is good news for fans of Mastrojanni Brunello since it means the new owners have no intention of changing day-to-day operations or the house style at their recently acquired winery, but they will make needed investments in both the vineyards and cellars to guarantee that quality remains steady. Illy has kept on agronomist and in-house enologist Andrea Machetti, who is now officially managing director although he had basically been running the estate for the Mastrojannis since 1992. Maurizio Castelli, one of the real experts in Sangiovese, has also stayed on as the firm's outside consultant.

The firm's 14.5 hectares of Brunello vineyards and 4 hectares of Rosso vines are situated on average at 350 meters (1,150 feet) above sea level, where they benefit from mixed soils of clay, limestone, and pebbles that lend their wines their structure and minerality. Sangiovese planted at the estate "is Sangiovese selected from within the denomination, which means it has had many years to adapt to Montalcino's growing conditions," explains Machetti. Vines are planted between 3,600 and 5,300 plants per hectare, while plant age for Brunello vines are between ten and thirty-five years old, generating natural concentration and balance. While the older vineyards are planted with spurred cordon, vines planted after 2002 are trained on a modified Guyot, which Machetti claims leads to more stable quality. Vinification is traditional, taking place in both cement and stainless-steel vats. Machetti tries to avoid selected yeasts, but as he admits, "in difficult vintages we will use selected yeasts if within a reasonable amount of time fermentation either doesn't start on its own, or blocks."

Mastrojanni's Brunellos are aged for thirty-six months in mid-sized botti of French oak, while the Rosso, made from both declassified Brunello as well as from younger vines planted in 2004, are aged six to seven months in larger French casks. While the Brunello and Rosso are excellent, archetypical expressions of Sangiovese, the firm's best and most celebrated bottling is Brunello Schiena d'Asino, named after a particular 1-hectare (2.47-acre) vineyard situated at 380 meters (1,247 feet) above sea level with perfect southeast exposure. Schiena d'Asino is vinified and bottled separately only in the best vintages, producing between five thousand and seven thousand bottles. In less than stellar years the grapes are blended in with the regular Brunello. A newly planted vineyard, Loreto, is also being bottled separately starting with the 2007 vintage that will be released in 2012.

Production

Total surface area: 90 ha (222 acres)
Brunello: 14.5 ha (36 acres), 38,000 bottles
Rosso: 4 ha (10 acres), 18,000 bottles

Brunello. These are quintessential Brunellos demonstrating all the beauty of Sangiovese's earthy, berry, and mineral nuances. In their youth, aggressive tannins and firm acidity balance the wine's rich fruit, meaning these wines bloom with aging and are best after ten years but can age even longer. Even in 2005, a lean vintage in much of the denomination, Mastrojanni made an outstanding Brunello that while already enjoyable upon release, will benefit with a few more years in the cellar. Best through 2020.

Brunello Schiena d'Asino. While this is not a Riserva, this single-vineyard cru is the glory of Mastrojanni, and one of the top Brunellos in the entire denomination. Aged for three and a half years in 15-hectoliter French casks and released only in the best years, this is more compelling and far more complex than the straight Brunello, and more elegant. The impeccably balanced 2004 has breathtaking depth and length, and should age well through the 2030s.

Rosso. Although this has the ripe but restrained fruit of the firm's Brunellos, it has a much more approachable structure and is highly enjoyable upon release.

Poggio di Sotto

Località Poggio di Sotto
Castelnuovo dell'Abate
53024 Montalcino (SI)
Tel. +39 0577 835502
www.poggiodisotto.com
palmucci@poggiodisotto.com

As he likes to tell it, when Piero Palmucci arrived in Castelnuovo dell'Abate in 1989, "there were no other wineries here yet . . . besides Mastrojanni." But Palmucci's love affair with Montalcino goes back much further. When he was a young schoolboy during World War II, his parents sent him to live with friends in Montalcino, deeming the small isolated town a safer haven than his hometown city of Grosseto, an important port on the Tuscan coast. Needless to say, his parents never expected that the Front would eventually pass through Montalcino, as it did in 1944.

Piero retained his memories of Montalcino, most of them decidedly good despite the tragedies he witnessed during the war; when he got tired of running a container-shipping company that dealt mostly with the Far East, he decided to fulfill his dream of returning to Montalcino and make Brunello. Palmucci spent years investigating every corner of Montalcino before finding the perfect location, which he eventually discovered at Poggio di Sotto. And what a beautiful spot it is. From the spacious terrace, exploding with fragrant herbs, one can take in brooding Mount Amiata in front and a sweeping panorama of the Orcia Valley below. Palmucci's manicured vineyards and olive groves, which he lovingly tends with the air of an overprotective father, surround the comfortable stone villa and cellars.

A stalwart traditionalist, Palmucci is even more protective of his Brunellos. While many other growers in Montalcino cultivate other grape varieties in areas not suitable for Sangiovese, Palmucci would just as soon leave those undesirable areas uncultivated rather than plant what in his opinion are equally undesirable grapes. "Why should I even bother making wine from international grapes when I should focus all my attention on Brunello and Rosso, which we can only make here?" he asks rhetorically.

Despite his sense of idealism, at least when it comes to Brunello, Palmucci took a distinctly business-minded approach to his new endeavor. One of his first orders of business was to have his soil analyzed, for which he engaged Attilio Scienza, from the University of Milan and one of Italy's most famous professors of viticulture. Based on the resulting studies, Palmucci chose a multiclonal approach, and planted his vineyards with Sangiovese F9A 548, JANUS 10, JANUS 20, I-TIN 10, I-TIN 50, all paired with the most suitable rootstocks for both the clone and the clay and limestone soils. He also preserved some of the older vines that were already on the property. Perhaps one of the secrets to the unusual depth of Poggio di Sotto's concentrated yet elegant Brunellos is the natural balance in almost every aspect of grape growing, starting with the commitment to organic farming. Vineyards all benefit from south and southeast exposures and are situated between 200 and 450 meters above sea level, guaranteeing both perfect ripening as well as intense perfumes and fine acidity. Vine density ranges between 3,000 and 4,200

FIGURE 27. Poggio di Sotto's vineyards face brooding Mount Amiata, which protects much of the denomination from violent storms and hail. Photograph by Paolo Tenti.

vines per hectare and plants are between ten and fifty years old, generating both vibrancy and an impressive concentration of flavors.

Palmucci also chose to work with Giulio Gambelli, who trained with the legendary Tancredi Biondi Santi and under whose tutelage became a master in the art of Sangiovese. Years ago other enologists, evidently jealous of Gambelli's sterling reputation, pointed out that because Gambelli never had any formal academic training he could not technically be called an enologist. Gambelli is therefore always referred to as *maestro assaggiatore,* or master taster, which in the end has given him even more respect and distinction, much to the ire of these same colleagues.

Gambelli, well into his eighties, strongly advocates minimal intervention in the cellar, and Palmucci has followed his advice, employing extended maceration and using no selected yeasts for fermentation, which takes place in wooden vats and stainless steel. Palmucci ages his Brunellos for a minimum of four years in 30-hectoliter Slavonian botti that he changes at least every ten years "to maintain intense perfumes," while the Riserva, which he only makes in stellar vintages, ages for longer. Even the Rosso spends two years in wood, as much time as most producers' Brunello. None of the wines are filtered.

Just as this book was going to print, Palmucci sold the estate to the Tipa family, owners of ColleMassari in Motecucco.

Production

Total surface area: 33 ha
Brunello: 12 ha (30 acres), 15,000 bottles
Rosso: 1 ha (2.47 acres), 15,000 bottles

Brunello. These wonderful Brunellos have intense floral aromas with hints of leather and a rich but elegant palate of wild cherry punctuated with tobacco and soothing licorice. They are dense but beautifully balanced, and benefit with aging. Palmucci's 2005, a vintage that produced more delicate Brunellos in the rest of the denomination, has remarkable structure for the vintage, and should age well through 2020 at least. The estate's 2004, 2001, and 1999 are also prime examples of quintessential Brunello.

Riserva. In exceptional vintages, Poggio di Sotto also releases a Riserva. The 2004, aged for six years in wood, is magnificent, with intense, complex aromas of earth, leather, and spice. The rich palate is dominated by concentrated and creamy cherry-berry flavors and licorice impeccably balanced with round velvety tannins and pleasing acidity. A focused, engaging wine. Will drink beautifully for decades.

Rosso. Thanks to its Brunello-like structure, enhanced by two years aging in botti, plus its easy drinkability and a more accessible price tag, this is one of the most sought-out Rossos in the denomination.

Ciacci Piccolomini d'Aragona

Località Molinello
53024 Montalcino (SI)
Tel. +39 0577 835616
www.ciaccipiccolomini.com
info@ciaccipiccolomini.com

The story of how Giuseppe Bianchini ended up at the helm of the Ciacci Piccolomini d'Aragona winery near Castelnuovo dell'Abate plays out like a modern-day fairy tale, or a Hollywood film script.

The estate's ecclesiastic origins date back to the seventeenth century, when Montalcino's bishop, who was also the abbot of nearby Sant'Antimo, constructed a palatial residence, the Palazzo del Vescovo, in Castelnuovo dell'Abate. Over time the palazzo and its surrounding land passed into the possession of the diocese of Montalcino, only to be auctioned off in 1868 under an Italian law that seized Church property after the unification of Italy. Francesco Ciacci eventually acquired the estate in 1877, and his daughter married into the noble Piccolomini d'Aragona family. Upon her death in 1985, having no direct heirs, the countess bequeathed the estate to her property manager, Giuseppe Bianchini, to his complete and utter surprise.

After installing his family in the lofty palazzo, Bianchini immediately began the long process of restructuring the firm to maximize quality Brunello production, which included selling off nearly half of the estate's holdings. In 1986 and 1990 Bianchini replanted the best vineyards, those situated between 240 and 360 meters (787 and 1,181 feet) above sea level near the Orcia River. Here southwest exposures and altitude create a particularly mild microclimate suitable for ideal ripening, while Eocene soil composed predominantly of marl lends structure. Bianchini immediately understood the exceptional merits of the 12-hectare (29.7-acre) Pianrosso vineyard, and the cru's grapes are vinified separately and bottled as the eponymous single-vineyard. In exceptional years, the firm also makes Brunello Riserva Santa Caterina d' Oro from the same vineyard.

After Giuseppe passed away in 2004, his grown son Paolo, an avid cyclist who in 1998 won the title of Italian Champion in the amateur class and who had been working alongside his father for years, and his daughter Lucia, took over the estate. Paolo, whose passion for quality means that in difficult vintages he harvests up to four separate times in each vineyard, to pick only when grapes are perfectly mature, is also passionate about guaranteeing every phase of winemaking. Starting with photo documenting grapes as they arrive in the cellar, quality control extends to wrapping an anticounterfeit hologram around the capsule. In 2007, Ciacci Piccolomini became the first firm in Montalcino to further protect its Brunellos from fraudulent reproduction, using the innovative Certilogo system, based on security codes that prove the wine's authenticity and pedigree.

Guided by famed Brunello expert Paolo Vagaggini, Paolo and Lucia keep things on the traditional side for Brunello, with long maceration and fermentation taking place in both glass-lined cement tanks and stainless steel under controlled temperatures. Aging takes place in traditional botti, ranging in size from 20 to 85 hectoliters. The Bianchinis have also acquired a farm further south in the Grosseto Province, where they produce Montecucco Sangiovese DOC.

Production

Total surface area: 170 ha (420 acres)

Brunello: 18 ha (45 acres), 40,000 bottles Annata +
  45,000 bottles Pianrosso

Rosso: 8 ha (20 acres), 45,000 bottles

Brunello. The straight Brunello boasts intense-violet and black-fruit aromas that carry over onto the palate along with stewed cherry and mineral. The Brunello is both vibrant and ripe, and bracing tannins will benefit with age. The 2005 showed impressive body and concentration for the vintage, with brooding tannins and fresh dark fruit, and will drink well through 2015.

Brunello Pianrosso. Aged for three years in botti, a year longer than the basic Brunello, this shows more concentration and stunning depth, all graced with restraint. This is best after ten years, but can age longer. In outstanding vintages, the firm also makes Brunello Riserva Caterina d'Oro from a selection of the best grapes in the Pianrosso vineyard that boasts more complexity and aging capability. The 2004 Riserva is outstanding, with an intense bouquet of rose, spice, and incense accompanied by a rich fruit, spice, and licorice palate. Powerful with bracing tannins. Best after 2014; will drink through 2025/2030.

Rosso. Earthy floral and berry aromas with vibrant flavors of raspberry jelly and mineral. Lively, lovely, and very approachable despite an impressive structure.

Uccelliera

Podere Uccelliera 45
Castelnuovo dell'Abate
53024 Montalcino (SI)
Tel. +39 0577 835729
www.uccelliera-montalcino.it
anco@uccelliera-montalcino.it

Andrea Cortonese's big, earthy Brunellos have a cult following among lovers of Italian wine thanks to their heady aromas, penetrating succulent fruit, and dense concentration. You can almost taste the mineral rich soils and sunshine that define this part of Montalcino's growing zone.

Andrea was born and bred in Castelnuovo dell'Abate and his family have always worked the land. Just when Andrea was a young man contemplating his path in life, a unique opportunity arose when an old farmhouse on the Ciacci Piccolomini property, along with a few hectares of land, went up for sale. Andrea leapt at the chance, buying the property in 1986, sealing his future as a grape grower and winemaker in what was a pivotal time for the denomination. Or as Andrea puts it, "I was still in time to be a part of the old-style farming here in Montalcino, before Brunello became an international phenomenon. Shortly afterward everything changed, but starting when I did allowed me to learn to have an intimate relationship with the land I cultivate and which gives me my living."

Andrea lovingly restored the farmhouse, built a new cellar, planted new vineyards, and eventually acquired 2 more hectares (5 acres) of vines next to Ciacci Piccolomini's excellent Pianrosso vineyard. Uccelliera, the original name of the small property (so named for the many birds that nest nearby), now consists of several hectares of Brunello vines, as well as centuries-old olive trees—among the few that survived the terrible frost that destroyed most of Montalcino's olive groves in 1985. Soil in all the vineyards, which are close to the farmhouse, is a complex mix of sand, clay, and rock fragments and is highly rich in minerals. Plant ages range from eight to thirty-five years old and are located between 150 and 350 meters (500 and 1,150 feet) above sea level in vineyards benefiting from varied sun exposure. Plant density is a conservative 3,000 to 5,700 vines per hectare, which Andrea feels is just right for optimal ripening and gives wines the perfect concentration in this warm, sunlit subzone.

Andrea mixes both traditional cellar practices with modern-day conventions. He doesn't use selected yeasts for fermentation, which starts spontaneously, and is carried out for twenty to twenty-five days in temperature-controlled steel tanks. Brunello is aged for a minimum of up to thirty-six months in botti of both Slavonian and French oak. In great vintages Uccelliera also makes a powerful and velvety Riserva from the oldest vines that is aged in Slavonian and French oak of varying sizes from thirty-six to forty-two months followed by eighteen months of bottle aging. The small firm also makes a wonderful, full-bodied but vibrant Rosso.

Production

Total surface area: 10.5 ha (26 acres)
Brunello: 6 ha (15 acres), 20,000 bottles
Rosso: 25,000 bottles

Brunello.   This is the mainstay of production, and is both full-bodied but vibrant, with intense, earthy, and often funky aromas of smoke, leather, and meat juices. It is a muscular Brunello, with juicy, black-fruit flavors, a hint of sweet oak, and big, voluptuous tannins. The 2004 has incredible intensity and length and will drink best 2012–20.

Riserva.   In outstanding years, Andrea rigorously selects the best grapes from the oldest and highest vineyards. It has more depth, brawn, and evident alcohol than the Brunello Annata. Its gripping structure includes an aggressively tannic backbone, and even the impressive 2004 needs some serious aging before blooming. Best 2015–30.

Rosso.   Made from the same Brunello vines and aged for nine months in oak, this intense Rosso is much friendlier than its siblings, though at fourteen degrees alcohol it is not as easy drinking as one might expect from what is after all Brunello's junior partner. A perfect example of those full-bodied Rossos many consider to be "baby Brunellos."

Belpoggio

Località Bellaria
Castelnuovo dell'Abate
53024 Montalcino
Tel. +39 0423 982147
www.belpoggio.it
belpoggio@belpoggio.it

When Enrico Martellozzo, whose family owns Bellussi, one of Italy's most important *Prosecco* houses, decided he wanted to invest in one of Italy's famed denominations and try his hand at red-wine making, he and his wife Renata naturally turned to their favorite red-wine region, Tuscany. After spending three and a half years scouting out every corner of the region, they had nearly given up when they unexpectedly came upon a small but lovely piece of land just up the street from the Abbey of Sant'Antimo. The Belpoggio property not only offers a stunning view of the Orcia Valley below but is also blessed with perfect sun exposure that hits vines all day, promoting ideal grape maturation while constant breezes keep vines dry and diseases at bay. The Martellozzos bought the estate in 2005, but with only 3 hectares (7.4 acres) under vine; in 2007 they acquired more vineyards directly across the street from the Biondi Santi's legendary Greppo estate where the calcareous soil has a high content of rock fragments.

The Martellozzos brought along their Bellussi enologist, Francesco Adami, from the Veneto; and the winemaker is as excited as his employers are about their Brunello adventure. "Our most difficult decision in the beginning was choosing what winemaking road we wanted to follow," Adami explains. "In other words, before we could begin fitting out the cellars, we had to determine right off if we wanted to make oak-driven, inky-black wines that were good but that were not in our opinion typical Brunellos, but that pleased the critics, or, if we wanted to make a more traditionally crafted Brunello that pleased wine drinkers and that we ourselves preferred." Thankfully for Brunello lovers, the Martellozzos and Adami chose what at the time was the road less traveled among Montalcino's newcomers: they opted to craft classic Brunellos that boast hallmark wild-cherry aromas and flavors, perfectly balanced with silky-smooth tannins and vibrant acidity. The estate's nascent Brunello production promises to yield elegant, age-worthy bottlings.

This is a young estate showing a lot of potential. Its first release, the 2003 Brunello, was already in barriques in the final stage of its mandatory aging period when Martellozzo and his wife bought the winery, and the 2004 had also been racked into barriques before the change in ownership. Belpoggio's 2005 vintage marks the change in production, and the first vintage fermented and aged in their brand new cellars. Starting with the 2008 vintage, which will be released in 2013, Belpoggio Brunellos will be a blend of the best grapes from the firm's two separate vineyard areas—Castelnuovo dell'Abate, where vines are situated at 350 meters (1,150 feet) above sea level, and the newly acquired vineyards closer to Montalcino at Poggio d'Oro, where vines average 450 meters above sea level. Tank and barrel samples in 2009 of the both the 2008 and 2009 vintages showed great depth and elegance even at these early stages of development.

Martellozzo and Adami keep it simple in the cellar. After temperature-controlled fermentation in steel vats, they age their Brunello for up to three years in traditional 30- to 40-hectoliter botti, one year for Rosso.

Production

Total surface area: 10 ha (24.7 acres)
Brunello: 2.5 ha (6.1 acres), 15,000 bottles
Rosso: 2.5 acres (6.1 acres), 10,000 bottles

Brunello. This is the focus of production seeing that Belpoggio does not make a Riserva, for now anyway, although they don't rule this out as a possibility for the future. These are quintessential and finely crafted Brunellos, with enticing aromas of violet, incense, and freshly tilled earth. The creamy palate shows marasca cherry, spice, tobacco, and mineral. Firm tannins and bright acidity should allow them to evolve beautifully for at least a decade or more after release. Their 2005 had impressive depth and creamy fruit for the vintage, which had much better results in Castelnuovo dell'Abate compared to other areas of the denomination. Will drink well through 2016.

Rosso. These offer pretty floral aromas with vibrant and rich cassis and spice flavors accompanied by a long, clean finish. Supple tannins make these more approachable than the Brunello, but the 2009 also possess good structure.

Stella di Campalto

Podere San Giuseppe 35
Castelnuovo dell'Abate
53024 Montalcino (SI)
Tel. +39 0577 835754
www.stelladicampalto.it
info@stelladicampalto.it

Stella di Campalto, the young proprietress of the small San Giuseppe farm, is an ambitious woman with set ideas about crafting Brunello that are carrying her onto a path less traveled than the one taken by Montalcino's more business-minded producers. Stella has set her sights on making Brunellos of balance and breeding in the most natural way possible. Her farming is not only certified organic, but as an ardent follower of Steiner she is also one of the first and so far few biodynamic winemakers in Montalcino. Showing remarkable determination and courage, Stella, along with fellow producers at Piano dell'Orino and Salicutti, has started the long process of legally divorc-

FIGURE 28. Stella di Campalto makes polished, well-balanced Brunellos from organically grown grapes and biodynamic farming methods on her San Giuseppe property. Photograph by Paolo Tenti.

ing from the Brunello Consorzio, despite that as a member of this Growers' Union she is part of a major vehicle for promoting the local wines around the world. According to Stella, the Consorzio is far more interested in satisfying the desires of the largest estates, those with the most political power within the union, than the small producers that individually have little influence or weight. "I don't feel the Consorzio is protecting the interests of the small, serious Brunello producers," argues Stella, a sentiment shared by many of Montalcino's estates. Keeping in mind that 66 percent of all of the denomination's estates possess 5 hectares (12 acres) or less, with 22 percent having less than 1 hectare (2.47 acres), the small estates that Stella feels are being neglected make up the vast majority of producers.

Stella's farm, a long drive through a sea of vineyards down a steep dirt road that dips beneath the magnificent Castello di Velona, was abandoned in the 1940s until her father-in-law acquired the property in 1992. As Stella points out, this long pause gave the soil a much-needed rest. When she began planting her vineyards a few years later, she found virgin soils laden with minerals, along with an intact and unspoiled ecosystem. This farm's pristine environment and isolated position motivated Stella to embrace certified organic farming methods in 1996 and biodynamic in 2002. Until the 2004 vintage, Stella made only Rossos, wisely preferring to let her vines reach maturity before making Brunello.

Stella's 2004 caught the attention of intrepid Brunello lovers for its intense concentration and flair, but success has not been an easy road. Stella clearly remembers the first time I tried her Rosso during the Benvenuto Brunello press tasting in February 2004, when I frankly commented on their massive tannins and almost scorching alcohol. "When you told me they were unbalanced and dominated by alcohol, you did me a great favor," remembers the winemaker when I visited her estate in 2009. "At the time I thought I wanted to make the big and bold style that everyone assumed the market wanted, but I realized after talking with you that those wines were difficult to drink. Since then, my goal has been to make Brunellos with elegance and balance," adds Stella, who, I am happy to say, has achieved her goal and more. In 2011, I tasted her latest vintages of Brunello and Rosso, and what were once muscular and bitterly tannic, high-octane offerings have been transformed into some of the most exciting, complex, and graceful Brunellos being made, with Stella's passion and commitment transmitted in every glass.

In 1998 Stella stopped using fertilizer in the vineyards because she noticed her varied soil, dominated by rock, schist, and chalk, becoming uniform. According to Stella, besides restoring the soil's former equilibrium, banning fertilizer had the added benefit of allowing her to drastically reduce bunch thinning and green harvesting. "Without fertilizer, the plants have regulated themselves and now naturally produce less grapes," explains Stella. She adds that banning fertilizer and not needing to resort to thinning out have been major factors in lowering the alcohol content. In keeping in tune with her attention to every facet of winemaking, Stella's six vineyards, located between 290 and 380 meters (950 and 1,247 feet) above sea level, are divided into twelve separate parcels based on soil, which are all vinified and aged separately.

Stella's simple cellar covers three floors and is designed to allow the must to naturally flow via gravity into awaiting barrels and eventually into bottles to avoid pumping. Starting in 2001, Stella stopped using selected yeasts, and firmly believes that wild yeasts have further helped her wines attain ideal balance. Fermentation takes place mostly in 35-hectoliter Slavonian oak vats, along with other barrels of varying capacities, while the firm ages the wines in 15- and 17-hectoliter French casks as well as a small amount, about 5 percent, of barriques and tonneaux that have already been used numerous times before. Although Stella makes all final decisions, she proudly admits that before bottling, Brunello's undisputed *maestro,* Giulio Gambelli, tastes the wines and shares his views on the final assembly of grapes from the various parcels for the Brunellos and Rossos.

Production

Total surface area: 13 ha
Brunello: 4.75 ha (12 acres), 7,000 bottles
Rosso: 1 ha (2.47 acres), 6,000 bottles

Brunello. The firm's debut Brunello 2004 is an impressive effort, more masculine than the 2005, with dense fruit, gripping tannins, and lovely minerality and menthol. This needs time to fully develop. The 2005 displays well-integrated oak but is elegant, with delicious strawberry fruit. This will improve with age, and should drink best between 2012 and 2015. The 2006 has striking depth with intense sour-cherry fruit and merely a whiff of oak that does not compromise the purity of fruit. Best 2016 to 2025.

Rosso. Aged for two years in wood, Stella's latest Rossos have been outstanding, thanks to their floral aromas, and the combination of finesse, structure, and restraint that has become the estate's trademark. Supple tannins make these more approachable than the Brunello, and these are perfect to enjoy young.

Tenuta di Collosorbo

Via Villa Sesta 25
Castelnuovo dell'Abate
53024 Montalcino (SI)
Tel. +39 0577 835534
www.collosorbo.com
info@collosorbo.com

After trying a Brunello from Collosorbo during lunch at the Il Pozzo trattoria in Sant'Angelo a few years ago, my husband, Paolo, and I were both so impressed with its floral, earthy aromas and ripe black-cherry and berry flavors that we stopped in unannounced at the winery, which lies midway between Sant'Angelo and Castelnuovo dell'Abate. Owner Giovanna Ciacci happily greeted us and showed us around her small jewel of an estate and opened up the latest vintages for us to try.

Giovanna's estate, with its entrance guarded by two ancient cypress trees, was originally part of the historic Sesta property, with various versions of the name going back all the way to documents from 715. Tenuta di Sesta was founded in the fifteenth century by a rich family from the Republic of Siena; after changing hands several times it was acquired by the Ciacci family in 1850. In 1994 the original estate was divided among family members and a year later Giovanna, formerly a professor of math and biology, founded Collosorbo on her inherited land. The area, known collectively as "Sesta," is in one of the most enviable areas in the denomination. The long hours of sunlight, and warm, dry microclimate that is protected from cold winds by Mount Amiata, favor ideal grape maturation. The harvest tends to occur earlier here than in nearby subzones, meaning that grapes are usually picked before the risk of autumn rain.

The Brunello vineyards average 300 meters (985 feet) above sea level and vines are between five and twenty-three years old. The loose calcareous soil is rich in rock fragments and covers deep layers of clay, lending structure to the wines. Giovanna, who is joined by her two daughters Lucia and Laura Sutera, keeps things straightforward in the cellar, with temperature-controlled fermentation in steel and aging in large oak casks from 12 to 54 hectoliters made of both Slavonian and French oak, three years for Brunello and one for Rosso.

Production

Total surface area: 140 ha (345.8 acres)
Brunello: 11.5 ha (28.4 acres), 50,000 bottles
Rosso: 7.3 ha (18 acres), 30,000 bottles

Brunello.   Intensely perfumed, and thanks to their big sweet-fruit flavors and supple tannins, with hints of spice, mineral, and earth, these Brunellos have wide appeal without being at all international in style. These Brunellos are almost always a great effort even in difficult vintages and are very approachable. This is not a wine I'd like to cellar for ages, though it should drink well for at least ten to fifteen years after the harvest. In exceptional years they also make a more structured and age-worthy Riserva made by first choosing the best grapes from two select vineyards that yield optimal grapes, as well as from a selection carried out in the cellar.

Rosso. This is a brighter version of their Brunello with intense floral aromas accompanied by a vibrant palate loaded with mouthwatering red- and black-fruit flavors and spicy notes. Delicious and easy to drink, thanks to silky tannins.

La Fiorita

Piaggia della Porta 3
Castelnuovo dell'Abate
53024 Montalcino (SI)
Tel. +39 0577 835657
www.fattorialafiorita.it
info@fattorialafiorita.it

La Fiorita makes rich, dense Brunellos loaded with black fruit and spice, and while these may be too round and forward for die-hard Brunello purists, their earthy aromas, juicy flavors, ripe tannins, and lovely acidity are equally hard for Sangiovese fans to resist.

The estate was founded in 1992 by three friends, all dedicated wine lovers, among them consulting enologist Roberto Cipresso, who guides the winemaking. Born in Veneto, upon finishing his agricultural studies in 1986, Cipresso moved to Montalcino, where he cut his teeth at some of the most upcoming estates. By 1987 he was the managing director at Ciacci Piccolomini d'Aragona, a position he had until 1995. Besides his role at La Fiorita, Cipresso consults for several other wineries in Italy and abroad. Lucio Gomero, who also owns a winery in the Colli Euganei denomination in Veneto, and Tiziano Siviero, a former world rally champion, complete the ownership team at La Fiorita.

The winery is in the heart of the tiny hamlet of Castelnuovo dell'Abate, housed in what was once an olive mill beneath a seventeenth-century palazzo that the firm perfectly restored while maintaining the building's original charm. The main vineyards are divided in two areas: Sesta, between Castelnuovo dell'Abate and Sant'Angelo about a mile and a half from the cellars; and Pian Bossolino, further up the road toward Montalcino, near Fattoria dei Barbi. A third, tiny parcel lies just outside the hamlet of Castelnuovo.

The Poggio al Sole vineyard, which translates into Hill in the Sun, in Sesta gives La Fiorita's wines their power and ripe fruit thanks to the lower altitude of 200 meters (656 feet), warmer climate, and calcareous clay soil. The Pian

Bossolino vineyard, in a cooler microclimate, reaches up to 350 to 370 meters (1,150 to 1,215 feet), where the soil is rock and marl, lending the wines their fine aromas, finesse, and fresh acidity. The firm's Sangiovese is the fruit of massal selection performed in vineyards at another Castelnuovo dell'Abate estate where Cipresso used to be in charge of winemaking. The offspring of these mother vines were replanted in La Fiorita's vineyards at high densities of 7,000 and 7,500 vines per hectare, which, along with exceedingly low yields, help create the remarkable concentration of La Fiorita's Brunellos.

Vinification takes place in conical Slavonian oak vats with maceration lasting never more than fifteen days. During fermentation Cipresso uses pump overs and *délestage,* the latter a two-part technique (rack and return of the must) that softens tannins via aeration and produces wines with more fruit character. Aging takes place for two years in wood, the first in 500-liter tonneaux of French oak, a third of which are new, while the rest have been used through one- and two-year aging cycles. The second and final year of mandatory wood aging takes place in Slavonian botti, followed by lengthy bottle aging.

Production

Total surface area: 20 ha (50 acres)
Brunello: 7 ha (18 acres), 25,000 bottles

Brunello. This has always been the focal point of production—La Fiorita makes no Rossos, and until now only a rare Riserva, though this seems to be changing now that the estate's vineyards have reached maturity. The firm's basic Brunellos are loaded with plum, black cherry, and spice, balanced by dramatically ripe, supple tannins and enough fresh acidity and minerality to keep them edgy. La Fiorita's Brunellos are best around ten years after the harvest.

Riserva. La Fiorita 2004 Riserva heralds an important turning point for the estate, since by this time both of the firm's primary vineyards had reached maturity and were in full production. The 2004 Riserva released in 2010 and the 2006 Riserva slated for release in 2012 are both made with grapes exclusively from the Pian Bossolino vineyard. "Our concept of Riserva is really more a concept of terroir. When and if one of the vineyards performs much better than the other, that vineyard will be designated as our Riserva," explains Luigi Peroni, the estate manager. Fermentation and wood aging are the same as for Brunello, though Riservas have one more year in bottle. The outstanding 2004 Riserva showed more complexity than the straight

Brunello, boasting a lovely nose with truffle, ripe berry, earth, and meat juices. Juicy, black-cherry, and plum flavors with loads of spice are well balanced with fresh acidity and big, velvety tannins. More age-worthy than the straight Brunello, will drink best 2015–25. A gorgeous wine.

Le Presi

Via Pantaneto 15
Castelnuovo dell'Abate
53024 Montalcino (SI)
Tel. + 39 0577 835541

Founded by Bruno Fabbri in 1970, this boutique winery handcrafts quintessential Brunello with charm, structure, and finesse. Bruno released his first Brunello in 1978, and in 1998 handed the reins over to his son Gianni. Like his father, Gianni shuns barriques, preferring to make polished but authentic Brunellos.

Grapes are organically farmed on two estate vineyards, Fosso and Piagge, located near Sant'Antimo Abbey. Situated at an altitude of 310 meters (1,017 feet) above sea level, vines have an ideal southeast exposure and are planted in mixed soils composed of stone and sand at densities ranging from 2,550 to 5,550 vines per hectare. Fermentation takes place in temperature-controlled steel tanks at the firm's recently built vinification cellar, while wood aging, exclusively in 10- to 20-hectoliter Slavonian casks, occurs in the family's ancient stone cellars in the heart of Castelnuovo dell'Abate.

Brunello. These are textbook bottlings, with all the floral, earthy, and mineral sensations one would expect from expertly, classically made Brunello. Unfiltered and aged for three years in large casks, these are vibrant wines with great depth.

Riserva. Since 1978, the family has released only six Riservas, made exclusively in outstanding vintages and from only the best grapes that are vinified and aged apart. Unfiltered and aged for four years in botti, the 2004 Riserva is compelling, with layers of cherry, leather, and mineral, and gripping tannins. Well balanced and fresh, this will easily age majestically. Best 2014 to 2034.

Rosso. Lovely, refreshing, and bright. Aged for six months in stainless steel and then ten months in large Slavonian oak.

PART THREE

Beyond Brunello

OTHER WINES AND LOCAL CUISINE

FOURTEEN

Montalcino's Other Wines

ROSSO DI MONTALCINO, MOSCADELLO, AND SANT'ANTIMO

While Montalcino is synonymous with Brunello, the commune's growing area is also home to three other denominations: Rosso di Montalcino DOC, Moscadello di Montalcino DOC, and Sant'Antimo DOC. Besides these three Montalcino-only denominations, some producers also make wine under the Chianti Colli Senesi DOCG and the loosely controlled IGT Toscana.

ROSSO DI MONTALCINO DOC

After Brunello, Rosso di Montalcino, which can be one of the best values in the Italian wine world, is the most important wine in terms of volume, with between 4 and 5 million bottles produced annually. Besides consumer demand for a more everyday alternative to Montalcino's flagship wine that still expresses Sangiovese and Montalcino, Rosso, often made by declassifying a percentage of Brunello production, plays a crucial role in keeping Brunello quality in check. Like Brunello, Rosso di Montalcino is made exclusively with 100 percent Sangiovese, as is stipulated under the regulations that govern its individual production code, but it undergoes far less mandatory aging than its senior partner. Created as the denomination's second wine to be drunk young and fresh, Rosso not only gives consumers a more approachable and economical version of Montalcino's famed Sangiovese for everyday enjoyment; it also closes the income gap for producers while Brunello ages for over four years in their estate cellars. And following in the footsteps of Montalcino's flagship offering, Rosso, aka "baby Brunello," has also generated its share of controversy, starting with its name.

Back in the mid-1960s when many of Montalcino's erstwhile sharecroppers began phasing out their mixed crops and other agricultural activities in order to specialize in Brunello production, the economic sacrifice of allowing newly planted vineyards several years to reach maturation followed by waiting nearly more than four years after the harvest before Brunello could be sold was not just deterring; it would have been economically crippling for all but the handful of already established producers. The solution was to have a second wine, made from the same vineyards, that could be sold one year after the harvest. Even though all the producers were in agreement over the concept of this subordinate bottling, the name of the new wine proved to be a battleground. Tancredi Biondi Santi proposed calling it Rosso di Montalcino, but the newly established estates, united in 1967 by their nascent consorzio, voted against Biondi Santi's proposal and voted instead to call the wine Vino Rosso dai Vigneti di Brunello (Red Wine from Brunello Vineyards). Tancredi, who had not only laid down the foundation for Brunello's strict DOC production code but was also poised to play a major role in the Consorzio, and his son Franco, firmly believed this was a blatant exploitation of the good Brunello name. They thought it would confuse consumers and trick them into mistaking this relatively humble wine for the famed Brunello itself. Tancredi and Franco refused to join the Consorzio over the matter, and the estate would remain outside the Growers' Union until Franco eventually joined nearly forty years later, in 2004, when it evidently made more sense to be part of this growers' union rather than remain outside.

In 1983, the Italian government upgraded Montalcino's lesser bottling, hitherto designated as a simple table wine, by ushering it into the DOC fold of wines regulated under the country's system of checks and controls. However, EU laws governing wine production strictly prohibit using the name of another controlled wine of origin in connection with other bottlings. Forced to drop any mention of Brunello from the label, local winemakers heeded the late Tancredi's advice and renamed the wine Rosso di Montalcino. Rosso di Montalcino DOC's debut hailed the first time in Italy that producers were allowed to obtain two wines of controlled origin from essentially the same vineyards, and set a precedent that paved the way for similar bottlings in other denominations, namely Rosso di Montepulciano and Rosso di Valtellina.

Rosso di Montalcino can be produced either from vineyards registered to Rosso di Montalcino or from vineyards registered to Brunello. It can also be produced by declassifying Brunello production. (Brunello, however, can never be made from Rosso vines, or by "promoting" Rosso production to Brunello production.) Registered Rosso vines are usually either the youngest vines on an estate, or vines located in areas where Sangiovese doesn't yield the cellar-worthy structure required for Brunello, but still yield delicious, lighter-bodied, more immediate wines. Grape yields for Rosso are also at a higher maximum of 90 quintals per hectare, as opposed to Brunello's maximum of 80, further enhancing its lighter style. Most producers make Rosso by combining the various options; they not only have Rosso vines but also declass a percentage of their Brunello production, either in the vineyard by demoting those registered Brunello grapes that don't reach perfect maturation, or more commonly, by declassifying vinified lots that don't have the structure required to sustain Brunello's mandatory aging period. Born to be drunk young and fresh, Rosso can be released starting from September 1 of the year following the harvest, although a number of producers age their Rosso for two years. Aging can take place in either steel or wood, with the majority of producers aging their Rossos between six and nine months in barrels, followed by three to four months in bottle.

A quintessential Rosso di Montalcino should be vibrant, with fresh, succulent fruit sensations, supple tannins, and crisp acidity that make it exceedingly food-friendly. Thankfully, many producers still adhere to this style. The decade since 2000, however, has heralded the advent of a new breed of Rossos—more structured, often with aggressive tannins that need time to soften, and evident alcohol teetering on 14.5 percent, effectively turning many new-generation Rossos into poor imitations of Brunello—packed with structure but lacking the balance and complexity of their more famous sibling. While part of the reason for making a more turbo-charged Rosso is undoubtedly an attempt to gain the attention of critics, the recent escalation in Brunello output is also a major factor. To combat having more Brunello than the market demands, producers are declassifying more Brunello than ever before into the cheaper-to-produce and better-priced Rosso, yet results are decidedly mixed.

Some top producers making outstanding, food-friendly Rossos with superb balance and serious but not overwhelming structure include Paradiso di Manfredi, Gianni Brunelli, Poggio di Sotto, Stella di Campalto, Pertimali, Lisini, Sesti, Altesino, Lambardi, Biondi Santi, and Mastrojanni.

Rosso di Montalcino played a unique part in the aftermath of the Brunellogate scandal, where its role as Brunello's fall guy was underscored.

As several leading producers publicly declared following the grape-blending scandal, the essential problem in the denomination is that not all estates have vineyards in areas where Sangiovese excels, and these estates evidently feel forced to add other grapes to make a quality wine which they still want to call Brunello di Montalcino. Seeing that this clearly violates the wine's production code, soon after the scandal broke there was fierce debate among local producers over relaxing the production regulations to allow other grapes into Brunello.

Back in the autumn of 2008, in the uncertain aftermath of the Brunellogate scandal and just before Montalcino's producers were set to vote on changing Brunello's production code, some influential producers, namely Franco Biondi Santi, supported by Col d'Orcia's Francesco Marone Cinzano, advocated relaxing the 100 percent Sangiovese rule for Rosso di Montalcino, allowing producers the option of adding other grapes to the denomination's second wine. This was quite obviously done with the best intentions. The thinking was that this solution would save Brunello, which would continue to be made exclusively with Sangiovese, but at the same time permit producers the freedom to use international grapes in a wine that was not only already famous but that also boasted the Montalcino name. As was to be expected, the recommendation stirred fierce debate and thankfully the proposal was shot down in October 2008 when producers voted overwhelmingly to leave both Brunello and Rosso di Montalcino as 100 percent Sangiovese.

While this seemed the end of it, just as this book was being wrapped up in September 2011, the issue was raised again but this time the stakes were much higher. The Consorzio's board of directors called for a new vote on September 7 to decide on changing Rosso's production code, and as Col d'Orcia's Francesco Marone Cinzano told me, there was no warning and no discussion between the Consorzio and its members on the matter before producers received a letter announcing the assembly just a few weeks before the vote.

Not only did the Consorzio's board of directors break the unwritten rule that such assemblies and votes never be called during the harvest and pre-harvest period, but the proposals themselves shocked producers and the media. The Consorzio proposed creating up to three tiers of Rosso di Montalcino—Rosso di Montalcino Sangiovese Superiore, Rosso di Montalcino Sangiovese, and Rosso di Montalcino, the latter of which would allow up to 15 percent other grapes. Not only would this have caused tremendous consumer confusion, but under the proposals, the wine currently known as

Rosso di Montalcino would have become a blended wine. Other proposed changes included permitting emergency irrigation and allowing lesser vineyard sites into the Rosso fold, opening the door to converting land currently registered to Sant'Antimo, IGT Toscana, and Vino da Tavola, to be upgraded to Rosso di Montalcino vineyards. Not only would these measures have compromised overall quality, but they would have increased the amount of Rosso di Montalcino in an already saturated market. But most importantly, the proposals would have dumbed down Rosso di Montalcino, turning it into just another blended wine in the plethora of Sangiovese blends coming out of Tuscany. Observers are convinced the move was initiated by the larger wineries who have hundreds of hectares of registered Sant'Antimo and IGT vineyards, which currently produce wines that do not sell.

While wine writers such as Nicolas Belfrage, who initially signaled the alarm, Franco Ziliani, and myself wrote letters and articles and implored producers to vote no, even the initial supporters of the measure three years ago, Marone Cinzano and Franco Biondi Santi, had changed their minds given the drastic conditions stipulated under the new proposals. "In 2008 I thought that permitting 3 to 5 percent of international grapes into Rosso would help producers who had Sangiovese vines in unsuitable places. But since then, it's clear that some producers are trying to find a solution for the 400 hectares registered to Sant'Antimo and 400 registered to IGT. Allowing 15 percent other grapes is unacceptable, as are all the proposed changes to vineyard prerequisites," explained Biondi Santi. Or as Marone Cinzano stated, it would be "the path to plonk." Fortunately, Montalcino's producers turned out in full force and threw out the proposed changes to Rosso, with 69 percent of producers voting no. So at least for now, as of 2011, Rosso remains 100 percent Sangiovese.

MOSCADELLO DI MONTALCINO DOC

Although vines that yielded this once legendary dessert wine had nearly died out by the mid-twentieth century, a small group of producers have painstakingly revived this native variety and wine, saving Moscadello di Montalcino from certain extinction. Production remains tiny, with only 50 hectares (124 acres) dedicated to Moscadello, translating into about 80,000 bottles annually.

As already mentioned in the discussion of the birth of Brunello in chapter 3, Moscadello was once the township's cherished nectar, lauded as far back as the sixteenth century when, according to both legend and documents, even several popes enjoyed a glass or two of the celebrated wine and ordered that quantities of it be shipped from Sant'Antimo to the Vatican. Poets also sang the wine's praise, and Francesco Redi's seventeenth-century dithyrambic ode to the greatest wines in Tuscany, *Bacco in Toscana,* sealed Moscadello's celebrity status both in Italy and abroad, resulting in albeit brief popularity at the English royal court, as narratives from the day attest.

Although Moscadello, made by a native strain of the Muscat grape or Moscato Bianco, thrived in the eighteenth and nineteenth centuries, by the late nineteenth century Brunello production was supplanting that of Moscadello. The Moscadello grape also proved extremely susceptible to oidium and peronospora (downy mildew), vine diseases that were inadvertently imported from America in the latter half of the nineteenth century, followed by phylloxera, which virtually wiped out production by the early twentieth century. While these maladies also wreaked havoc on Sangiovese and other vines, farmers replanted the latter while Moscadello, by all accounts a very difficult and delicate grape to cultivate and vinify, was left to languish into near oblivion.

In the 1960s, very few producers possessed any of the original vines or produced the once legendary wine. Tancredi Biondi Santi's 1969 Moscadello, of which only 80 bottles now remain, was the last produced by the estate before Franco pulled up what few vines remained, and his father's late-harvest version was still exquisite when tasted in 2009. In the early 1960s, Il Poggione began planting new vines from old plants it had discovered on the estate, and in 1965, Caprili also planted 60 plants of Moscadello di Montalcino clones culled from an old vineyard near Poggio alle Mura. Using clones selected from these 60 plants, Caprili then planted a new Moscadello vineyard in the early 1990s; today they make a lovely, refreshing Moscadello made to be consumed young.

Encouraged by the Brunello Consorzio to resurrect the area's historic wine, today nearly a dozen firms produce Moscadello di Montalcino, which became DOC in 1984. Col d'Orcia is another prime Moscadello maker, and the firm has planted an experimental vineyard with 80 presumed Moscadello clones native to Montalcino for research that should eventually lead to improving and expanding production. While this impressive recovery bodes well for the wine's future, not all of the Moscadello di Montalcino made today comes from Montalcino's original clones, but descends from clones and plants originating in other areas, namely Piedmont. Unsurprisingly, Montalcino's native clones that have had centuries to conform to their environment generate the most fascinating results. Moscadello di Montalcino must be made solely with the Moscato Bianco grape cultivated in Montalcino, and the wine can be produced in three different versions; sparkling, late-harvest, and a still version. Il Poggione is currently the sole estate making a sparkling Moscadello, produced using the Charmat method whereby a second fermentation takes place in a steel tank. Redolent with intense floral and Muscat grape aromas, it also has surprising structure along with a sweet but crisp palate that makes it perfect to pair with creamy desserts or dry pastries. The still version also boasts intense varietal aromas and flavors, and Caprili's is my favorite. Delicious and refreshing, its lovely acidity and long, clean finish keep it from being too sweet. This is a wonderful wine with which to top off a meal, with or without the fruit tart usually recommended as the ideal pairing. Capanna also makes a wonderful still Moscadello, and Pertimali's is quite good as well. The late-harvest version, for the most part made by cutting the vine branches and then leaving grapes on the vine to dry or raisin out, is the most popular style today. Deep golden yellow, this rendition has impressive structure, and floral, honey, and apricot sensations with hints of herbs and spice. Late-harvest Moscadellos boast concentrated palates, though once again fresh acidity saves them from being cloying, making late-harvest Moscadello a perfect *vino da meditazione* to sip after dinner or to pair with dry biscuits and tarts.

SANT'ANTIMO DOC

Of all of Montalcino's wines, Sant'Antimo DOC, created in 1996, are the least interesting. This almost open-ended designation has little to do with Montalcino, Tuscany, or even Italy for that matter. Made from virtually any grape variety or blend of varieties from the long list of grapes, red or white, that are authorized to grow in Tuscany, wines made under Sant'Antimo DOC are direct descendants of the once rebellious but now passé Super Tuscans. Although Tuscany's cult bottlings, such as Sassicaia and Tignanello, which shook up Italy's stagnant wine scene in the late 1970s, 1980s, and 1990s, and were once deemed innovative, Italy has since become inundated with wines made partially or entirely with international grapes. New World countries, including the United States, Australia, and Argentina, have gained a large market share of wines made with the so-called international grapes, leaving Tuscany's expensive Merlot, Cabernets, and Syrahs largely abandoned by consumers who now look to similar but much cheaper New World alternatives of wines made with the same grapes.

During the height of the Super Tuscan craze, Montalcino's producers voted to have a new wine that would allow them to make wines with international grapes. Even if, in theory, producers can make Sant'Antimo DOC with Sangiovese that either does not excel enough for Brunello or Rosso production, or a Sangiovese wine that doesn't adhere to Brunello or Rosso's strict production codes, the main idea behind the appellation was to give producers a viable option to make so-called Super Tuscans with grapes other than Sangiovese. Sant'Antimo allows so much flexibility in terms of grapes, vinification, and aging that there are no defining styles or characteristics for wines made under this designation. They can run the gamut from vapid Pinot Grigios to full-bodied, new world–styled Bordeaux blends, and if anything, the only common denominator is a clear lack of identity. While some Sant'Antimos, mostly red, are technically of good, some even very good quality, consumers' preference for Italy's terroir-driven wines made from indigenous grapes makes Sant'Antimo DOC a hard sell these days, as can be seen from the downward spiral in its production. If in the beginning of 2008 there were 900 hectares (2,224 acres) of Sant'Antimo vines that produced 700,000 bottles, these numbers plummeted to 600 hectares (1,483 acres) producing 500,000 bottles by early 2010. By 2011 there were only about 450 hectares (1,112 acres) of registered Sant'Antimo vines, clearly demonstrating the lack of interest on the part of both consumers and producers. In 2011, Ezio Rivella, the president of the Consorzio and Banfi's enologist and managing director from 1978 until 2000, and a huge supporter of Sant'Antimo DOC in 1996, admitted that it "never really took off."

Disregarding the fundamental problems facing what is now an unfashionable denomination, some producers believe that a name change might be just the answer to the designation's woes. Ever since the 2008 Brunellogate grape-blending scandal, Montalcino's winemakers have debated substituting Sant'Antimo with a different designation. Several prominent producers that had invested heavily in Sant'Antimo, many with large tracts of land in the south of the denomination that they planted with international vines, are apparently advocating to change the name of the Sant'Antimo DOC to one that would promote Montalcino, arguing that Sant'Antimo does not provide immediate consumer recognition—hence the sluggish sales. One proposal was "Montalcino DOC," which would have united (and replaced) the three current DOCs of Sant'Antimo, Rosso di Montalcino, and Moscadello di

Montalcino. Even though producers voted this idea down in 2008, most of Montalcino's producers fear the issue will resurface, and that certain estates will push for an umbrella Montalcino denomination, resulting in labels such as Montalcino DOC Merlot for example. It goes without saying, however, that an umbrella Montalcino DOC would create consumer confusion especially in regard to Rosso di Montalcino DOC, prompting several key players to propose changing the name of the latter to Rosso di Montalcino Superiore or Rosso di Montalcino Sangiovese. However, rather than help sell Merlot or Syrah, an umbrella Montalcino DOC would only dent the prestige of both Brunello and Rosso as well as that of Montalcino. Giving Sant'Antimo a more prestigious name would not change the simple fact that consumers simply don't want to purchase Cabernet, Merlot, Bordeaux blends, or Pinot Grigio, made in Montalcino's vineyards, not only because they would be overpriced compared to the New World offerings due to Italy's labor laws that ensure high costs, but because these wines don't excel here, as does Sangiovese when planted in the right areas.

CHIANTI COLLI SENESI DOCG

Besides having its own denominations, Montalcino also lies within the enormous Chianti DOCG-producing area, and specifically in the large Chianti subzone Colli Senesi, or Siena's hills. Under its production code, Chianti Colli Senesi must be made from at least 80 percent Sangiovese. Chianti Colli Senesi is made by the some of largest wineries in Montalcino, although a few of the mid-sized and even a few small estates also make this designation. However, most producers in the denomination put their efforts into Brunello and Rosso or IGT Toscana.

IGT TOSCANA

IGT (Indicazione Geografica Tipica) is the most flexible of Italy's designations. As the name IGT Toscana suggests, wines falling under this specification can be produced anywhere in the entire region. While Sant'Antimo DOC has limited controls over yields and, more importantly, stipulates that grape origin must be from within the denomination, grapes for IGT Toscana can be sourced from throughout the region.

At the time of this book's writing, a number of Montalcino's producers were pulling their vines from the Sant'Antimo DOC registers and enrolling them as IGT because they felt that IGT Toscana offers more name recognition for consumers than does Sant'Antimo. IGT is also a completely elastic designation and far less controlled than DOC.

Following the national trend, more Montalcino producers than ever are also adding to their range of wines a *rosato* made from rosé vinification of Sangiovese grapes or by bleeding the must during Brunello or Rosso production (commonly done to concentrate color). Since Sant'Antimo DOC covers only red or white wines, Montalcino's winemakers are forced to label their *rosato* under IGT Toscana.

FIFTEEN

Brunello, Rosso, and Food Pairing

Brunello, like Italian wines in general, is a food-friendly wine, but unlike most other full-bodied, age-worthy red wines, Brunello is surprisingly flexible with what it can be paired with. Barolo, for example, needs the heady aromas and flavors of truffle and porcini mushrooms or rich beef dishes, while Brunello, which also pairs wonderfully with such big, rich dishes, also makes an exquisite companion to lighter fare—everything from gnocchi with four-cheese sauce, to white meats, to (believe it or not) some fish dishes. Here, however, I do have to put in a disclaimer: densely concentrated and wood-driven wines—whether they be Brunello, Chianti Classico, or Super Tuscans—are extremely difficult to pair with food. All of the pairings recommended in this section are for full-bodied but brighter, less extracted Brunellos and of course Rossos that are not dominated by oak.

With the exception of a glass of spumante or prosecco as an aperitif, the Italian approach to wine is that it be consumed at the table. At the risk of scandalizing gastronomists, when pairing such great, structured wines like Brunello, and even the more approachable Rosso di Montalcino with dishes, I often choose my wine first, and then decide what I want to eat with it, but of course the more common approach is to choose your dish, then your wine. Fortunately Sangiovese is very versatile, so the task at hand is relatively easy. Brunello and Rosso di Montalcino cover a very wide spectrum of pairings. While they match particularly well with traditional dishes from Montalcino and Siena, they also work perfectly well with Italian and international cuisine.

As a rule of thumb, Rosso di Montalcino is the perfect accompaniment for pasta and tomato dishes, soups, and white meat. Brunello, more complex, pairs better with richer dishes, including those with a lot of cheese, dense Tuscan soups like *ribollita,* red meats, and pecorino cheese, although some of the more refined Brunellos make a divine match with *baccalà* or cod. Brunello Riservas, especially when they are in the prime of youth, up to fifteen or twenty years old, should be paired with more demanding dishes such as the classic Florentine steak. However, contrary to what many would expect, as Riservas reach advanced age they become more delicate; once-aggressive tannins turn silky and bracing acidity tames down. As a result, older Riservas should be paired with more delicate foods without strong sauces or condiments. The oldest Riservas, those from the 1950s, 1960s, and 1970s, also make wonderful *vino da meditazione,* to be sipped at the end of the meal in place of dessert, or as some would suggest, in front of a crackling fire on an autumn or winter night. But part of the fun of food and wine pairing with Brunello is experimenting. Thanks to its food flexibility, you'll come up with surprising matches.

ORDERING BRUNELLO AT A RESTAURANT

One of the most misguided assumptions is that Italians eat something under every category found on a typical Italian menu: antipasto, primo piatto, secondo piatto, contorno, dolce (appetizer, first course, second course, side dishes, dessert). This could not be further from the truth, although it is undoubtedly true that when visiting journalists (or visiting relatives for that matter) spend time in Italy, the red carpet of Italian cuisine is rolled out. However, Italians, as a rule, never eat all this, either at lunch or dinner, except perhaps at a wedding, or when they are wine producers hosting hungry international journalists. So when visiting Italy, feel free to mix and match the categories and order as much or as little as you wish.

Given that Brunello does need time to aerate, although I don't usually like to decant wines, it may be necessary at a restaurant.

GREAT BOTTLES AT HOME: TO DECANT OR NOT DECANT?

One of the beauties of an older Brunello and, even more so, an aged Riserva is the evolution of wine over a number of hours after the bottle is opened. Decanting interrupts this natural evolution, and although the procedure is almost unavoidable at restaurants, opening a bottle three to four hours ahead of time is my preferred method at home. Decanting is a controversial subject, but most winemakers who produce wines destined for long cellaring prefer that the bottle be opened hours beforehand as opposed to decanting, which many winemakers feel can cause shock. Or as Maria Teresa Mascarello, daughter of famed Barolo maker Bartolo Mascarello, puts it, "Decanting an older or old vintage is traumatic for the wine. It's like going up to an eighty-five-year-old person and shaking him or her violently. It is harmful, if not to say life-threatening."

TYPICAL MONTALCINO DISHES

It is hard to distinguish Montalcino cuisine from that of Siena because their respective histories are so intertwined. There are some variations and preferences in Montalcino, however, that are worth noting, the most prominent being that more emphasis is placed on ingredients coming directly from the countryside, such as the fresh aromatic herbs that are widely used in many Montalcino dishes:

basilico (basil): generally used crude in sauces

rosmarino (rosemary): used with red meat and fish, often seen on Montalcino estates in wild bushes with their characteristic purple flowers

salvia (sage): used in roasts and wild game

pepolino (thyme): also known as *timo* in the rest of Italy, used crude in salads or cooked in sauces

dragoncello (tarragon): found growing abundantly near Sant'Antimo Abbey, often used raw as seasoning to accompany salami and cold meats

borrana (wild borage): also grows around Sant'Antimo, blue leaves used in salads, also fried or cooked as fritters usually with anchovies and served as a side dish

Many dishes are amazingly simple to prepare, and their extraordinary quality is very much a result of the freshness of the ingredients and their unusual but insightful combination. In general, the Sienese cooking makes a larger use of garlic and aromatic herbs, such as dragoncello, when compared to the rest of the region.

Given that wine is the absolute protagonist in Montalcino, not enough is said about the denomination's olive oil but it too is outstanding. Many wine producers have olive trees in select plots near their vineyards, and just by looking at the manicured olive groves it is easy to imagine the great results they yield. Extra virgin, the most precious in the olive oil hierarchy, is also the healthiest and the most naturally produced. The taste and overall quality of olive oil is influenced not only by the soil on which the olive trees grow but also by the moment when the olives are harvested and milled; unripe olives produce bitter oil while overripe olives produce rancid oil so it is extremely important to only pick when the olives are perfectly ripened. Thanks to the bounty of the excellent local produce, extra virgin olive oil plays a major role in Montalcino's local cuisine, while other vegetable fats and butter are almost nonexistent.

Antipasti

Crostini alla senese (Rosso di Montalcino). Crostini are thin slices of toasted bread, topped with a vegetable or meat spread. It is the standard Sienese antipasto in a wide variety of flavors:

crostini di fegatini: Chicken liver cooked in extra virgin olive oil and onions. Usually cooked with a little Vin Santo, crushed capers, and black pepper.

crostini di milza (also called *crostini neri*): Beef spleen dipped in extra virgin olive oil and onions, crushed and slowly cooked in white wine, then cooked in broth. Anchovies and capers are added later.

crostini con i funghi: Usually done with fresh field mushrooms *(prataioli)*, which enjoy a longer growing season than more precious porcini or *ovoli*. The mushrooms are cooked in extra virgin olive oil along with garlic, onion, parsley, and then pureed.

crostini al pomodoro: Chopped fresh tomatoes, minced garlic, capers, and olive oil. Fresh *dragoncello* is sometimes put on top of each crostino right before serving.

Bruschetta (Rosso di Montalcino). Grilled Tuscan (unsalted) bread with fresh garlic and a drizzle of extra virgin olive oil. A common variation to the basic but very tasty version involves topping with fresh tomatoes cut in small pieces, garlic, and basil.

Salumi senesi (Rosso di Montalcino). There is a wealth of handcrafted products of unusual cold cuts in Tuscany, locally known as *soppressate, salami, finocchiona, capocolli, salsicce*. There are also versions made from *cinta senese* and *cinghiale* or wild boar. The *cinta senese* is the only pig native to Tuscany to survive extinction. It is so called because of the white strip around the middle (*cinta* means "belt").

Primi Piatti

Pinci all'aglione (Rosso di Montalcino). *Pinci* (called *pici* in Siena) are thick, handmade strands of pasta. *Aglione* is browned garlic sautéed with a little shredded hot pepper, diced fresh tomatoes, peeled and without seeds, added at the end.

Ribollita (Rosso or Brunello di Montalcino). *Ribollita*, whose name literally means "reboiled," was originally made by slowly reheating the leftover soup from the previous day. Slow cooking is the secret of this hearty and thick vegetable soup that is best made on wood stoves or back burners. There are many variations but the main ingredients always include leftover Tuscan bread (unsalted), beans (preferably white varieties like *cannellini* or *toscanelli*), *cavolo nero* (black Tuscan kale), onion, and garlic. It is served hot with freshly ground pepper and extra virgin olive oil.

Pappardelle al sugo di cinghiale (Brunello di Montalcino). The wild boar sauce used for serving over this dish is a lighter version of the *scottiglia di cinghiale* described below, with smaller pieces of meat and more tomatoes. *Pappardelle* is a flat pasta cut into broad ribbon shapes about one inch wide, traditionally served with very rich sauces, most commonly wild boar.

Pappa col (al) pomodoro (Rosso di Montalcino). This thick and delicious soup is made with lightly cooked fresh tomatoes and basil, stale bread, garlic, served with extra virgin olive oil, and black pepper. Usually served hot, in the summer this refreshing soup can also be served cold.

Acquacotta alla senese (Rosso di Montalcino). A soup made with mushrooms, usually *ordinali* or *prugnoli*, lightly sautéed in extra virgin olive oil and garlic, mixed with lightly cooked fresh tomatoes.

Risotto al Brunello (Brunello di Montalcino). Risotto is a typical dish of northern regions such as Lombardy and Piedmont, where rice is cultivated. *Risotto al Barolo* is a classic northern dish made with rice cooked with Barolo, Parmesan cheese, and butter. Replacing butter with olive oil, Barolo with

Brunello, and Parmesan cheese with seasoned pecorino turns this Piedmont specialty into a delicious Brunello-inspired meal.

Secondi Piatti

Scottiglia di cinghiale (Brunello di Montalcino).   This hearty wild boar stew is a classic match with Brunello di Montalcino. Made with wild boar that has been marinated in Rosso di Montalcino and then cooked in extra virgin olive oil with onion, garlic, tomato sauce, rosemary, and sage.

Pollo con le olive (Brunello di Montalcino).   Chicken breast cooked in extra virgin olive oil, garlic, and sage leaves, topped with green olives.

Lesso rifatto (Brunello di Montalcino).   So-called *lesso rifatto,* or recooked boiled meat, is a by-product of making broth, very common in households before the advent of bouillon. Made with fresh tomatoes, extra virgin olive oil, onion, garlic, and carrot.

Frittata con gli zoccoli (Rosso di Montalcino).   Senese (and other Tuscan) *frittate* or omelets differ from French omelets in that they are cooked slowly in extra virgin olive oil rather than butter and are served when they are firm but still soft. This version is very popular in Montalcino and consists of small cubes of prosciutto added to the eggs together with some grated pecorino cheese. Other typical *frittate* are made with wild asparagus, zucchini flowers, or porcini mushrooms.

Baccalà alla livornese (Rosso or Brunello di Montalcino).   Salted cod (*baccalà*) that is dusted with flour then cooked with garlic, onion, extra virgin olive oil, together with chopped basil, parsley, tomatoes, and a little red wine. Although white wine is almost universally suggested to pair with fish, this savory dish cries out for Rosso or one of the more elegant Brunellos.

Contorni e Formaggi

Fagioli all'uccelletto (Rosso di Montalcino).   Cannellini beans cooked with garlic and sage leaves in extra virgin olive oil and served with a drizzle of extra virgin olive oil and black pepper.

Pecorino di Pienza (Rosso or Brunello di Montalcino).   This sheep's milk cheese gets its name from the ancient city of Pienza, located just a few miles from Montalcino. It is widely agreed that the best Pienza pecorino is produced in the Crete Senesi. Sheep were probably being raised in Tuscany since before the Etruscans; Pliny the Elder documented their presence during the Roman age. Pecorino di Pienza is a cheese made with whole, raw milk from Sardinian sheep or sheep from the Apeninnes. The sheep are raised out in the open and graze on local grass and herbs. The aromas of rare plants that grow in the clay soil of the Crete Senesi (wormwood, meadow salsify, juniper, broom, burnet, etc.) can be sensed in the sheep's milk and are the reason why raw milk is still used by some producers, in the belief that pasteurization destroys flavor-producing bacteria and the subtle fragrances that the sheep's open pasture diet imparts to milk. Some artisans use a vegetal rennet made from the stamen of wild cardoon (instead of veal rennet), a feature that might appeal to strict vegetarians.

Marzolino (Rosso or Brunello di Montalcino). Named after the first grass appearing in March, this famous cheese is produced with pure sheep's milk. The still sparse spring grass often contains thyme and other aromatic herbs that carry over into this tangy cheese.

Other Dishes

Ravioli maremmani (Brunello di Montalcino). These oversized ravioli are filled with sheep ricotta and chard or spinach and usually served with freshly grated pecorino cheese and extra virgin olive oil infused with sage.

Bistecca alla fiorentina (Brunello di Montalcino). Often compared to either a Porterhouse steak or a T-bone, the real difference with the Florentine steak is the *chianina,* one of the oldest and largest existing beef cattle breeds in the world. Because of the size reached by the animals, the steaks can easily exceed six pounds.

Peposo (Brunello di Montalcino). *Peposo* is a traditional, slow-cooked beef shank. Numerous sources attribute its origins to the 1430s, when Brunelleschi was supervising the construction of Santa Maria del Fiore, the Duomo in Florence. The original recipe is amazingly simple and prepared with four local ingredients: beef shank, garlic, red wine (most likely what we now know as Chianti), and salt, with the addition of an unusually generous quantity of black pepper, at the time a very expensive and exotic spice. At the end of the workday on the Duomo, the ingredients for *peposo* were put in a clay pot and placed in the kiln that during the day had fired the terra-cotta tiles for the dome. Overnight, the residual heat cooked the stew and by the morning the smaller bits of meat and pepper had broken down into a thick and dark sauce giving it a characteristic flavor of wine, lean meat, and pepper. Cooks now add mushrooms, onions, and other ingredients not available at the time, including tomatoes. *Peposo* is usually served on toasted bread or mashed potatoes.

APPENDIX A

Vintage Guide to Brunello

The star rating in this section is taken from the Consorzio's vintage rating guide, bestowed at least in the past few decades after chemical and physical analysis carried out by a tasting committee of twenty industry professionals who work in Montalcino. However, particularly since 2000, many vintage ratings appear to be overly optimistic; it is clearly in the Consorzio's short-term interests to boost vintage classification, even if by doing so the ratings have lost some credibility. I have added notes where I want to add any relevant information, and where I disagree with the official vintage ratings. Starting with 1990, I also suggest drink or hold. For detailed tasting notes on many older vintages please see the profiles of Biondi Santi, Costanti, Il Poggione, Col d'Orcia, and Lisini.

1945 *****	1951 ****	1957 ****	1963 ***	1969 **
1946 ****	1952 ***	1958 ****	1964 *****	1970 *****
1947 ****	1953 ***	1959 ***	1965 ****	1971 ***
1948 **	1954 **	1960 ***	1966 ****	1972 *
1949 ***	1955 *****	1961 *****	1967 ****	1973 ***
1950 ****	1956 **	1962 ****	1968 ***	1974 **

1975 ***** A breathtaking vintage still going strong. See profiles on Biondi Santi and Lisini.
1976 *
1977 **** A surprising vintage that has aged very well. Drink.

1978 ****	1981 ***	1984 *	1987 ***
1979 ****	1982 ****	1985 *****	1988 *****
1980 ****	1983 ****	1986 ***	1989 **

1990 ★★★★★ An excellent vintage. Drink.

1991 ★★★★ Drink.

1992 ★★ Drink.

1993 ★★★★ Drink.

1994 ★★★★ Drink.

1995 ★★★★★ An outstanding vintage. Drink or hold.

1996 ★★★ Drink.

1997 ★★★★★ With very few exceptions, this is an extremely overrated vintage. A very warm year yielded wines that were soft, ripe, and approachable in their youth. Wines hailing from the higher reaches and closer to Montalcino fared the best and are aging well, but with few exceptions, this is to drink now. A horizontal tasting of 1997 in 2006 also showed that those Brunellos aged in barriques had not held up at all, with wood and alcohol dominating, while Brunellos from the classic zone and those offerings aged in large casks were aging the best. Drink. (Biondi Santi's 1997: hold.)

1998 ★★★★ A sleeper vintage. Austere when first released, this evolved very slowly and bloomed after ten years. Drink or hold for another decade.

1999 ★★★★ An excellent vintage that is starting to bloom now but can be aged for another decade. Drink or hold.

2000 ★★★ A very hot, dry year that produced warm, forward wines, especially exaggerated in the far south. Not a vintage for aging. Drink now.

2001 ★★★★ This is one of the few underrated vintages that deserved five stars. Well balanced and cellar-worthy across the denomination. Hold.

2002 ★★ A terrible vintage due to torrential rains at harvest time in September, though areas further south fared better. The higher reaches closer to the Montalcino fared the worst. Drink now.

2003 ★★★★ Overrated. One of the hottest, driest vintages ever in all of Italy. In Montalcino, Brunellos from the highest reaches closest to Montalcino fared better thanks to more elevated acidity. Other areas suffered from cooked fruit and low acidity, and had bitter tannins because the plants, which shut down during the severe heat and water stress, could not reach ideal ripening. Lowest vineyards in the deep south of the denomination suffered the worst. Drink now.

2004 ★★★★★ A gorgeous vintage. Sangiovese reached perfect maturation throughout the growing zone. The 2004s are defined by their impeccable balance and serious aging potential. Hold.

2005 ★★★★ Rain during the harvest compromised the crop in most of the denomination. While these Brunellos are not complex, and do not have age-worthy structures, they are perfect to enjoy now while the 2004s age. The 2005s are surprisingly elegant, almost delicate. When compared to the excellent 1999 and 2001 harvests, this should be a three-star vintage. Drink.

2006 ★★★★★ Overrated. If some 2006s boast exceptional structure and balance, many more are unbalanced, with massive tannins, low acidity, and soaring alcohol, sometimes topping 15 and 15.5 percent. While tannins need time to tame, due to lack of acidity, many will not age well. Drink or hold.

(2007 ★★★★★) To be released in 2012. Based on Rosso and barrel samples, looks to be a very good if somewhat forward and warm vintage.

(2008 ★★★★) This won't be out until 2013, so evolution in wood during the aging process will be crucial. At the moment quality appears to be good but not exceptional. An intense hailstorm that steamed through the denomination in mid-August wiped out 40 percent of the crop in much of Sant'Angelo, so quantity will be down. This, and warm dry weather afterward, kept rot at bay and generated better-than-expected quality.

(2009 ★★★★) To be released in 2014. Rainy weather lasted through July, followed by very hot and dry summer, though vines had enough water reserves to avoid heat and water stress. Based on Rosso 2009, this promises both structure and finesse with firm tannins and good acidity.

(2010 ★★★★★) To be released in 2015. A wet and cold spring delayed bud break and overall yields were down 10 percent. The hot summer allowed for good ripening and the vintage shows unusually high extract, as well as high alcohol content.

APPENDIX B

Brunello at a Glance

BRUNELLO ESTATES

Brunello estates are for the most part tiny, with 22 percent of estates having less than 1 hectare of vines, 29 percent have between 1 and 3 hectares, 15 percent possess between 3 and 5 hectares, 15 percent have between 5 and 15 hectares, 9 percent between 15 and 100 hectares, and only 1 percent own more than 100 hectares. Nine percent are solely commercial enterprises.

A hectare of Brunello vines cost the equivalent of €15,537 in 1967; in 2007 the same land cost €350,000—an increase of 2,153 percent.

VINES AND TERROIR

Brunello can be made from vines that are three years old, although until vines are five years old maximum grape yields are lower than for mature vines five and over. (Barolo's recent modifications stipulate a scale of reduced grape yields for vines from three to seven years old, as is already the case in Barbaresco, while vines must be at least four years old in Chianti Classico.)

Brunello and Rosso vines are dry-farmed, no irrigation is allowed, not even emergency irrigation during severe heat stress.

Brunello and Rosso cannot be made from vines situated over 600 meters (1,969 feet) above sea level, yet there is no established minimum altitude for the denomination. Vino Nobile, on the other hand, can only be produced from vines between 250 meters (820 feet) and 600 meters (1,969 feet), while recent modifications for Barolo stipulate that vines have to be between 170 meters (558 feet) and 540 meters (1,772 feet).

According to the Brunello production code, vines must be on land originating from the Cretaceous period to the Pliocene epoch, which basically covers most terrain in the Montalcino denomination. (Chianti Classico restricts land deemed not suitable for vines. Vines on humid terrain, valley floors, and land with a strong presence of Pliocene clay or predominantly dense clay are prohibited from producing Chianti Classico, while Barolo's regulations categorically prohibit vines on flat terrain and valley floors.)

BLENDING VINTAGES

Producers can add up to 15 percent of another Brunello vintage in the cellar to another vintage, younger or older, that is also in the cellar, in order to add freshness or structure, as the case may be. This is a measure allowed at the EU level for all wines.

AGING

Brunello must age for just over four years (five for Riserva) in estate cellars before release, and cannot be released before January 1 five calendar years (six for Riserva) after the harvest with the calculated period including the harvest year. (For example, 2004 Brunellos were released starting in January 2009, while the 2004 Riservas were released starting in January 2010.) This is the longest mandatory aging period for Italian wines. (Barolo has three years mandatory cellaring before release, eighteen months of which must be in wood.)

Brunello must be aged for at least two years in wood and four months in bottle (six months in bottle for Riserva).

PRODUCTION

There are 250 growers and 200 producers making Brunello from 2,100 hectares (5,189 acres) of registered Brunello vines. Annual bottle production is approximately 8 million bottles a year, 25 percent of which is exported to the United States.

LABELING

Brunello grower-producers (as in all of Italy) write *imbottigliato all'origine,* which corresponds to estate bottled in the United States, while *imbottigliato dal viticoltore* means that the wine was bottled by the grower. *Imbottigliato all'origine dal viticoltore* states that not only do the grapes come from the same estate where the wine is made, but it is bottled by the grower himself or herself. However, most growers who make the wine and bottle use the first version out of simplicity.

The phrase *imbottigliato da,* followed by an estate or producer name, means that the bottler bought the wine in bulk from a grower or another producer.

FOUNDING FATHERS OF THE CONSORZIO

The following people were the founding members of the Brunello Consorzio in 1967, and the names appear in the order in which they appear in official documents relating to the incorporation of the Consorzio: Nello Baricci, Silvio Nardi, Siro Pacenti, Gino Zannoni, Lucia Perina, Milena Perina, Orazio Machetti, Elina Lisini, Dino Ciacci, Guglielmo Martini, Emilio Costanti, Sabatino Gorelli, Assunto Pieri, Manfredi Martini, Ivo Buffi, Giovanni Colombini, Rev. don Leopoldo Bianchi, Loffredo Gaetani Lovatelli, Giuseppe Cencioni, Bramante Martini, Leopoldo Franceschi, Pierluigi Fioravanti, Silvano Lambardi, Annunziato Franci, and Ferruccio Ferretti.

CONSORZIO PRESIDENTS

1967–69	Leopoldo Franceschi
1969–70	Pier Luigi Fioravanti
1970	Elina Lisini
1970–73	Paolo Fioravanti

1974–82	Bruno Ciatti
1982–88	Enzo Tiezzi
1988–92	Ermanno Rosi
1992–95	Sante Turone
1995–98	Andrea Costanti
1998–2007	Baldassarre Filippo Fanti
2007–8	Francesco Marone Cinzano
2008–10	Patrizio Cencioni
2010–	Ezio Rivella

ESTATES TO WATCH THROUGHOUT THE DENOMINATIONS

Baccinetti	Fattoi	Pietroso
Citille di Sopra	Ferro	San Giacomo
Colleceto	Fornacina	Sesta di Sopra
Col di Lamo	Lazzeretti	Solaria
Domus Vitae	Palazzo	Verbena

NOTES

CHAPTER 1. MONTALCINO

1. Costantini, ed., *Zonazione viticola ed olivicola.*
2. Caprioli, *Montalcino: Diecimila anni di vita.*
3. Donati, *Gli etruschi su Poggio Civitella.*
4. Raffaelli, *Montalcino e il suo Brunello.*

CHAPTER 2. TEMPERAMENTAL SANGIOVESE

1. Soderini, *Trattato della cotivazione delle viti.*
2. Mainardi, *Storia di un grande protagonista.*
3. Ibid.
4. Ibid.
5. Molon, *Ampelografia.*
6. Di Vecchi Staraz et al., "Genetic Structuring and Parentage Analysis for Evolutionary Studies in Grapevine: Kin Group and Origin of the Cultivar Sangiovese Revealed."
7. Nencini and Pratt, "Clemente Santi."
8. Mainardi, *Storia di un grande protagonista.*
9. Ibid.
10. As cited by Boselli, *Il "Sangiovese."*
11. Calò et al., *Caratterizzazione molecolare.*
12. Moretto, "Comportamento vegeto-produttivo del Sangiovese."

CHAPTER 3. BIRTH OF A NEW WINE

1. Montanari et al., *Trama poderale.*

2. Degli Abbizi, "Sulla produzione del vino in Italia," republished in Nanni, *Storia della vite e del vino.*
3. *Bollettino del Comizio agrario di Siena* (1876), cited in Raffaelli, *Montalcino e il suo Brunello.*
4. Nencini and Pratt, *Alle origini del Brunello.*
5. *Bollettino del Comizio agrario di Siena.*
6. As reported in Nencini and Pratt, *Alle origini del Brunello.*
7. Raffaelli, *Un pioniere.*
8. *Relazione della Commissione interministeriale.*

CHAPTER 4. BRUNELLO COMES OF AGE

1. Gabbrielli, "Giulio Gambelli: Maestro assaggiatore."
2. Official bottle numbers are not available for the 1967 vintage, but based on total hectoliters and factoring in the common practice especially in the early days of declassifying much of the Brunello production to a table wine, the precursor of Rosso di Montalcino, this is the Consorzio's estimate.
3. Ferrazza and Giannelli, "Montalcino: Uno scenario strategico."

CHAPTER 5. BOOM YEARS AND THE LOSS OF *TIPICITÀ*

1. Suckling, "The Greatest Brunellos Ever."

CHAPTER 6. THE BRUNELLOGATE SCANDAL

1. Asimov, "Some See a Wine Loved Not Wisely."
2. Suckling, "Smoke and Fire in Montalcino."
3. Winenews.it, "Ezio Rivella: Enologo e grande conoscitore."
4. Winenews.it, "Il manager-enologo Ezio Rivella."
5. Fumagalli, "L'intervista al produttore Angelo Gaja."
6. Gaja, "The Case for Brunello di Montalcino."
7. Department of the Treasury, Alcohol and Tobacco Tax and Trade Bureau, *Brunello di Montalcino Wine.*

CHAPTER 7. BRUNELLO TODAY AND TOMORROW

1. Macchi, "Intervista a Rivella."

CHAPTER 8. MONTALCINO

1. O'Keefe, *The Gentleman of Brunello*.

CHAPTER 9. BOSCO AND TORRENIERI

1. Santi, "Sulle Crete Senesi."

CHAPTER 12. SANT'ANGELO

1. Anderson, *Vino*.
2. Gabbrielli, *Pierluigi Talenti*.

ACKNOWLEDGMENTS

I would like to thank the following people for the help and time they gave to me while I was writing this book:

Stefano Campatelli and the staff of the Brunello Consorzio for answering many questions and for supplying crucial statistics;

Francesco Belviso, Ilio Raffaelle, Ivo Caprioli, and Montalcino Ieri for all their help re-creating Montalcino and Brunello history for me;

Dr. Roberto Bandinelli of the University of Florence and Professor Maurizio Boselli of the University of Verona for their expertise in clonal research and ampelography;

Paolo Vagaggini for his insight on Sangiovese and Montalcino;

Professor Edoardo Costantini of CRA-ABP Florence for sharing his research into pedology and geology;

Alessandro Benvenuti for his description of local geology;

Alessandra Gemmiti of ARSIA for documents on Sangiovese, Guila Zoi, and the Museo di Brunello for statistics;

the many producers who spent hours on end answering my barrage of questions, walking me through their vineyards, and opening numerous bottles of Brunello.

And most of all I would like to thank my husband, Paolo Tenti, for his photos, for reading the manuscript, and for his overall support, moral and technical, of the project.

GLOSSARY

AGRITURISMO. Holiday apartments on a farming estate.

ANNATA. Vintage, or vintage wine that is not the Riserva bottling.

APPASSIMENTO. Method for drying grapes, either in ventilated rooms, as with *vin santo,* or partially on the vine for late-harvest wines like Moscadello.

ARGILLA. Clay.

ASSEMBLAGGIO. Blending the different lots of wine, before aging or, more commonly, before bottling.

AZIENDA, AZIENDE. Firm(s) or estate(s).

BARRIQUE. Barrel, 225 liters, usually made with French oak, though is sometimes made with other oak including American and Austrian oak. French wood is by far the most common in Italy.

BORGO. Hamlet.

BOTTI. Large barrels, the most traditional being made of Slavonian oak with capacities anywhere from 7 to 100 hectoliters. The most common being used today are usually 20 to 50 hectoliters.

CANTINA, CANTINE. Cellar, cellars.

CANTINA SOCIALE. Cooperative cellar.

CASA COLONICA. Traditional Tuscan stone farmhouse.

CASTELLO. Castle.

CILIEGIA. Cherry, which is a typical aroma or flavor of Sangiovese.

CLASSICO. Term used to indicate the historical or original part of a growing zone.

COLLINA. Hill.

COLTURA PROMISCUA. Mixed cultivation of crops prevalent in rural Italy, and in particular Tuscany, which preceded specialized vineyards.

COMUNE. Commune or municipality. May incorporate several villages.

CONSORZIO. Consortium or growers' union.

CONSULENTE. In Italian wine terms, consulting enologist.

CORDONE SPERONATO. Spurred cordon vine training system, the most prevalent in Montalcino and popular in most of Tuscany for Sangiovese.

CRETE SENESI. Lunarlike landscape created by dense, compact clay.

CRU. Italianization of the French cru concept, usually meaning wine that comes from a single vineyard, or a special selection.

CUOIO. Leather, an aroma or taste often found in aged Brunellos, though hints of it can be detected in younger, traditionally crafted wines.

DÉLESTAGE. Also known as rack-and-return method of aerating fermenting wine by pumping it out of the fermenting vat and into awaiting receptacles (or another tank), and then back into the fermenting tank.

DIRADAMENTO. Thinning out of the bunches.

DISCIPLINARE. Legally binding regulations that govern a specific denomination.

DOC. Denominazione di origine controllata. An appellation whose origin is controlled and regulated by the Italian government equivalent to France's AOC.

DOCG. Denominazione di origine controllata e garantita. The most rigidly controlled appellation, guaranteed by a tasting commission.

DOP. Denominazione di origine protetta. The new EU regulations that will eventually supplant Italy's current DOC and DOCG designations, though at present (2011) how this will be implemented into Italy's current system, and how it will appear on labels, is not clear.

ENOLOGO. Enologist.

ENOTECA. Wine bar, wine shop.

EQUILIBRIO/EQUILIBRATO. Balance/balanced.

ETICHETTA. Label.

FATTORIA. Farm.

FECCE. Lees.

FORTEZZA. Fortress.

FRAZIONE. A small part of a commune.

FRIZZANTE. Sparkling (e.g., wine with tiny bubbles).

GALESTRO. Flaky schist.

GOUDRON. Tar aromas, a tertiary aroma sometimes found in aged wine.

GOVERNO. A largely defunct technique of enhancing wine structure by refermenting via the addition of dried or partially dried grapes that was very popular in the late nineteenth and early twentieth centuries.

IGT. Indicazione geografica tipica. A more flexible designation that is not as strictly controlled as DOC and DOCG.

IMBOTTIGLIATO ALL'ORIGINE. When written on the label means the wine was made entirely by a single estate that grew the grapes, produced the wine, and bottled it. Equivalent to "estate bottled" on U.S. labels.

IN PUREZZA. In Italian winespeak signifies a wine made solely with 100 percent of a single varietal, as Brunello is made with Sangiovese *in purezza*.

LIEVITI. Yeast used for fermentation.

MASSAL SELECTION (SELEZIONE MASSALE). Propagation method whereby cuttings are taken from a number of the best-performing vines on the estate to propagate a new generation of vines. Unlike clonal selection, where vines are propagated from a single "mother vine" and have identical DNA, massal selection involves a number of vines. Hence, while the new vines are all from the same family with the same genes, individual plants are not identical.

MEZZADRIA. Sharecropping.

MEZZARDO. Sharecropper.

NORMALE. Usually used to describe a given wine in a firm's range that is not designated as a single vineyard or a Riserva. For Brunello, often referred to as Annata.

PASSITO. Dried. In wine terms a wine made from dried grapes that have undergone *appassimento*.

PODERE. Small estate or farm.

POTARE. Pruning.

RESA. Yield.

RIMONTAGGIO. Pumping over of the wine or must during fermentation to break up the solid cap (*capello*) that forms on the top.

RISERVA. A strictly controlled designation that means the wine has been aged longer than the Annata.

SABBIA. Sand.

SALASSO. Bleeding of the must whereby some of the wine in a tank is siphoned off to concentrate the remaining wine, especially in terms of color. These days the siphoned-off wine is often bottled as a *rosato*.

SFUSO. In wine terms, wine that is sold or bought in bulk.

SPUMANTE. Sparkling wine.

SUOLO. Soil.

SUPER TUSCAN. Term that defined the renegade wines, born in the 1970s and 1980s, that broke away from the miserably outmoded and quantity-inspired regulations of the era. Referring to wine usually made from a blend of international grapes or Sangiovese and international grapes, the term is now considered largely passé.

TENUTA, TENUTE. Large estate(s) or holdings.

TERRENO. Land or soil.

TERRITORIO. Territory, but largely used in Italian wine terms as terroir.

TERROIR. Originally a French term now used universally to signify the natural environment of a viticultural area or specific vineyard, it underscores the crucial role "place" plays in certain grape varieties and therefore wines. Soil, topography, and microclimate are key factors of terroir. It is perhaps the most discussed and controversial of all wine terms.

TINO/TINI. Vat used for fermentation. Usually refers to conical wooden vats although the term can also be used for stainless steel vats as well.

TIPICITÀ. A quintessential expression of a particular type of wine, of its grape variety or varieties and terroir.

TONNEAU, TONNEAUX. In Italian wine terms, refers to 500-liter French oak barrels, although they occasionally come in 700 liters as well.

TRACCIABILITÀ. Traceability. System that enables consumers to check on a series of data that help verify the wine's authenticity. By going to www.consorziobrunellodimontalcino.it, clicking on "Traceability," and inserting the code numbers on every pink paper strip around the capsule of Brunello, consumers can find carefully documented information on the producer and a link to the estate's website, the individual batch of wine in the bottle, and analytical data resulting from tests on the wine.

VIGNA/VIGNETO. Vineyard.

ZONAZIONE. An in-depth analysis of soil, climate, sun exposure, and other considerations, often undertaken before planting a vineyard.

BIBLIOGRAPHY

Anderson, Burton. *Biondi Santi: The Family That Created Brunello di Montalcino.* Pomezia: Union, 1988.
———. *Vino: The Wines and Winemakers of Italy.* Boston: Little, Brown, 1980.
———. *The Wine Atlas of Italy.* New York: Simon and Schuster, 1990.
———. "Wines for People with Patience." *International Herald Tribune,* Paris, 1971.
ARSIA (Agenzia regionale per lo sviluppo e l'innovazione nel settore agricolo e forestale). *Il Sangiovese.* Proceedings on the First International Symposium on Sangiovese, Florence, 2000.
———. *Il Sangiovese vitigno tipico e internazionale: Identità e peculiarità.* Proceedings on the Second International Symposium on Sangiovese, Florence, 2004.
Asimov, Eric. "Some See a Wine Loved Not Wisely, but Too Well." *New York Times,* February 15, 2006.
Belfrage, Nicolas. *Brunello to Zibibbo.* London. Faber and Faber, 2001.
———. *The Finest Wines of Tuscany and Central Italy.* Berkeley: University of California Press, 2009.
Belviso, Francesco, Ivo Caprioli, Sergio Lambardi, Mario Marri, and Ilio Raffaelli. *Montalcino ieri.* Montalcino: Edizioni Alessio Machetti, 1988.
Boselli, Maurizio. *Il "Sangiovese": Importanza e diffusione.* Florence: Atti Arsia dal Simposio Internazionale, 2000.
Breviglieri, Nino, and Enrico Casini. "Sangiovese." In *Ministero dell'agricoltura e delle foreste, Commissione per lo studio ampelografico dei principali vitigni da vino coltivati in Italia.* Treviso: Tip. Longo and Zoppelli, 1965.
Calò, Antonio, Attilio Scienza, and Angelo Costacurta. *Vitigni d'Italia.* Bologna: Edagricole, 2001.
Calò, Antonio, et al. *Caratterizzazione molecolare, ampelografica e ampelometrica di 30 accessioni di Vitis Vinifera L. riferibili al 'Sangiovese.'"* Florence: Atti Arsia dal Simposio Internazionale, 2000.
Caprioli, Ivo. *La liberazione di Montalcino, 27 giugno 1944.* Montepulciano: Le Balze, 2003.

———. *Montalcino: Duemila anni di vita alla luce dei ritrovamenti archeologici.* Montalcino: Comitato Ricerche e Studi Etruschi ed Italici, 1994.

Ciacci, Mario. *Il Brunello e gli altri vini di Montalcino.* Siena: Nuova Immagine Editrice, 2000.

Ciuffoletti, Zeffiro, ed. *Storia del vino in Toscana.* Florence: Edizioni Polistampa, 2000.

Consorzio del vino Brunello di Montalcino. *Brunello: I produttori.* Colle di Val d'Elsa: AL.SA.BA., 2008.

Costantini, Edoardo, ed. *Zonazione viticola ed olivicola della Provincia di Siena.* Colle Val d'Elsa: Grafiche Boccacci Editore, 2006.

Degli Albizi, Vittorio. *Sulla produzione del vino in Italia.* Atti Accademia dei Georgofili, 1867. Republished in *Storia della vite e del vino in Italia Toscana,* ed. Paolo Nanni. Florence: Edizioni Polistampa, 2007.

Department of the Treasury, Alcohol and Tobacco Tax and Trade Bureau. *Brunello di Montalcino Wine.* Industry Circular No. 2010-03, March 29, 2010.

Di Vecchi Staraz, D. M., et al. "Genetic Structuring and Parentage Analysis for Evolutionary Studies in Grapevine: Kin Group and Origin of the Cultivar Sangiovese Revealed." *Journal of the American Society for Horticultural Science* 132 (2007): 514–24.

Donati, Luigi. *Archeologia Viva,* March–April 1998, 64–69.

Ferrazza, Giuseppe, and Tommaso Giannelli. "Montalcino: Uno scenario strategico per la valorizzazione del patrimonio territoriale." Ph.D. thesis, University of Florence, 2002.

Fumagalli, Marisa. "L'intervista al produttore Angelo Gaja." *Corriere della Sera,* August 23, 2008.

Gabbrielli, Andrea. "Giulio Gambelli: Maestro assaggiatore." *EV,* no. 78, September 2004.

———. *Pierluigi Talenti: L'altro Brunello.* Bergamo: Veronelli Editore, 2005.

Gaja, Angelo. "The Case for Brunello di Montalcino: An Open Letter." *World of Fine Wine,* no. 20, 2008.

Guardia di Finanza. Press release, July 18, 2009. Published by the news agency Ansa on its website, www.ansa.it.

Lechmere, Adam. "Outrage as Montalcino Proposes Blended Rosso." *decanter.com,* August 30, 2011.

Macchi, Carlo. *Giulio Gambelli: L'uomo che sa ascoltare il vino.* Bergamo: Veronelli Editore, 2007.

———. "Intervista a Rivella" (www.winesurf.it, www.youtube.com), July 22, 2010.

Mainardi, G. *Storia di un grande protagonista dell'enologia italiana: Il Sangiovese, in ARSIA 2000.* Florence: Atti Arsia dal Simposio Internazionale, 2000.

Malenotti, Ignazio. *L'Agricoltore istruito dal padron contadino.* Colle Val d'Elsa: Eusebio Pacini, 1815.

"Masterpieces of Italian Wine: Brunello di Montalcino." *Italian Wines and Spirits,* October–December 1985 (16 pages reprint numbered from 1 to 16 by Editoriale Lariana, Milan).

Mencacci, Stefania. *Piano strutturale: Relazione geologica.* Montalcino: Comune di Montalcino, 2009.

Ministero d'Agricoltura. *Ampelografia italiana.* Turin: Litografia Fratelli Doyen, 1879.

Molon, Girolamo. *Ampelografia.* Vol. 2. Milan: Hoepli Editore, 1906.

Montanari, Massimo, et al. *Trama poderale, colture, e allevamento in età moderna: Piano strutturale; Indagine storica, memoria storica.* Montalcino: Comune di Montalcino, 2009.

Moretto, Alessandro. "Comportamento vegeto-produttivo del Sangiovese in 'Chianti Classico' in funzione della forma di allevamento e della densità di piantagione." Ph.D. thesis, University of Pisa, 2006.

Nanni, Paolo, ed. *Storia della vite e del vino in Italia Toscana.* Florence: Edizioni Polistampa, 2007.

Nencini, Roberto, and Jeff Pratt. *Alle origini del Brunello: Studi e ricerche sull'agromontalcinese: Montalcino; Itinerario nell'agricoltura d'autore.* Rome: Union for Agrimontalcino '88, 1988.

———. "Clemente Santi e l'agricoltura montalcinese nell'800." Unpublished manuscript containing several articles and letters by Clemente Santi, 1987.

O'Keefe, Kerin. "Biondi Santi, Frescobaldi Protest Rallies Montalcino, but 40% Abstain." *decanter.com,* October 16, 2008.

———. "Brunello De-con-struct-ed." *Wine News,* October–November 2007.

———. "Brunello: Image or Substance, Truth or Dare?" *World of Fine Wine,* no. 20, 2008.

———. "Brunello's Moment of Truth." *World of Fine Wine,* no. 11, 2006.

———. "Brunello: No Change in Rules, Producers Vote." *decanter.com,* October 28, 2008.

———. "Brunello on the Brink." *Decanter,* August 2008.

———. "Brunello Producers Rally to Save Beleaguered Denomination." *World of Fine Wine,* no. 22, 2008.

———. "Brunello: 2005 Now, 2004 Later." *Decanter,* May 2010.

———. *Franco Biondi Santi: The Gentleman of Brunello.* Bergamo: Veronelli Editore, 2005.

———. "Government and Consorzio Clash over Brunello." *decanter.com,* June 9, 2008.

———. "Montalcino Changes Demanded by Markets, Says Consorzio." *decanter.com,* September 6, 2011.

———. "Montalcino Throws Out Rosso's Changes." *decanter.com,* September 8, 2011.

———. "Trend vs. Tradition: Italian Wine Styles under Siege." *Wine News,* April–May 2004.

———. "Vintage of a Lifetime." *Wine News,* February–March 2003.

———. "War of Words Breaks Out in Montalcino." *decanter.com,* September 26, 2008.

O'Keefe, Kerin, and Howard G. Goldberg. "US Threatens to Block All Brunello Imports." *decanter.com,* May 12, 2008.

Ottavi, Edoardo, and Arturo Marescalchi. *Guida vinicola della Toscana.* Casale Monferrato: Cassone, 1902.

Paccagnini, Riccardo. *Trattato teorico: Pratico di agricultura ed enologia.* Bari: Tipografia e Riproduzione Fotomeccaniche M. Samele, 1907.

Parenti Righi, Giovanni. *La cucina toscana.* 4th ed. Rome: Newton and Compton, 2006.

Parzen, Jeremy. "US Officially Lifts Brunello Certification Requirement." *decanter .com,* April 6, 2010.

Pellucci, Emanuele. *Il Brunello e gli altri vini di Montalcino.* Fiesole: Vipsul Edizioni, 1999.

Raffaelli, Ilio. *Montalcino e il suo Brunello.* Colle di Val d'Elsa: Vanzi Editrice, 2008.

———. *Un pioniere del Brunello: Riccardo Paccagnini.* Massa: Type Service Editore, 1990.

———. *Prima dell'economia del Brunello.* Montepulciano: Le Balze, 2001.

———. *Ricordando la supremazia enologica della nostra terra.* Colle di Val d'Elsa: Vanzi Editrice, 2010.

Ray, Cyril. *The Wines of Italy.* New York: McGraw-Hill, 1966.

Redi, Francesco. *Bacco in Toscana: Ditirambo.* Florence: Pier Matini, 1685.

Relazione della Commissione interministeriale per la delimitazione del territorio del vino Chianti. Bologna: Tipografia Antonio Brunelli, 1932.

Santi, Clemente. "Sulle Crete Senesi." *Bollettino del Comizio Agrario di Siena* (1864). Republished in "Clemente Santi e l'agricoltura montalcinese nell'800," unpublished manuscript containing several articles and letters by Clemente Santi, 1987.

Santi, Luigi. *Lettera storico-critica sull'origine di Montalcino.* Florence: Filippo Marchini, 1822.

Soderini, Gianvettorio. *Trattato della coltivazione delle viti, e del frutto che se ne può cavare.* Florence: Luigi Giunti, 1590.

Soldati, Mario. *Vino al vino.* Milan: Mondadori Editore, 1969.

Suckling, James. "The Greatest Brunellos Ever." *Wine Spectator,* July 3, 2002.

———. "Smoke and Fire in Montalcino." *Wine Spectator,* March 21, 2008.

Toscani, Cesare. *Sulla cultura dell'agro montalcinese e specialmente quello che sono e che potrebbero essere le vigne.* Siena: Tipografia Moschini, 1866.

Veronelli, Luigi. *Guide Veronelli all'Italia piacevole: Toscana.* Milan: Garzanti Editore, 1970.

"Villa Banfi Builds on Success Importing Italian Wine." *Time,* January 9, 1984.

Wilson, James E. *Terroir.* Berkeley: University of California Press, 1998.

Winenews.it. "Ezio Rivella: Enologo e grande conoscitore dei problemi di Montalcino." *Winenews.it,* September, 12, 2008.

———. "Ezio Rivella propone cambio delle regole per il Brunello." *Winenews.it,* September 12, 2008.

———. "Il manager-enologo Ezio Rivella: 'Sul Brunello di Montalcino inutili e deleterie polemiche.'" *Winenews.it,* April 5, 2008.

Ziliani, Franco. "Rumors from Montalcino." At vinoalvino.org website, March 21, 2008.

INDEX

Abbadia Ardenga, 180, 184–86
Angelini, Tenimenti (Val di Suga), 168–70
Altesino, 95, 137, 154, 160, 162–64, 259

Baccinetti, 281
Bandinelli, Roberto, 23–24, 26–28, 30, 211, 287
Banfi, 11, 27–28, 55–57, 71–74, 77, 85, 205, 209, 217–22, 264, 296. *See also* Castello Banfi
Barbi, Fattoria dei, 47–49, 55, 95, 111–14, 116, 166, 251. *See also* Stefano Cinelli Colombini
Baricci, Nello, 53, 137, 159–61, 280
Belpoggio, 244–46
Bernini, Laura, 32, 34, 117. *See also* Brunelli, Gianni
Benvenuti, Alessandro, 171, 196, 198
Biondi Santi, 27, 34, 48–50, 54, 76, 95, 97, 109, 114, 125, 138, 144, 147, 150–51, 154, 157, 245, 259, 275
Biondi Santi, Ferruccio, 42, 44–47, 98
Biondi Santi, Franco, 45, 47, 65, 69, 75, 77, 98–102, 147, 181, 258, 260, 261–62
Biondi Santi, Jacopo, 99
Biondi Santi, Tancredi, 16, 45–48, 51–53, 98, 147, 149, 154, 239, 258, 262
Bosco, 91, 171–77
Boselli, Maurizio, 22, 287

Brunelli, Gianni, Laura (Le Chiuse di Sotto), 32, 115–18, 119, 259
Brunellogate, 70–80

Camigliano (subzone), 61, 91–92, 187*map*, 196–204
Campatelli, Stefano, 53, 90, 287
Campogiovanni, 229–30
Canalicchio (area), 95, 137, 149
Canalicchio, Pacenti, Franco, 142–44
Canalicchio di Sopra, 137, 142, 145–46
Cantina Sociale Biondi Santi e C., 16–17, 46–47, 149
Capanna, 137, 157–59, 263
Caprili, 193–95, 262–63
Casale del Bosco, 173–75. *See also* Nardi, Silvio, Tenute
Case Basse, 52, 186, 188–89, 191. *See also* Soldera Gianfranco
Casisano Colombaio, 133–34
CastelGiocondo, 55, 78, 171, 197–99, 209. *See also* Frescobaldi, Marchesi de'
Castello Banfi, 55, 74, 221–22
Castelnuovo dell'Abate, 13, 14*fig*, 61, 91–92, 108–10, 117, 120–21, 129–30, 132, 154–55, 162, 173, 223, 232–53
Castiglion del Bosco, 175–76, 197–98
Cerbaiona (Diego Molinari), 122–24
Chiuse, Le, 147–48
Ciacci Piccolomini d'Aragona, 240–42, 251

Cinelli Colombini, Donatella (Casato Prime Donne), 85, 86, 111, 166–68, 184
Cinelli Colombini, Stefano, 111–13, 166
Citille di Sopra, 281
Col di Lamo, 281
Colleceto, 281
Col d'Orcia, 27, 47, 55, 75, 77, 205–9, 211–15, 260, 262, 275. *See also* Marone Cinzano, Francesco
Costanti Andrea, 104–7, 281
Costanti, Conti, 104–7
Costanti, Emilio, 104, 280
Costanti, Tito, 42, 46
Costantini, Edoardo, 12–13, 56, 95, 97, 134, 181, 219, 287
Colle, Il, 52, 107–8
Collosorbo, Tenuta di, 249–50
Crete (Senesi), 35, 178–80, 272–73
Crocedimezzo, Tenuta, 113–15

Di Campalto, Stella, 109, 246–49, 259
Domus Vitae, 281

Fattoi, 281
Fattoria Sant'Angelo in Colle, 47, 211, 214
Ferrini, Carlo, 89–90, 167
Ferro, 281
Fiorita, La, 251–53
Fornacina, 281
Frescobaldi, Marchesi de', 41, 61, 72, 176, 197–99
Fuga, Tenuta La, 200–202
Fuligni, 95, 137–39

Gaja, Angelo, 75, 191–93
Gambelli, Giulio, 52–54, 108, 122–23, 152, 184, 186, 189, 224, 239, 249
Geology, 11–12, 97, 134, 171, 178, 196, 207, 219
Gerla, La, 153–55
Gode, Le, 137, 145, 164–66
Gorelli, Giuseppe, 32, 35, 126–28. *See also* Potazzine, Tenuta Le
Greppone Mazzi, Tenuta, 131–33

Innocenti, 183

L'Aietta, 130–31
Lambardi, Maurizio (Canalicchio di Sotto), 65, 137, 143–45, 259, 280
Lazzeretti, 281
Leanza, Francesco, 109, 118–20
Lisini, 65, 208, 223–25, 259, 275, 280

Machetti, Andrea, 33, 236. *See also* Mastrojanni
Marchesato degli Aleramici, 202–4
Marroneto, Il, 65, 134, 139–41
Mastrojanni, 33, 235–37, 259
Montosoli, 47, 105, 137, 145–46, 157–60, 162–65
Mori, Alessandro, 65, 66, 139–41
Marone Cinzano, Francesco, 76, 207, 209, 211, 260, 281
Montalcino: history, 13–18; overview, 9–13; subzone, 95–170

Nardi, Silvio Tenute (Nardi, Emilia), 173–75, 235, 280

Padalletti, 45, 46, 47, 148–50
Palazzo, 281
Paradiso di Manfredi, Il, 136*fig.*, 137, 150–53, 154, 259
Pertimali (Sassetti, Livio), 136, 156–57, 259, 263
Pian dell'Orino, 109–11
Pietroso, 281
Pieve Santa Restituta, 191–93. *See also* Gaja, Angelo
Poggio al Vento, 206, 208, 209, 211–14. *See also* Col d'Orcia
Poggione, Il, 27, 34, 47, 49, 55, 86, 205, 208, 211, 214–17, 227, 262–63, 275
Poggio di Sotto (Palmucci, Piero), 52, 65, 235, 237–40, 259
Potazzine, Tenute, Le, 126–28
Presi, Le, 253

Salicutti, 109, 118–20, 246
Salvioni, Giulio (La Cerbaiola), 83, 122, 124–26, 209
San Giacomo, 281

Sangiovese: 10, 13, 19–26; clones, 27–31; diseases, 37; harvesting, 35–37; planting densities, 33–35; rootstocks, 35; training systems, 31–33, 130–31
Sant'Angelo (in Colle, Scalo), 3, 11, 36, 56–57, 61, 91–92, 205–31
Santi, Clemente, 39–42, 46, 178
SassodiSole, 181–83
Sesta di Sopra, 281
Sesti, Giuseppe Maria (Castello di Argiano), 226–27
Soil, 11–13, 56, 91–92, 95, 97, 100, 134, 136*fig,* 171, 178–81, 186, 196, 198, 207–8, 219, 232. *See also under individual producer profiles.*
Solaria, 281

Soldera, Gianfranco, 65–66, 154, 186, 188–91
subzones, 3–4, 11, 84, 87–92

Talenti, Pierluigi, 215
Tavernelle, 61, 91–92, 126, 129, 186–96
Terralsole, 120–22
Torrenieri, 16, 91, 171–72*map,* 178–85, 192, 196

Uccelliera, 242–44

Vagaggini, Paolo, 20, 114, 117, 121, 133, 138, 140, 142, 144–45, 152, 158, 194, 241, 287
Verbena, 281
Villa I Cipressi, 128–30

TEXT
11/14 Garamond Premier Pro
DISPLAY
Garamond Premier Pro
COMPOSITOR
BookMatters, Berkeley
CARTOGRAPHER
Lohnes+Wright
PRINTER AND BINDER
Thomson-Shore, Inc.